JLS

ANOTHER BEAT

POSY EDWARDS

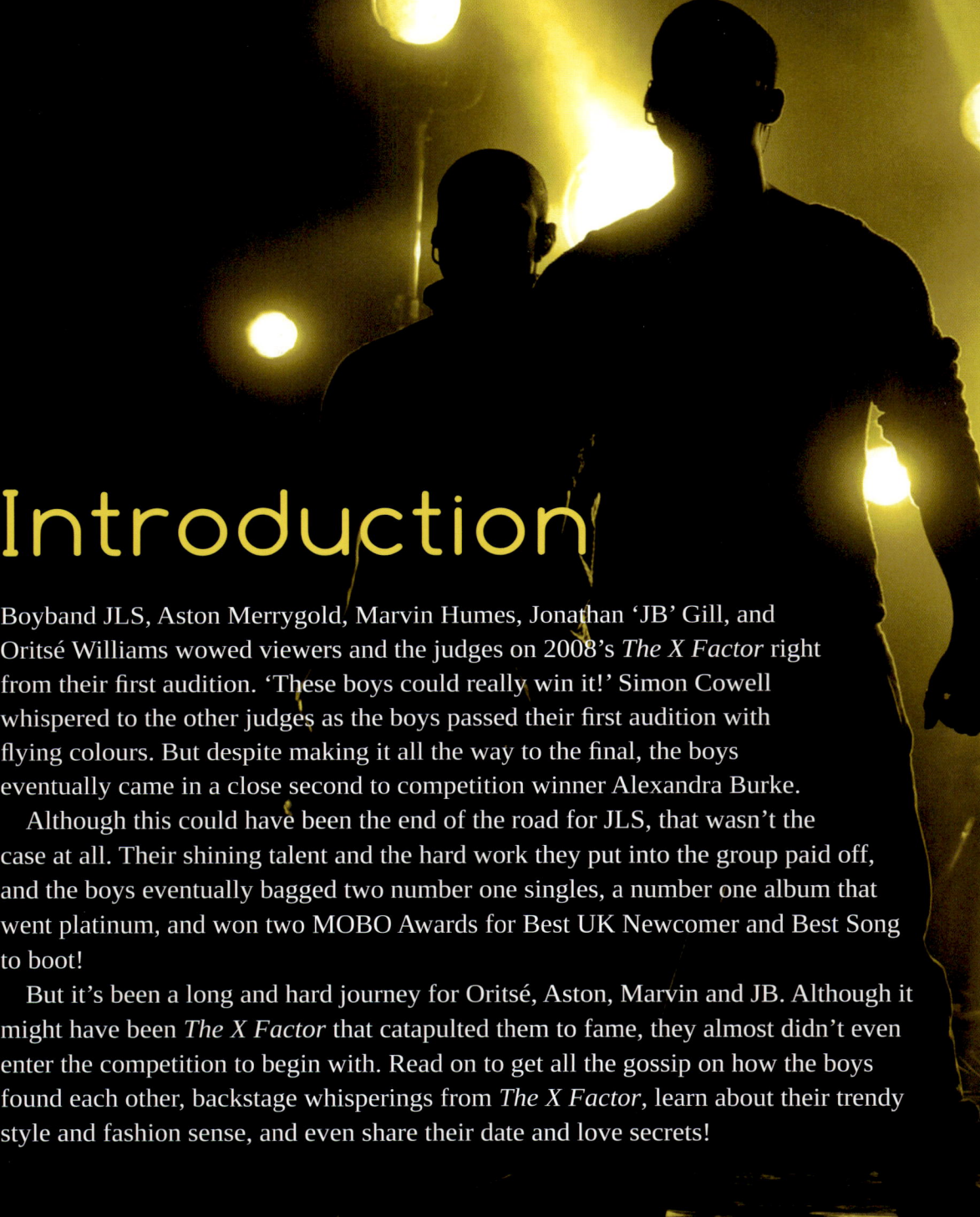

Introduction

Boyband JLS, Aston Merrygold, Marvin Humes, Jonathan 'JB' Gill, and Oritsé Williams wowed viewers and the judges on 2008's *The X Factor* right from their first audition. 'These boys could really win it!' Simon Cowell whispered to the other judges as the boys passed their first audition with flying colours. But despite making it all the way to the final, the boys eventually came in a close second to competition winner Alexandra Burke.

Although this could have been the end of the road for JLS, that wasn't the case at all. Their shining talent and the hard work they put into the group paid off, and the boys eventually bagged two number one singles, a number one album that went platinum, and won two MOBO Awards for Best UK Newcomer and Best Song to boot!

But it's been a long and hard journey for Oritsé, Aston, Marvin and JB. Although it might have been *The X Factor* that catapulted them to fame, they almost didn't even enter the competition to begin with. Read on to get all the gossip on how the boys found each other, backstage whisperings from *The X Factor*, learn about their trendy style and fashion sense, and even share their date and love secrets!

oritsé

marvin

aston

jb

chapter 1

Meet The Boys!

'Everyday I have to pinch myself . . . This is closer than I ever could've imagined to the original idea for JLS.'

Oritse's dream has become a reality.

Aston

JLS   Aston   Marvin   JB   Oritsé

What would you like to ask ASTON?

NAME – Aston Merrygold

BORN – 13th February 1988

HOMETOWN – Peterborough, England

STAR SIGN – Aquarius

EYE COLOUR – Brown

WHAT WAS YOUR NICKNAME AT SCHOOL? – Lil' Man, A.S.

FAVOURITE COLOUR – Blue

FAVOURITE FOOD – Tuna and Pasta or Pizza

FAVOURITE SPORT (to watch or to play) – Football

WHAT IS YOUR IDEAL WEEKEND? – Waking up late, partying all weekend

WHAT IS YOUR FAVOURITE HOLIDAY DESTINATION? – Florida, America

IF YOU WERE AN ANIMAL, WHAT WOULD YOU BE? – A cheetah or a little monkey

WHAT'S YOUR MOST EMBARRASSING MOMENT? – I don't really get embarrassed. I embarrass people!

TELL US ONE SECRET ABOUT YOU OR A FELLOW BAND MATE – JB likes to stand next to a window, look up on the horizon and put lotion on himself. HA!

WHAT WAS THE FIRST ALBUM YOU EVER BOUGHT? – Usher – *My Way*

WHAT IS THE BEST CONCERT YOU HAVE EVER ATTENDED? – Boyz II Men

Marvin

JLS | Aston | Marvin | JB | Oritsé

What would you like to ask MARVIN?

NAME – Marvin Humes

BORN – 18th March 1985

HOMETOWN – Woolwich, England

STAR SIGN – Pisces

EYE COLOUR – Brown

FAVOURITE COLOUR – Green

FAVOURITE FOOD – Nando's

FAVOURITE SPORT (to watch or to play) – Football

WHAT'S ON YOUR IPOD? – Beyoncé – *I am … Sasha Fierce*

WHAT IS YOUR IDEAL WEEKEND? – Somewhere hot with beaches, cocktails, good shopping and great clubs!

WHAT IS YOUR FAVOURITE HOLIDAY DESTINATION? – Thailand

WHO ARE YOUR HEROES? – Martin Luther King, Michael Jackson, Mum and Dad

WHAT MAKES YOU LAUGH? – Adam Sandler movies and Eddie Murphy stand up

DO YOU PLAY ANY INSTRUMENTS? – A little piano!!

IF YOU WERE AN ANIMAL, WHAT WOULD YOU BE? – A lion

TELL US ONE SECRET ABOUT YOU OR A FELLOW BAND MATE – Aston lives on tomato ketchup – literally!

WHAT WAS THE FIRST ALBUM YOU EVER BOUGHT? – Michael Jackson – *Bad*

WHAT IS THE BEST CONCERT YOU HAVE EVER ATTENDED? – Michael Jackson – Dangerous 1994

factbook JB

JLS | Aston | Marvin | JB | Oritsé

What would you like to ask JB?

NAME – Jonathan Benjamin Gill

BORN – 7th December 1986

HOMETOWN – Croydon, England

STAR SIGN – Sagittarius

EYE COLOUR – Brown

WHAT WAS YOUR NICKNAME AT SCHOOL? – Gilly, Gillster & JG

FAVOURITE COLOUR – Yellow

FAVOURITE FOOD – Chinese

FAVOURITE SPORT (to watch or to play) – Playing rugby and watching football

WHAT'S ON YOUR IPOD? – The Script

WHAT IS YOUR IDEAL WEEKEND? – Sleeping and Nando's

WHAT IS YOUR FAVOURITE HOLIDAY DESTINATION? – The Caribbean

WHAT MAKES YOU LAUGH? – Aston!!

DO YOU PLAY ANY INSTRUMENTS? – Yes, the flute and the piano

IF YOU WERE AN ANIMAL, WHAT WOULD YOU BE? – A koala

WHAT WAS THE FIRST ALBUM YOU EVER BOUGHT? – Backstreet Boys – *Backstreet's Back*

WHAT IS THE BEST CONCERT YOU HAVE EVER ATTENDED? – Prince

13

Oritsé

JLS | Aston | Marvin | JB | Oritsé

What would you like to ask ORITSE?

NAME — Oritsé Williams

BORN — 27th November 1986

HOMETOWN — Fulham, England

STAR SIGN — Sagittarius

EYE COLOUR — Hazel

WHAT WAS YOUR NICKNAME AT SCHOOL? — Glitzy Ritzy and Music Boy

FAVOURITE COLOUR — Red

FAVOURITE FOOD — Nando's

FAVOURITE SPORT (to watch or to play) — Table tennis. 'Ask Marvin about that, he'll let you know our match score to date'

WHAT'S ON YOUR IPOD? — Lauryn Hill – *The Miseducation of Lauryn Hill*

WHAT IS YOUR IDEAL WEEKEND? — A weekend in the Caribbean

WHAT IS YOUR FAVOURITE HOLIDAY DESTINATION? – The Caribbean

IF YOU WERE AN ANIMAL, WHAT WOULD YOU BE? — An eagle

TELL US ONE SECRET ABOUT YOU OR A FELLOW BAND MATE — JB needs a minimum of 8 hours sleep

WHAT IS YOUR BIGGEST AMBITION FOR THE FUTURE? — For JLS to become the biggest band in the world!

WHAT WAS THE FIRST ALBUM YOU BOUGHT? — Sisqó – *Unleash the Dragon*

WHAT IS THE BEST CONCERT YOU HAVE EVER ATTENDED? — Tina Turner

15

chapter 2

Life Before Fame

According to Marvin, the name JLS came from the group's British identity. 'Jack the Lad Swing' was a combination of the New Jack Swing (an American genre that groups like Jodeci and Boyz II Men belonged to), and the boys' own cheeky charm.

The Dream

Although JLS came to be one of the best loved and most successful boybands of the decade, people only found out about the group through 2008's *The X Factor*. In reality, the JLS dream started years before that as the bright idea of a young Oritsé, who was studying at university in London in 2007.

He had always been musical as a child, and while at university he had been thinking about launching a career as a solo R&B artist. However, when Take That reunited, he realised there was a gap in the market for a young boyband, and decided to form one.

Family First

But Oritsé's motivation was personal as well as musical. He wanted to earn some money for his mum Sonia who suffers from multiple sclerosis. Oritsé's family had suffered some very hard times, and he was determined to raise cash to help pay for her treatments.

Looking For Talent

When he began the hunt for other members of the group, Oritsé spread the search as far as he could. The ambitious singer started looking through hundreds of MySpace pages of local talent, and placed adverts in music shops all over London's West End. Yet it was recommendations from his friends that eventually contributed to the group's final line up: Aston, JB, and Marvin.

A friend of Oritsé's put him in touch with Marvin, who he arranged to meet in London's Oxford Circus. Thinking that there was no time like the present, Oritsé decided to audition Marvin right there in the middle of the street. Fortunately for him, Marvin was a born performer, and wasted no time in singing his heart out, even pulling a few dance moves that made passers-by cheer him!

The Dream Team

Marvin already knew Aston, who he met at an audition for a TV advert. When Oritsé told Marvin he was still looking for members, Marvin handed over his mobile with Aston's number, and told Oritsé he had to call him, right then and there. The group was almost complete – they just needed one more future superstar to create the magic number of four. And the second Oritsé met JB he knew that his charisma and charm meant he would fit in perfectly.

Before Oritsé finalised his dream team, he sat for hours, pouring through all the potential group members he had met. He put photographs of different boys next to each other, working out the group dynamic, seeing what combination worked. But as soon as he put his photograph next to Marvin, Aston and JB, it was magic. He knew he had found the secret formula!

The Next Step

Immediately after the group formed, they felt a special bond with each other. Oritsé opened up to the boys about his tough home life. Instantly, the other three said they would always look out for him.

The four were soon devoting all their spare time to rehearsing at a dance studio in London's West End. They began playing gigs around London, though often they'd come away with less than £50 for their night's work. But it didn't matter – they knew that the hard work they put in and all the practice would pay off in the end. So they put plenty of thought into how they sounded as a group – and how they looked.

Keeping up the Studies

Although they were serious about the group, they also knew how few bands actually made it, so they were all working and studying hard outside the studio, just in case. Oritsé was studying events management, JB was studying theology, and Marvin was a property developer. But as it started looking like they had a chance of a serious shot at the music industry, they became less interested in their studies.

The X Factor

Friends and families of the boys began suggesting they take the group to try out for *The X Factor*. At a band meeting, the boys discussed whether they thought it was a good idea or not. They didn't want to try out, thinking that they could get there with their effort and determination alone.

But – even though things were going well for the band – they talked and talked about it, then made a group decision to try out for *The X Factor*. Things were looking good for the group anyway – so if they didn't get through, they would just carry on. After all, what did they have to lose?

chapter 3

The X Factor

'If you'd asked us who we wanted to guide us, we might have said Simon, or Cheryl, as she was a new judge. But luckily for us, as it turned out, we had Louis. Remember the success he's had with Westlife, Boyzone and even Girls Aloud in the early stages. He worked really hard for us … he got quite emotional!'
JB

Band from the Start

From day one, JLS had something that set them apart from almost every other group that had auditioned for *The X Factor*. They were already a real group. They hadn't just formed for the competition – they had been singing and dancing together for over a year, and formed a brotherly bond that worked hugely in their favour.

'At the auditions, when we were lining up to see the judges, everything was going wrong,' Oritsé remembers. 'JB had cut his hand on glass, Aston was desperate for the toilet, Marvin was the most nervous I'd ever seen him, and I was the same. When we went in, I was thinking: "You know, this can go totally wrong . . ." We saw Simon sighing, with his head in his hands, and we thought he was going to hate us. But thankfully we had a good start and that set us up!'

As Louis Walsh had to mentor the groups in the competition, JLS were relying on his knowledge and experience with groups to steer them to victory. But just two weeks into the show, JLS were Louis's last remaining act in the competition. To try and get some public support behind the boyband, Louis walked the streets of London in a bright green JLS hoodie, handing out flyers and asking people to support JLS!

Saved by Simon!

But the boys showed they were more than capable of making pop gold out of a number of different styles of music. Although they gave tight performances of tracks like *I'll Make Love to You* by Boyz II Men, *The Way You Make Me Feel* by Michael Jackson, *Ain't That a Kick in the Head?* by Dean Martin, *Baby One More Time* by Britney Spears (and other songs by Mariah Carey, The Beatles, The Isley Brothers and Take That), they were sometimes criticised by the judges for making poor decisions in their music choice.

As Aston sings many of the group's lead vocals, he would blame himself if things went badly on the show. On a few occasions, Oritsé had to run after him and tell him to pull himself together. 'Aston – we can get through this if we deliver a phenomenal second performance.'

This led to them finishing in the bottom two in week seven, but they were saved by the judges after Simon Cowell told the boys they didn't deserve to be at the bottom of the list. They went on to the semi-finals of the competition, in a nail-biting finale that had the nation on the edge of its seat!

Fans' Favourite

As if being in the competition wasn't stressful enough, the boys had drama surrounding them away from *The X Factor* studios. At a free show in Surrey, nearly 3,000 screaming fans turned up to watch JLS. However, when the venue filled up, disappointed fans rushed forwards, trying to stampede inside to see their beloved JLS. People in the crowd even witnessed rival girl gangs in the crowd fighting!

It was a chaotic scene, but it hinted at how popular the boys had already become before the competition had even finished.

As the show approached the semi-final, JLS had decided to sing Rihanna's *Umbrella* – and were due to perform alongside princess Rihanna herself! But a matter of days before the final, Rihanna cancelled, sending all the contestants and the production crew into chaos.

It was a real mess up. JLS – who had been extremely confident about their performance – were suddenly worried that they couldn't prepare enough. But they didn't show it onstage. The boys gave such strong performances that even Simon Cowell said to them: 'I'm gonna make a prediction, you could actually win this competition!' JLS ended up with the most votes in the semi-final, sailing through to the final.

'We work hard. That's our ethos. It's important to do things properly. JLS is all about excellence!'
JB

Finals Time!

If the semi-final was stressful to watch, the final was a million times worse! All around the country, devoted JLS fans were glued to their TVs, watching their boys team up with Westlife to sing their hit single *Flying Without Wings*. They watched as the boys managed to get through the first public vote (which saw Eoghan Quigg voted off). The boys then performed their own version of *Hallelujah*, but in the second public vote that night, Alexandra Burke came out on top, with JLS coming in second, only the fourth group ever to make the final on the show.

As gracious and respectful as ever – even in defeat – the boys immediately surrounded Alex and congratulated her on her win.

Though they were disappointed not to have won, they had no time to mope. *The X Factor* tour was about to set off around the UK, and the boys were about to show everyone exactly what they were made of. The JLS steam train was just about to pick up some steam!

29

chapter 4

Beyond The X Factor

'I never thought we would be here! I never
thought we'd get nominated, and I never
thought we would win two awards!'
Marvin on winning two MOBOs.

Although Alexandra Burke had won *The X Factor*, it seemed increasingly as if JLS were winners too. As *The X Factor* tour played to sold out arenas around the UK, crowds of screaming fans turned out to cheer JLS on. The boys sang a handful of Michael Jackson's hits, and with their soulful harmonies, slick moves and good looks, they were a smash hit.

Rumours circulated that the boys were jealous of the star treatment that Alex was receiving on the road, but they knew that was just the media trying to stir up trouble. In reality they were grateful to be getting the exposure that they were on the tour. 'The show opened up so many doors for you that you didn't even know existed before,' said Marvin. 'Without that platform it would've taken us much longer to get to where we are now.'

Record Contract Beckons . . .

Part of that was hooking up with Epic Records' Managing Director, Nick Raphael, who was the man behind stars like Lemar and Jay-Z. Although rumour had it that Simon Cowell's record company, Syco, was set to sign the boys, that deal fell through, and JLS found themselves signed to Epic Records.

The boys worked super hard on their music and their performances at Epic,

and they were rewarded in July 2009 when their debut single *Beat Again* went straight in at number one, and sold 100,000 copies in a week – becoming the fastest selling debut single of the year!

Instead of blowing a load of cash on a lavish party, they decided to celebrate in a more low-key way. Aston spills, 'When we had a party to celebrate reaching No. 1 in the charts, we went to Tesco and bought champagne on a buy-one-get-one-free deal and took it back to mine!'

Supporting a Hero

Riding on the wave of popularity since appearing on *The X Factor*, the boys spent the summer playing a number of

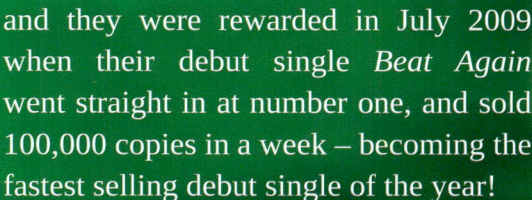

big shows around the UK. However, their biggest thrill came when R&B soul star Lemar asked the boys to support him on his tour. Lemar had noticed the boyband on *The X Factor*, and had been really impressed with their performances. JLS jumped at the chance of appearing on the road with one of their biggest heroes!

The tour definitely spread the JLS love to a much wider audience. And suddenly, before they knew it, there was even more good news – the boys had been nominated for two MOBO Awards! They were over the moon just to be nominated – but totally stunned to pick up not one, but both awards at the show, for Best Song with *Beat Again*, and Best Newcomer, beating *The X Factor* rival and pal, Alex Burke.

But JLS had no time to enjoy the win – they immediately returned to work, preparing for their 2010 tour, and releasing their second single. *Everybody in Love* not only went to number one in the singles chart but knocked Cheryl Cole off the top spot!

Riding High

They spent many months at work on their debut album, and were rewarded for their hard work when it went straight into the chart at number one, again knocking Cheryl Cole off the top spot and beating Robbie Williams. Not bad for a debut album!

However, it wasn't all good news. Disaster struck when thousands of screaming fans turned out to see the boys turn on the Christmas lights in Manchester. So many fans turned up that the entrance was completely blocked, meaning that JLS couldn't actually get into the building!

'We had to change in the car then go straight onto the red carpet. We never thought it would be anything like that. It was crazy,' says Aston. Thankfully no one was seriously hurt.

Back to their Roots

Following their chart success and growing popularity, Oritsé, Marvin, Aston and JB were invited back onto *The X Factor* to perform in the 2009 series, as the most successful group ever to graduate from the show.

When they returned to the set, it was just like the old days. In fact, the boys completely forgot to head to their own luxury performer's dressing room – and started heading for the contestants' dressing rooms instead! The boys eventually found where they were supposed to go, and got on stage to perform their second single *Everybody in Love*, to the sounds of wild screaming from the crowd. It was awesome! And it just went to show the huge phenomenon that JLS had become in just two short years!

chapter 5

Style & Looks

From day one, it wasn't just their smooth dance moves or killer harmonies that got us hooked on JLS. It was their unique group style and cheeky smiles too!

Although each of the boys likes to rock their own look, they also make sure they're wearing complimentary outfits when they perform onstage, and even when they're seen out on the town!

ASTON

Aston describes his own personal style as pure JLS – or 'Jents Looking Sick!'. He loves the colour grey, and although he doesn't have a favourite item of clothing, he's often seen rocking his trademark beanie. If you fancy catching Aston when he's out shopping, you can bet he'll be found in All Saints or Topman – his favourite high street shops!

'We're all equal – and there's no jealousy about Aston emerging as the focus of the group'
Oritsé

MARVIN

Marvin's favourite designer is Vivienne Westwood, and he can often be spotted sporting VW chains and other accessories. He describes his own personal style as 'cool, chilling, sophisticated, slick, and sweetboy!', and he likes wearing slinky fitting tops to show off that killer bod!

'I train as I believe it's part of the whole package: you've got to look good and feel good – plus it's nice for the ladies to see us at our peak,' says Marvin about the group's dedication to physical fitness.

JB

JB loves a nice fitting leather jacket, and says that his style is 100 per cent pure 'Urban Gentleman'. Although he's got a soft spot for a lot of designers and high street stores, his favourite is Burberry, every time.

'It's not always about winning, it's not always about beating someone, it's about us establishing ourselves in the market-place and having a career in music,' says JB, about how the group were thankful for all their success since The X Factor.

ORITSÉ

Oritsé calls his fashion sense 'sexy, cool, retro, different, unique, Oritsé!' And although he loves labels too, he knows that there's nowhere better to grab those one-off pieces of fashion than from Camden Market in London.

'Every element, from styling to sound to vocals, we did it with ambition, determination and dedication,' says Oritsé. 'We became an unshakeable force from the beginning.'

chapter 6

Romance

The boys started receiving fan mail when they were on *The X Factor*, but it was the fans outside the studio who presented them with the weirdest gifts. 'We've had charm bracelets, a dance DVD, lollipops, jumpers and a money box!' said Aston.

Romance and Rumours

If you believed everything you read in the papers, you would think all the boys must be romantically linked to every woman they stand within ten feet of!

In reality, the boys live a much more restrained life. When they formed as a group, they made a commitment to their careers that, unfortunately, meant that they had to break up with their long term girlfriends.

But as soon as they were performing on *The X Factor* they wasted no time in attracting potential girlfriends. They started working out every day, and even stripped off for a raunchy photoshoot in *Heat* magazine!

But having dedicated so much time to their careers meant the boys just didn't have time to find girlfriends, regardless of how tight their six packs may be!

So, while they were on *The X Factor*, they signed up for speed dating sessions! The hunky boys had been warned by protective mentor Cheryl Cole that they better keep their eyes off her mentees, Diana Vickers and Alex Burke. But we can all rest easy – although they had a lot of fun, none of the boys found girlfriends through speed dating. Phew!

After the show finished, the boys were even busier, and had even less time to spend looking for girlfriends. That didn't stop them – particularly Aston and Marvin – being linked to new partners almost on a weekly basis. 'We all like to go out and have a good time, because we work very hard – but work comes first, not play,' says Aston.

But what about all those screaming girls? 'There are girls out there who will just chuck themselves at you for your status,' admits Aston. But the boys are careful to look after each other, and watch each other's backs.

You have to hand it to the JLS fans – those girls can really be persistent! One dedicated fan even risked suffocation trying to meet her idols – hiding inside a zipped bag, which she got a friend to leave at a hotel that JLS were staying in!

So although these may be some of the most eligible bachelors on the market, they're remaining single for the time being – because they're married to their music!

chapter 7

The Future

Well, it's clear that Oritsé's dream of 'taking elements of the members of the greatest boybands of all time . . . and you'd end up with a supergroup' has come true – how could these guys get any bigger?

The boys have come so far in such a short time. It's a real rags to riches tale – four talented boys who found each other through Oritsé's masterplan, and have since become closer than brothers. They've managed chart success with hit singles, a platinum debut album, sold out arenas across the country, performed alongside some of the most famous urban artists around today, and even won top awards!

Keeping Both Feet on the Ground

You might expect some of this success to have gone to their heads, but the truth couldn't be further from that. These four boys heeded the advice of everyone they spoke to on *The X Factor* who told them to keep their wits about them and stay grounded. As a result, they've become more successful than any of them ever had dreamed of.

But the best thing of all is that the boys are sharing the most incredible journey of their life with each other, and with a shared ambition and love for what they do.

These four talented guys always knew they were destined for greatness, and they dared to dream. Just look where it got them! For these boys, the sky truly is the limit. Who knows what incredible things they will achieve next!

Picture Credits

Getty: 4, 5, 6, 16, 20-21, 25, 26-27, 30, 32, 33, 34, 39 left top and bottom, 41 bottom left and right, 43 top right and bottom left, 45 top left and right, 46-47, 59.

Rex: 9, 11, 19, 22, 24, 28-29, 39 right top and bottom, 41 top left and right, 43 top left and bottom right, 45 top right, 48, 50, 51, 52-53, 56, 58, 60-61.

PA: 13, 15, 38, 40, 42, 44, 45 top left, 54-55.

Acknowledgements

Posy Edwards would like to thank Helia Phoenix, Jane Sturrock, Helen Ewing, James Martindale, Viki Ottewill and Rich Carr.

First published in hardback in Great Britain in 2010 by Orion Books an imprint of the Orion Publishing Group Ltd.

Orion House, 5 Upper St Martin's Lane
London WC2H 9EA

An Hachette UK Company

10 9 8 7 6 5 4 3 2

A CIP catalogue record for this book is available from the British Library.

ISBN: 978 1 4091 2245 6

Designed by Viki Ottewill

Printed in Spain by Cayfosa

The Orion Publishing Group's policy is to use papers that are natural, renewable and recyclable and made from wood grown in sustainable forests. The logging and manufacturing processes are expected to conform to the environmental regulations of the country of origin. Every effort has been made to fulfil requirements with regard to reproducing copyright material.

The author and publisher will be glad to rectify any omissions at the earliest opportunity.

www.orionbooks.co.uk

reece
Turkey
Kurdistan
Syria
Israel Lebanon
Iraq
Iran Baluchistan
Afghanistan
Pakistan
North-South
Yemen
(Gulf War)
ad Sudan
Burma Thailand
Laos
China-
Vietnam
Ethiopia (Eritrea,
Ogaden, & Tigray)
India
(Assan
& Punjab)
Kampuchea
Sri
Lanka
Malaysia
Philippines
Uganda
Zaire
gola
Mauritius
East Timor
mibia
South
Africa
Mozambique

The World in Conflict
1989

War Annual 3

Brassey's titles of related interest

JOHN LAFFIN
Brassey's Battles: 3,500 Years of Conflict, Campaigns and Wars from A–Z
JOHN LAFFIN
War Annual 1
War Annual 2

Also by John Laffin

Military
Middle East Journey
Return to Glory
One Man's War
The Walking Wounded
Digger (The Story of the Australian Soldier)
Scotland the Brave (The Story of the Scottish Soldier)
Jackboot (The Story of the German Soldier)
Tommy Atkins (The Story of the English Soldier)
Jack Tar (The Story of the English Seaman)
Swifter than Eagles (Biography of Marshal of the R.A.F. Sir John Salmond)
The Face of War
British Campaign Medals
Codes and Ciphers
Boys in Battle
Women in Battle
Anzacs at War
Links of Leadership (Thirty Centuries of Command)
Surgeons in the Field
Americans in Battle
Letters from the Front 1914–18
The French Foreign Legion
Damn the Dardanelles! (The Story of Gallipoli)
The Australian Army at War 1899–1975
The Israeli Army in the Middle East Wars 1948–1973
The Arab Armies in the Middle East Wars 1948–1973
Fight for the Falklands!
On the Western Front: Soldiers' Stories 1914–18
The Man in the Nazis Couldn't Catch
The War of Desperation: Lebanon 1982–85
Battlefield Archaeology
The Western Front 1916–17: The Price of Honour ⎫
The Western Front 1917–18: The Cost of Victory ⎬ Australians at War
Greece, Crete & Syria 1941 ⎭
Holy War: Islam Fights
World War 1 in Postcards
Scotland's Soldiers (with John Baynes)

General
The Hunger to Come (Food and Population Crises)
New Geography 1966–67
New Geography 1968–69
New Geography 1970–71
Anatomy of Captivity (Political Prisoners)
Devil's Goad
Fedayeen (The Arab-Israeli Dilemma)
The Arab Mind
The Israeli Mind
The Dagger of Islam
The PLO Connections
The Arabs as Master Slavers
Know the Middle East

And other titles

The World in Conflict 1989

War Annual 3

*Contemporary warfare described
and analysed*

JOHN LAFFIN

BRASSEY'S DEFENCE PUBLISHERS
(a member of the Maxwell Pergamon Publishing Corporation plc)

LONDON · OXFORD · WASHINGTON · NEW YORK · BEIJING
FRANKFURT · SÃO PAULO · SYDNEY · TOKYO · TORONTO

U.K. (Editorial)	Brassey's Defence Publishers Ltd., 24 Gray's Inn Road, London WC1X 8HR, England
(Orders)	Brassey's Defence Publishers Ltd., Headington Hill Hall, Oxford OX3 0BW, England
U.S.A. (Editorial)	Pergamon-Brassey's International Defense Publishers, Inc., 8000 Westpark Drive, Fourth Floor, McLean, Virginia 22102, U.S.A.
(Orders)	Pergamon Press, Inc., Maxwell House, Fairview Park, Elmsford, New York 10523, U.S.A.
PEOPLE'S REPUBLIC OF CHINA	Pergamon Press, Room 4037, Qianmen Hotel, Beijing, People's Republic of China
FEDERAL REPUBLIC OF GERMANY	Pergamon Press GmbH, Hammerweg 6, D-6242 Kronberg, Federal Republic of Germany
BRAZIL	Pergamon Editora Ltda, Rua Eça de Queiros, 346, CEP 04011, Paraiso, São Paulo, Brazil
AUSTRALIA	Pergamon-Brassey's Defence Publishers Pty Ltd., P.O. Box 544, Potts Point, N.S.W. 2011, Australia
JAPAN	Pergamon Press, 5th Floor, Matsuoka Central Building, 1–7–1 Nishishinjuku, Shinjuku-ku, Tokyo 160, Japan
CANADA	Pergamon Press Canada Ltd., Suite No. 271, 253 College Street, Toronto, Ontario, Canada, M5T 1R5

First edition 1989

A CIP catalogue record for this book is available from the Library of Congress and the British Library.

ISBN 0 08 036265 6

Printed in Great Britain by A. Wheaton & Co. Ltd., Exeter

Contents

WAR TRENDS

Introduction

Anybody who writes about war can never be short of material; therefore as many wars are described in **WAR ANNUAL 3** as in **WAR ANNUAL 2**. Two conflicts had a predictably short fighting period and are no longer in these pages. They are: the US raid on Libya in April 1986 and the 'small war' of Togo in September 1986. However, new wars or subsidiary actions to existing wars took their place.

In two major wars, moves towards peace were made during 1988. The Soviet Union began to withdraw its troops from Afghanistan on 15 May and Vietnam started a withdrawal from Kampuchea. The Soviet Union expects to have all of its men out of Afghanistan by early 1989 while Vietnam named 1990 as the final withdrawal date.

In neither case does this mean the end of fighting. In Afghanistan war will continue, probably with greater ferocity, between the Mujahideen guerrillas and the Communist government. In Kampuchea, conflict between the parties of democratic moderation and the infamous and murderous Khmer Rouge army seems inevitable.

A lull occurred in the long war between Libya and Chad but given the unpredictable nature of Libya's President, Colonel Gaddafi, it could break out again at any time. Genuine and determined efforts were made to restore peace in Central America, especially in Nicaragua, but they achieved little more than a temporary cessation of hostilities. In Central America, it seems, peace cannot come about unless one side in a war is completely subjugated.

Talk of negotiation and peace—rather than talks about peace—raised hopes concerning the wars in Angola and Sri Lanka but they were short-lived. When opposing armies have been at each other's throats for years compromise has little meaning.

In Israel's administered territories of the West Bank and Gaza a new type of war—*intifada*—erupted. *Intifada* is Arabic for uprising and this particular Palestinian uprising is described in the book. Israel, the Palestinians and the Arab states see it as a war. It is a peculiar kind of war and I might assess it as serious and sustained civil disobedience, but when the parties concerned refer to it as a war, then a war it must be. Much the same comment could be made about the conflict in New Caledonia, which the French army and the opposing Kanaks refer to as a war.

Following publication of **WAR ANNUAL 2**, I was several times asked to name the 'worst war'. All wars are 'worst' wars. Guatemala has been called the 'dirtiest war' because of its many murders, massacres and 'disappearances'. It is no dirtier than the cluster of conflicts which afflict Lebanon or Indonesia's war in East Timor or the IRA's massacres in Northern Ireland. Indeed, the Guatemalan war may be a little less dirty than the vicious war which ravages Mozambique and the genocidal wars waged by the armies of Bangladesh and Burma against their minorities.

The most surprising war in the period covered by this book is that waged by

Ethiopia against the fighters of Eritrea and Tigré. Astonishingly, the 'guerrillas' of these regions inflicted major defeats on the Ethiopian army in pitched battles.

The biggest and most dangerous war was undoubtedly that between Iran and Iraq, the Gulf War. It was big in the size of the forces involved and the area over which they fought, dangerous in the risk it posed to world peace. It, too, was a dirty war with frequent use of gas by Iraq and of teenage martyrs by Iran.

To understand all the wars in real depth I advise readers to refer back to **WAR ANNUAL 1** and **WAR ANNUAL 2**, both of which are available.

War remains a growth industry. Despite the superpowers' negotiations on arms control—which have had some success—there are few negotiations about 'conventional' weapons. Arms control talks concern nuclear weapons, which have not killed anybody since old-fashioned atom bombs were dropped on Hiroshima and Nagasaki in 1945. Small-arms fire and grenades kill soldiers and civilians, somewhere, every day. The use of nuclear weapons *is* controlled. Control of lesser weapons is not yet contemplated and may be impossible.

London   JOHN LAFFIN

The Wars

Afghanistan Resistance War

Background Summary

The Soviet Union invaded Afghanistan in December 1979, for the stated reason of helping the Afghan government and army to 'maintain control over rebellious elements'. President Hafisullah Amin was killed in the fighting and Babrak Karmal succeeded him. Groups of Mujahideen or holy war warriors, mostly tribesmen from the mountains, opposed the allied Soviet forces and the Afghan regular army. These combined armies controlled parts of Afghanistan and caused a large-scale flow of refugees to Pakistan, but they were unable to subdue the Mujahideen. At the end of 1985 the two armies dominated only 35% of the country. The Soviet High Command built up a vast military infrastructure to help the 'Democratic Republic of Afghanistan' (DRA).

Summary of the War in 1987

Throughout this period virtually all the Soviet's military and political actions were based on its 'three preconditions for victory'. They were: neutralization of the guerrilla leadership; destruction of the popular base of the revolution by inflicting intolerable suffering on the civilian population; isolation of guerrilla groups from lines of supply.

The existence of the countrywide resistance depended primarily on the ability of the political leadership in Peshawar, Pakistan, to infiltrate commanders, instructions and weapons into the interior. Well aware of this, the Afghan regime and Soviet leaders attempted to destroy or render inoperable the few centres of logistical support in Paktia, near the Pakistan border.

However, the Mujahideen surprised their enemies by their ability to sustain their resistance. Several guerrilla leaders not only held out against all pressure but inflicted military defeats on the combined DRA and Soviet forces. The major leaders of the period were Abdul Haq, Ismael Khan, Rakhim Wardak, Jalaluddin Haqqani and Ahmad Shah Massood.

With Babrak Karmal unable to make progress against the Resistance, the Soviet High Command replaced him with Dr. Muhammad Najibullah, former head of the KHAD or security police and known to his followers as Comrade Najib. Presented as a figure of genuine national reconciliation, Najib worked hard to project this image but did not convince the Mujahideen. He also unavailingly tried to weaken Pakistan's help for the guerrillas. Even so, there was growing domestic pressure on the government in Islamabad to make a deal with the Kabul regime.

The Kabul government permitted the Soviet Union to annex the Wakhan corridor, the thin strategic finger of Afghanistan which reaches east to the Chinese

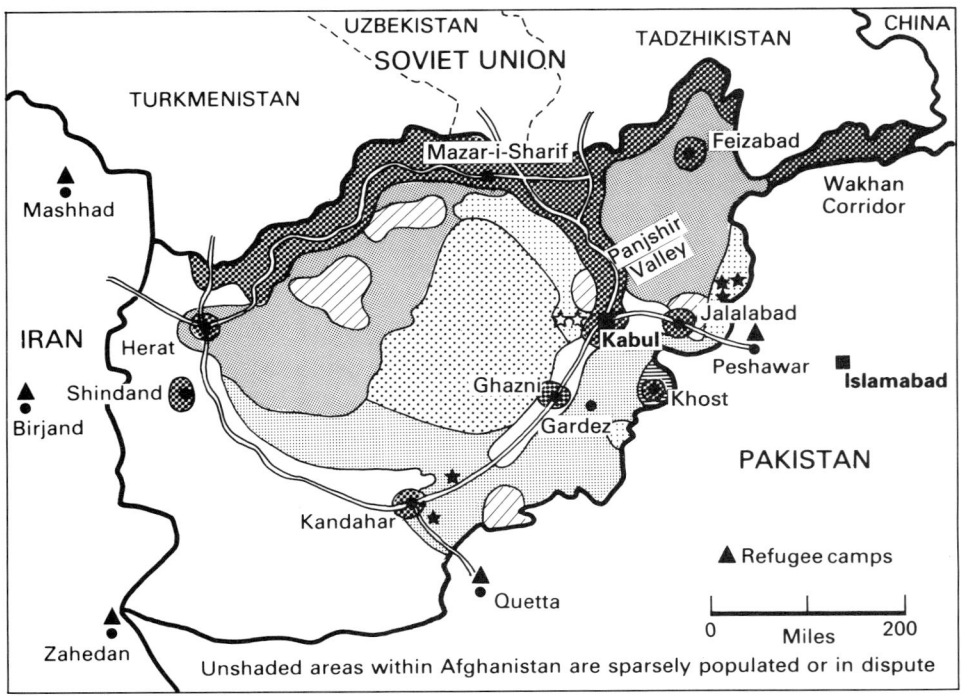

Unshaded areas within Afghanistan are sparsely populated or in dispute

The Afghanistan Resistance

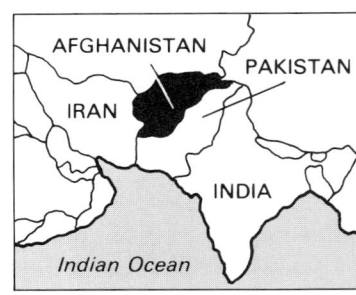

Fundamentalists

Jamiat-i-Islami; led by Barhannudin Rabbani. Regarded as the best fighters.

Hezb-i-Islami; led by Younis Khalis. Second only to Jamiat in quality.

Hezb-i-Islami breakaway faction; led by Gulbuddin Heckmatyar. Receives the most arms but has third best fighting strength.

☆ Ittehad-i-Islami; led by Rasul Sayyaf; backed by Saudis.

Traditionalists

Harakat-i-Inqilib; led by Nabi Mohammedi. An inefficient group.

National Islamic Front of Afghanistan; led by Pir Sayyed Ahmed Gailani; many religious followers.

★ National Front for the Rescue of Afghanistan; led by Sigbatullah Mojadedi, a monarchist.

Minor Resistance Groups

Shia Muslims. Much talk but little action.

Other groups, either non-aligned or with mixed loyalties.

The Communists

The People's Democratic Party of Afghanistan, with Soviet support. The PDA is an amalgam of the Parcham and Khalq factions. President Najibullah (Comrade Najib) is a Parchamite. The second most important figure is Muhammad Gulabzoi, a Khalqi and the Interior Minister. Parcham-Khalq enmity is notoriously bitter.

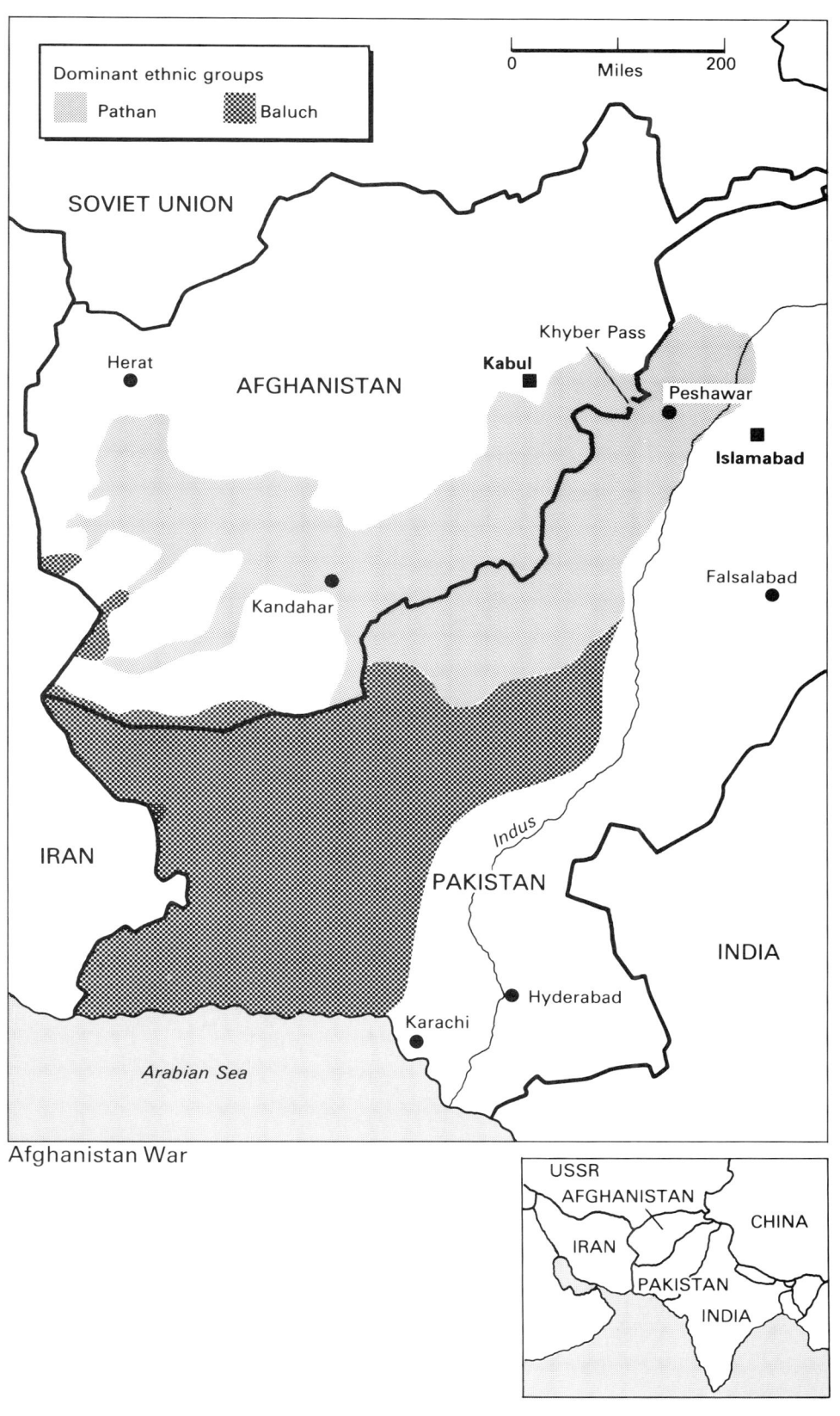

Afghanistan War

Legend: Dominant ethnic groups — Pathan, Baluch

Scale: 0 — Miles — 200

Labels: SOVIET UNION, AFGHANISTAN, Herat, Kabul, Khyber Pass, Peshawar, Islamabad, Falsalabad, Kandahar, IRAN, Indus, PAKISTAN, INDIA, Hyderabad, Karachi, Arabian Sea

Inset: USSR, AFGHANISTAN, IRAN, PAKISTAN, CHINA, INDIA

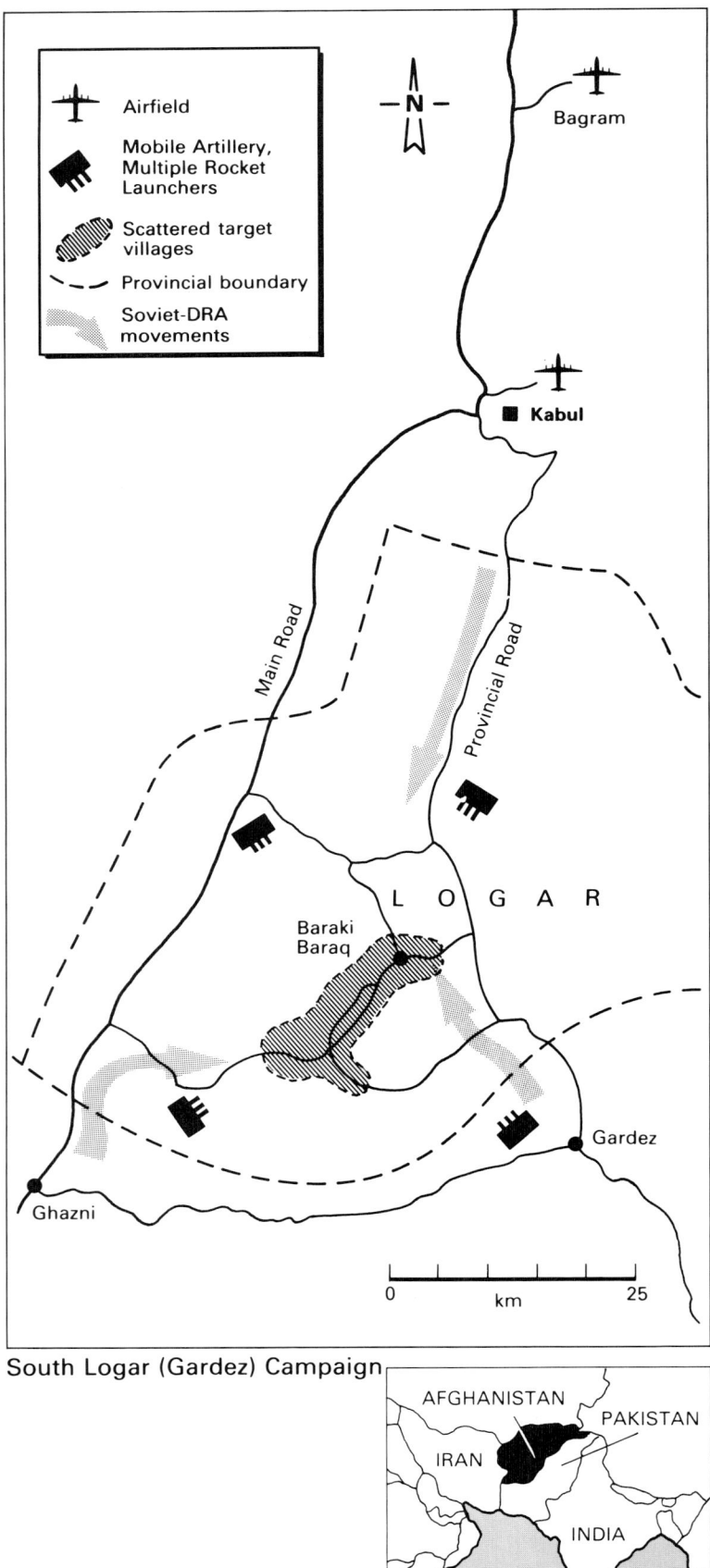

South Logar (Gardez) Campaign

border. This gives the Soviet command a 288 km border with Pakistan and cuts off China from Pakistan.

The Soviet sense of desperation about the expensive and politically embarrassing campaign was shown by their use of chemical warfare but this had no discernible effect in reducing the guerrillas' capacity to fight. At the same time, the guerrillas were counter-attacking with US Stinger and British Blowpipe missiles. The Soviet forces lost several helicopters and even some jet fighters to these missiles.

The Soviet army's General Staff had valued the Afghanistan campaign as a proving ground for matériel and as a training area for troops and air force personnel. By mid-1987 more than 400,000 Soviet personnel, including 33,000 officers, had rotated through Afghanistan. Without Afghanistan experience, promotion became virtually impossible in the Soviet army. The Afghanistan venture resulted in major changes in Soviet organization by 1987. For instance, the command structure was decentralized, with the intention of bringing about more rapid responses to enemy movements. At the same time, area commanders were given greater authority to act on their own initiative.

The War in 1987-88

Foreign Support for Guerrillas

On several occasions during 1988 the US administration assured the Resistance leaders that Washington would not reduce its support. In the twelve months to the end of May 1988, the US gave the Mujahideen more than $630 million in military aid. US Under-Secretary of State for Political Affairs, Michael Armacost, made a special trip to Islamabad to meet guerrillas. Later, one of them, Pir Sayyed Ahmed Gailani, leader of the moderate National Islamic Front, said: 'The US has explicitly assured us that they will not cut any deal with the Soviets behind our backs and that no settlement can take place which is not to our full satisfaction.'[1]

At this time the US supported the proposal to set up an elected *Shura* or Islamic council among the four million refugees in Pakistan, as well as exiles in Europe and fighters in Afghanistan.

Jihad has become an even stronger element in the fighting in Afghanistan. A young *Hezb-i-Islami* commander, Hashem Hafni, told an American correspondent: 'The most important thing in the Koran is *jihad*. For us religion is more important than land. We are fighting for Islam.'[2]

In the Persian-speaking West, which is a mostly non-tribal area, the *Jamiat-i-Islam* commander, Ismael Khan, operating in Herat Province, has achieved an impressive degree of military organization. His main problems have been the long supply lines from Pakistan and the unco-operative attitude of Iran. The Iranians, being Shi'a Muslims, have been reluctant to help the Sunni Muslims of Herat.

At the beginning of 1988 the President's brother, Sidiq, aged 36, defected to the Resistance movement. Sidiq, interviewed in the Panjshir valley, called Najib a 'charlatan and a power-mad Nero unable to tolerate people with different opinions'. The defection was not politically significant as Sidiq was not known to be active in the People's Democratic Party of Afghanistan (PDPA), but it was personally embarrassing to Najib.[3]

Afghan Mujahideen rebels having knocked out a Soviet tank, face towards Mecca in prayer. The guard on the tank watches their rear in case government troops should appear.

Mujahideen Resistance fighters wearing Soviet-made chemical warfare equipment captured from Russian soldiers. Since the Mujahideen have no gas or other chemical weapons, the masks suggest that the Soviet army in Afghanistan was ready to use them. (Courtesy Express Newspapers.)

The Soviet Union and Pakistan

The political climate in Pakistan does not displease the Soviet leaders, despite rumours to the contrary. They observe with satisfaction that the country is anti-American because the US objects to Pakistan's nuclear policy. Similarly, the Pakistani regime is interested in Russian hints that, should American aid dry up, Soviet aid could be forthcoming. Unrest in Pakistan itself encourages the Russians to believe that they will be able to manipulate certain factions in the country.

Occasionally, Soviet criticism of Pakistan is savage. For instance, the daily *Soviet Russia* declared on 5 January 1988: 'Pakistan is the Trojan horse of the Pentagon strategists in Asia. It has become a tool in the undeclared war of imperialism against Afghanistan.'

The Russians intend to get what they can out of the Baluchistan card. Leaders of a movement for an independent Baluchistan—which is part of Pakistan—have been given sanctuary in Afghanistan. If the Soviet leaders wanted to put more pressure on Pakistan to stop aiding the Afghan rebels it could give arms to the Baluchis and encourage them to use them. For the moment, the Baluchis are controlled, perhaps because the Soviet leaders believe that they can make Pakistan compliant without stirring up rebellion.

Looking south from Moscow, they can see a line of generally co-operative states. Syria is very friendly, India is friendly, Pakistan is becoming more friendly and Iran is responding to friendly gestures. Afghanistan is forbidden to be unfriendly.

As Russians See the War

Beginning on 1 January 1988, Soviet television began to give the war extensive coverage. Relief supplies were shown reaching Khost. In February a programme which dealt with the Afghan government's attempt to drag the country out of its mediaeval stagnation admitted that the Soviet Union had helped it to go too far, too fast. Other programmes allowed servicemen to complain that Russian reporters had given a false impression of the fighting; it had been much more serious than reports indicated. In March 1988 a young soldier criticized the 'stereotyped propaganda which shows the guerrillas as bandits waging war against their own people while Russian troops protected the women and children'.

A *Pravda* commentator admitted that the Soviet Press had been unprepared for the war's length. Many people, writing to newspaper editors, complained about official indifference to the difficulties of returning home from the war. One soldier, inquiring about the benefits to which his service entitled him, was told that this was classified information. Since no official memorials to the war dead of the Afghanistan fighting were being built, ex-servicemen in Ashkhabad, near the Afghan border, built a monument themselves, with official approval. All these signs of openness are regarded as startlingly unusual. Only days after the Soviet army began to pull out of Afghanistan, on 15 May 1988, the Army HQ in Moscow announced that 15,000 serviceman had so far been killed.

Rebuilding a Guerrilla Base

During 1988 a systematic attempt was made by the Supervisory Council of the North, founded by Ahmad Shah Massood, to establish bases within Afghanistan for the conduct of guerrilla war. No previous attempt had been successful, hence the dependence of the resistance movements on bases in Pakistan. Since sole bases had not survived enemy attack, Massood and his colleagues have been building economically mutually supporting bases. The more the bases proliferate, the Council leaders believe, the more difficult it is for the Soviet or Afghan government troops to deal with. Most of the bases are in the valleys of the northern Hindu Kush, one of the wildest parts of Asia. The Council has encouraged local people to take over the leadership of the communities.

The Council is co-ordinating military and civil activities of the *Jamiat-i-Islami* groups more efficiently than ever before. It exercises general control over most rural areas of Parwan, Kapisa, Takhar, Baghlan and Kunduz provinces, together with large portions of Badakhshan Province in the extreme north-east. North-eastern Afghanistan is inhabited mainly by ethnic Tajiks and Uzbeks gathered into farming communities. The non-tribal nature of their society has enabled the creation of a unified command structure.

In contrast, in Afghanistan's south and south-east, dominated by rival ethnic Pathan tribes, no effective military and civil organization exists. Most of Afghanistan local commanders, even those belonging to the same resistance party, operate independently of each other.

Massood and the Supervisory Council of the North foresee a protracted war of resistance, regardless of the withdrawal of the Soviet troops. Massood himself wants the war to continue until Afghanistan becomes a completely Islamic state on the Iranian model. He is one leader who sees no rule, not even a temporary one, for King Zahir, the former monarch of Afghanistan. Massood's strategy appears to owe something to Chinese and Vietnamese guerrilla experience, but in an interview[4] he said that this was not a paramount factor. He and his colleagues had studied the lessons from China, Vietnam and elsewhere but no blueprint fitted the problems of Afghanistan.

According to Massood's analysis of the war, the resistance is going through a long 'active defence' phase. During this period, which might last for years, it is necessary to expand and develop base areas, to educate the populace in Islamic ideology and to refine the military organization. The overall objective is to deny the countryside to the government forces and squeeze them into the provincial cities. Fear would keep them there.

Massood believes that 'within a few years' resistance forces, trained and experienced in conventional fighting, will be able to take the offensive. In this phase of the war the Resistance movement's objective will be to cut all communication between the regime-held towns and cities. The end effect would be collapse of the government and a popular uprising.

This change from guerrilla warfare to a type of conventional warfare obviously requires the guerrillas to be much more mobile, with armoured personnel carriers, self-propelled guns and even light tanks. Massood sees no difficulty in obtaining supplies and little danger of his forces being brought to the point of a pitched conventional battle, which he acknowledges they could not win. His troops will disengage before the enemy can properly deploy for battle.

The Abdul Haq Interview

While passing through London in March 1988 the redoubtable military commander of the *Hezb-i-Islami* group, Abdul Haq, was received by Mrs. Thatcher, a significant indicator of British support for the Afghanistan Resistance. In an exclusive interview with *Jane's Defence Weekly*,[5] Haq made several important observations about aspects of the war and, as he has had nine years' combat experience, they must be considered important.

Haq said that Soviet *Spetsnaz* troops, for all their training and skill, were not suited for warfare in Afghanistan. While conceding the *Spetsnaz* soldiers' formidable skills, Haq pointed out that they were not needed for reconnaissance because the Russians could see all they needed to from reconnaissance aircraft. They could not safely parachute in the rugged mountains and they could not move at night because that was when the Mujahideen moved. The Afghanistan experience must have proved to the Soviet High Command that *Spetsnaz* men are much more useful in conventional warfare than in fighting guerrillas.

Haq has found that ordinary Soviet conscript troops have been taught how to attack but not to defend. This is in keeping with the Soviet doctrine of paramount offensive; defence is given little consideration.

According to Haq, some Western accounts have exaggerated the effect of Stinger and Blowpipe missiles on the course of the war. 'How could we stop all the Soviet aircraft because we have twenty-five or thirty Stingers?' he said. However, the Mujahideen have used many hundreds of Stingers and Haq's assessment of them differs sharply from that of Massood, who is as experienced as Haq. Haq's comments may have been disinformation for the purpose of inducing the Americans to give him even more Stingers.

Haq criticized the Soviet leaders as two-faced. They demanded impossible conditions. In any case, they did not need nine months to withdraw. He believed that even when they did leave they wanted an excuse to come back. He opposed any agreement reached in Geneva, if only because the Mujahideen were not party to discussions.

Abdul Haq leaves nothing to chance. In the building which serves as a military school, films and slides of battle are methodically analysed and discussed. Miniature tanks in a sandbox reproduce battle movements, just as in any Western army academy. Haq has a network of informers in every ministry; most of them belong to the *Khalq*, one of the two groups forming the PDPA. He has detailed plans showing how Kabul's water, electricity and transport systems work and claims that he can cut electricity to any given district depending on the requirements of the Resistance.

Mujahideen Commanders Trained in Iran

Iran's Revolutionary Guards or Pasdaran began to train Resistance commanders at the beginning of 1987 but this did not become known until May 1988. A course lasts six months and is attended by up to 100 senior and middle-ranking Resistance leaders.

Training consists of exercises in both urban and guerrilla warfare, including demolition, use of medium and heavy arms and the laying of mines. Lengthy lectures in the theory of guerrilla warfare and anti-Western political indoctrination are included. Students on the course which finished in May 1988 believed that they could teach the Pasdaran instructors something about guerrilla warfare in the field but they were impressed by the Pasdaran's equipment and facilities.

While most Afghan Resistance men who attend the Iranian courses are Sunni Muslim—Sunnis make up eighty-eight per cent of the population—the Iranians prefer to teach the Shia Muslims. Iran is a Shia nation and the government hopes that Afghan Shias will become powerful in the army and in politics. Ayatollah Khomeini enjoys much support among the Mujahideen, whether Sunni or Shia, because they see in him a man who has united his nation against foreign interference and exploitation.

Nasr, a Shia fighting group in the central Hazarajat highlands, has received weapons and military advice from Iran since the early 1980s. *Nasr* commanders frequently make armed attacks against their less zealous Sunni allies of the Resistance. During much of 1987 and 1988 Shia ambushes of Sunni guerrillas in the region of Kurram, near the Pakistani border, disrupted rebel supply routes.

According to Sunni sources, about 6,000 Afghan Shias are subsidized by the Iranian government to study Islamic ideology in the city of Qom, one of Iran's holiest cities. Most of them will become mullahs and therefore influential in government and society.

It seems likely that Iran has supplied weapons to some of the prominent Resistance leaders, such as Massood. Some of these weapons may have found their way to Afghanistan through the tortuous pipeline opened by the Reagan administration's covert arms-for-hostages negotiations.

The long-term result of Iran's efforts to enlist support for an anti-Western Islamic revolution in Afghanistan remains to be seen, but nearly all the students return home to Afghanistan convinced that the US is more dangerous to Afghanistan than Iran is. After indoctrination, they are certain that it is US policy to divide the guerrilla groups and to change their Islamic way of life.

Role of the Stinger

During 1987 and 1988 the American-supplied anti-aircraft missile, the Stinger, did more than anything else to change the course of the war and to accelerate a Soviet withdrawal from Afghanistan. Until 1987 the Soviet High Command believed that air power was at least containing the war and in the end would win it. This was a reasonable assumption, since the Russians were unchallenged in the air. Then a plentiful supply of Stingers, used by guerrillas trained to fire them, changed everything. Late in 1987 Stingers were bringing down Soviet aircraft at the rate of one a day. This rate of loss was one of the Russians' most closely guarded secrets. Garrisons were cut off, sometimes for months, because the danger from the Stinger grounded the aircraft which would normally have protected relief columns.

The fear of missiles, even in regions where they do not exist, prompted the Russians to reduce severely and even to halt aerial attacks. Helicopter support used to be considered essential to any ground operation but during 1988 troops were deployed with little or no air cover. Instead, the Soviet command conducted slow-moving advances backed by long-range artillery and multiple rocket bombardments. They also made more night or high-altitude bombing attacks, both of which are less precise than low-level daylight raids.

In operations where helicopters are still deployed the Soviet army uses swift, hedge-hopping tactics, sometimes flying below guerrilla positions in the mountains. While this makes them difficult targets for Stingers, they become more vulnerable to conventional weapons such as heavy machine-guns, rocket-propelled grenades and even Kalashnikovs.

The Afghans have a natural understanding and feel for weapons and none of the imported weapons systems has been difficult for the guerrillas to handle. Some learnt to use the Stinger within a few hours, whereas the US manufacturers consider that several months' instruction and practice are necessary.

Realization of the Stinger's potency changed the Russians' strategic thinking and their political objectives. It made them aware of a parallel with Vietnam and they did not want to suffer the humiliation of the Americans. Several specialist analysts of the Soviet Union believe that it was the Stinger, aided by the Blowpipe missile, which determined the Russians to get out of Afghanistan, and sooner rather than later.

Islamic International Brigade

A Muslim international brigade of volunteers fought with the Mujahideen throughout 1987 and 1988. It mostly consists of Saudis, Egyptians, Pakistanis, Kuwaitis and Moroccans. They joined the brigade as a religious duty and to get experience for future revolution in their own countries. Many of the Egyptians in the Brigade are sympathizers of the Muslim Brotherhood fundamentalist movement. They were imprisoned during the crackdown that followed President Sadat's assassination and were released in 1987.

In units of roughly platoon strength, they were shared out among several Mujahideen factions. Most appear to be in their late teens and early twenties and are generally middle-class boys recruited by a fundamentalist Muslim group which provides air tickets, AK-47 rifles and preliminary training in Pakistan. Foreign observers say that their morale is high, even in the bitter cold of the Afghan mountains.

About thirty volunteers, the majority of them Saudis and Egyptians, took part in the guerrilla attack on the Soviet fortified outpost of Sumungkay, near Khost, in March. The attack, a conventional infantry assault, began with a Mujahideen artillery barrage. The Soviet commanders brought in six Sukhoi twenty-five fighter-bombers which dropped 500-kilo incendiary and cluster bombs. The guerrillas suffered no casualties and after a second abortive air attack the local Resistance commander, Abdul Manan, decided on a frontal attack.

Among the International Brigade volunteers was a former Egyptian military engineer who now prepared a Chinese-made anti-mine rocket. It screeched up Sumungkay hill towards the Soviet post, exploding all the mines in a 15 ft-wide strip. The Muslim volunteers made the first charge up the hill. Not one of them would have reached the enemy positions had the Afghan army soldiers opened up with their machine-guns. The charge was made with such spirit that the defenders' morale broke and they were soon embracing their attackers. Watching from a distance, Russian officers ordered Soviet tanks to open fire on Sumungkay, despite the presence of Afghan troops. The first round caused chaos and casualties and some Afghan soldiers ran towards Khost, while the guerrillas fired at them.

Under the barrage, the young Saudi who commanded the international contingent ordered evacuation. Since it was too dangerous to evacuate the wounded, they were quickly declared *shaheeds* or martyrs and left behind. Nevertheless, the Soviet post and its commander had been captured.

Afghan resistance leaders who command International Brigade volunteers say that they have much to learn as guerrillas but that as conventional infantry they perform well.

Western Victims of the War

Western journalists and aid workers suffered their heaviest casualties in the 1987-88 period. Many were wounded or killed in Afghan army ambushes and by the guerrillas whose cause they supported or were trying to publicize. British television cameraman Andy Skrzpkowiak, aged thirty-six, was killed by members of the *Hezb-i-Islami* led by Gulbuddin Hekmatyar. Skrzpkowiak, who had already made twelve trips to Afghanistan, was on his way to the Penjahir valley to interview Ahmad Shah Massood when he was attacked, robbed and killed.

Lee Shapiro and Jim Lindelhof, both Americans, were killed in an Afghan army ambush in Wardak province as they were returning to Pakistan after spending five months making a documentary of the war. A French freelance photographer, Alain Guillo, was captured thirty miles from the Soviet border and sentenced, in Kabul, to ten years' gaol. An Italian journalist, Fausto Biloslovo, was captured when he stumbled into an Afghan army post after becoming separated from the guerrilla group he was accompanying. Some guerrilla groups have deteriorated from resistance fighters into bandit gangs.

As a war, Afghanistan is one of the most difficult to cover. A reporter never has a complete overview of the situation. Australian film-maker Chris Hooke said: 'What you are seeing in one valley or province may only be the case in that particular area. The situation might be completely different in one or two valleys over. And then, by the time you get out, everything has changed.'

Even after more than eight years, Afghanistan remains one of the least reported conflicts of the century. No more than a hundred Western journalists report from inside Afghanistan each year. This does not include the foreign journalists allowed to visit Kabul but whose movements are restricted to the capital and a few other government-controlled areas. In contrast, 2,000 reporters, photographers and cameramen covered the Vietnam conflict at its height.

Diplomats, international relief workers and journalists are worried that the lack of coverage means that the public is not receiving reliable information. Peter Gilapin of 'Freedom Medicine', a US relief agency which is training Afghan paramedics for work in Resistance-held areas, said: 'When you realize what's going on out here it's pretty terrifying.'

Reporting in Afghanistan is hazardous. Most journalists have experienced ambushes, air bombardments and land mines. They travel in extreme discomfort and have to worry about informers who might report their presence to the authorities. Both the Soviet Army and the DRA threatened to execute journalists entering Afghanistan 'illegally'.

Despite the obstacles, individual journalists work with great enterprise and enthusiasm. Some, dressed in Afghan garb, roam for months with packhorses through the remote northern and north-eastern regions. Edward Gorman of *The Times* was smuggled into Kabul by guerrillas on reconnaissance and, dressed as a Soviet officer, driven around the city in a jeep.

During 1987 and 1988 efforts were being made to train Afghan nationals to report the war. Boston University runs a programme in Peshawar to train Afghan journalists and cameramen in an attempt to improve the war's coverage.

Among the most experienced of reporters in Afghanistan is Edward Girardet, a French journalist, who writes for *Christian Science Monitor* as well as French newspapers.

Reporting from Zadran Valley, early in 1988, Arthur Kent of *The Observer*, London, found the guerrillas with frayed nerves, inadequate equipment and supplies, and lacking in incisive leadership. 'Response to enemy ground movements', he reported, 'was slow and tentative'. Commander Nezmuddin, second-in-command to Jalaluddin Haqqani in the Zadran Valley, bemoaned the guerrillas' lack of artillery which would fire up to fifteen miles. Kent believed that the 'ragged irregulars were just hanging on'. However, in other areas, equally competent reporters found the guerrillas in good heart and militarily dominant.[6]

The Southern Logar Offensive

On 9 October 1987 guerrillas ambushed and killed an Afghan government militia commander, in southern Logar Province, sixty miles from Kabul. Soviet/Afghan air and ground forces mounted a major campaign of reprisal. Armoured columns with air cover converged on the sparsely populated farming region, intending to trap the guerrillas responsible.

The guerrillas avoided the assault force by taking to the hills or by creeping out of the area under cover of darkness. In small groups, they clashed by night with enemy patrols. Frustrated with lack of progress in capturing or killing guerrillas, the Soviet commander ordered daytime searches of many small settlements around the town of Baraki Baraq. In one village an Mi-8 helicopter carrying a squad of troops touched down on a land mine and exploded in flames. Thirty-six paratroopers died.

Fearing that they were under attack, other pilots quickly withdrew. The Soviet-DRA attackers then set up a heavy artillery barrage from mobile artillery and BM-27 Multi-Rocket System batteries. Following this attack the Soviet leader sent in tank columns which destroyed any buildings missed by the shellfire.

After twelve days, the Russian and government troops withdrew, having lost five tanks, six helicopters and perhaps 100 men. They had killed 260 civilians but no more than a score of guerrillas. The expensive offensive graphically showed the difficulties faced by the Soviet and DRA troops in coming to grips with the elusive guerrillas.

Capture of Koran

The tactical skill and fighting ability of the Mujahideen has rarely, if ever, been better shown than in the capture of the garrison town of Koran, in the Monjan Valley, north-east of Kabul, at the end of 1987. The attack plan was the work of Ahmad Shah Massood. With his senior lieutenants, he prepared the operation in meticulous detail, using videotapes and enlarged photographs of the target area. In addition, Massood had built a table-top scale model of the fortress area which showed every building and weapon position. From defectors he learnt that the garrison consisted of 298 men, what weapons they possessed and their daily routine.

In a series of planning sessions attended by a small group of Western reporters, Massood briefed the commanders of his 550-man assault force and gave each of them a specific mission. A man of great authority, Massood is more methodical in his military tactics than all the other faction leaders. He covered his attacking troops by putting support units in the mountains above Koran. They included crews armed with US-supplied Stinger missiles to defend against Afghan jets or helicopter gunships that might be called in to hit Massood's force.

The surprise attack at dawn caught the garrison commander in bed, where he was killed. The main army post, the military police compound and the protecting posts fell one by one. The government's conscript troops threw down their weapons. Only a unit of KHAD, the secret police, resisted throughout the morning before being overrun at midday. Massood's casualties were fourteen killed and eleven wounded, while the government lost twenty-nine killed and 266 captured. Massood regarded his own casualties as unacceptably high and said that they had resulted from the failure of some support weapons to reach mountain positions under cover of darkness before the assault.

Relief of Khost

The DRA army, helped by the Soviet forces, put a strong garrison into Khost as far back as 1981 and the Mujahideen at once laid siege to the town, which had a total population of 40,000 including the garrison of 8,000. The significance of Khost in the war cannot be overestimated. Its importance is strategic, psychological and tactical. Strategically, it commands the mouth of a frontier pass, only twenty-five miles from the Pakistan border. The Resistance need the route through the wide, scrubby valley to transport supplies to the guerrillas deep in the country. During 1987-88 it became ever more important as vast supplies of ammunition passed through to feed the build-up of heavy weapons.

Khost became a symbol for both sides. For the Soviet and DRA forces it was a matter of pride and prestige not only to hold the town, which has 40,000 civilians, but to break the siege. For the Mujahideen, Khost became almost sacred in its significance.

The relief of Khost became the Soviet Army's most ambitious winter offensive since the invasion in 1979. A joint Soviety-DRA ground and air force of more than 20,000 set out from Gardez, fifty-five miles away, to force its way through guerrilla-held country to relieve the garrison and drive off the guerrillas. Operating under the orders of Jalaluddin Haqqani, the Mujahideen were fighting more as regular soldiers than guerrillas, since they had established fixed positions from which to threaten the town and prevent movement in and out.

In December 1987 Soviet commanders used armour, artillery and air support to protect a large convoy of supply trucks along the dirt road. T-72 tanks manoeuvred over the Zadran plain ahead of the trucks, artillery was positioned in the foothills and DRA soldiers were sent as skirmishers into the hills. Soviet SU-25 ground-attack planes also sought out guerrilla positions in the hills. In principle, the Soviet-DRA advance was using the same methods of approach as had the British in many Afghan campaigns before aircraft and tanks existed.

Having only light guns and multi-barrel rocket launchers of short range, the guerrillas could not hit the targets on the plain, but themselves came under fire from Soviet heavy artillery. The guerrilla leaders took on the only targets left to them, the DRA units pressing into the hills. During mortar and machine-gun duels, the DRA troops suffered heavy casualties, since they were operating in country which the guerrillas knew well.

The greatest danger to the guerrillas were the 1,000lb bombs dropped by the SU-25 warplanes. Up to 300 were killed in these attacks but the survivors moved to fresh positions. To force them out, the Soviet command sent in Red Army airborne soldiers. One group was landed by helicopters close to hidden guerrillas, who held their fire until the helicopters were lifting off. Then they opened up with light machine-guns and rifles. Not one of the forty-four Russians was left alive and the helicopters were damaged.

As in other operations during 1988, the Soviet air force dropped by night huge flares suspended on parachutes, in an effort to catch guerrillas moving into position.

The action to relieve Khost was successful but it took six weeks, cost probably 150 Soviet and DRA dead and left the guerrillas still holding the heights. They were unable to impede further enemy movement in the valley below but the DRA and Soviet army abandoned all attempts to drive them from the hills. Heavy fighting continued as up to 10,000 guerrillas continued to ambush Soviet convoys on the road from Kabul through Gardez to Khost. Rebel leaders claimed to have shot down twelve Soviet warplanes and helicopters, mostly with Stinger missiles.

The relief of Khost in no way damaged the morale of the besieging guerrillas or reduced their ability to operate. Camel caravans arrived daily from the Pakistan border, bringing in fresh arms and supplies. Trained paramedics treated the wounded and evacuated the badly wounded to hospitals in Pakistan. Mujahideen casualties were probably 120 dead and 250 wounded.

The troops who forced their way through to Khost found that this was not the end of the action. The trucks had to leave Khost and run the gauntlet of Mujahideen fire before they reached safety. Many were destroyed in the open valley.

Massacre at Kolalgu

On 16 January 1988 about 200 guerrillas, mostly from the *Hezb-i-Islami* party, were asleep in the village of Kolalgu, seventeen miles east of Ghazni. En-route to the northern provinces of Takhir and Badakhshan, with a long mule and horse train of arms and ammunition, they were waiting for nightfall to resume their dangerous journey.

The place has a population of only 1,000 and, being a remote farming community, the people had seen little of the war. The Soviet command in the garrison town of Ghazni had been tipped off about the presence of the guerrillas in Kolalgu and sent in about forty tanks and armoured personnel carriers, with two helicopter gunships low overhead.

When they heard the noise of the approaching Soviet column the peasants were terrified. The village chiefs urged the guerrillas to leave quickly and a few did. Most, however, preferred to fight the Russians from the village, which was soon surrounded. Afghan soldiers, familiar with the area, led the Russians across the fields and into the narrow lanes. In exchanges of fire, the Soviet troops killed some guerrillas and captured thirteen of them.

These were taken to the mosque in the village square. Two, hands tied behind their back, were machine-gunned outside a house as a warning to villagers that helping the Resistance was dangerous. Meanwhile the soldiers built up a great heap of mines, rockets, mortar shells and explosives in the mosque. The bound prisoners were forced to sit beside the pile, which was then detonated by a cable mine. The enormous blast demolished the mosque and blow most of the guerrillas to pieces. Two, though terribly injured, survived. The house next to the mosque collapsed, killing seven children. The raiding force roared off back to Ghazni.

It is almost certain that the raiders were from the Soviet 191st Motorized Rifle Regiment. The Kolalgu massacre was a small one compared with others during the Afghan war but it assumes greater importance than the others because there is so much evidence about it. In the village at the time was a young Afghan reporter, Ahmad Masoud, who had been trained by the Peshawar-based Afghan Media Resource Centre, founded by the Boston University School of Journalism. Masoud had a camera with him and recorded the results of the Soviet attack.

The Observer, which first reported the massacre,[7] speculated that it could become as notorious as My Lai in Vietnam. This seems unlikely, since nobody is in a position to identify the individual Soviet soldiers responsible. World opinion forced the US administration to investigate My Lai but the only body capable of pressing for an inquiry into Kolalgu is Amnesty International. In time an Islamic government taking over from Najib might wish to make political capital out of the massacre but punishment of Soviet personnel is inconceivable.

Soviet Withdrawal

The Geneva agreement on Soviet withdrawal from Afghanistan was signed on 14 April 1988. Its main provision was that between 15 May 1988 and 15 February 1989, the Soviet army of 115,000 would leave Afghanistan, half of them before 15 August.

The Soviet withdrawal was not as politically damaging to the Soviet leadership as the US withdrawal from Vietnam to the Americans. The Soviet army never committed itself fully in Afghanistan. Its main military mission was always the holding of certain key points and the roads which connect them. It was hoped that from these bases a friendly Afghan élite army could be trained and then sent out to bring more of the country under government control.

Even after the agreement was signed, the Mujahideen groups were suspicious of Soviet promises of total withdrawal. During the week before the withdrawal began guerrilla groups hit targets wherever they could find them. They themselves suffered so many casualties that in Peshawar, Pakistan, the hospitals were crammed with more war wounded than at anytime for years. The groups swore to take reprisals until all Soviet troops were out of Afghanistan.

Najib showed no unease about the departure of the Soviet army. He said that he would not allow the formation of a coalition government. He would remain president until his seven-year term expired in 1994 and his DRA army was ready to deal 'a heavy blow' against the Mujahideen if they refused to stop fighting.[8]

The Soviet Union, many Afghans say, wants to leave behind a civil war which would justify Soviet claims that it had entered Afghanistan only to bring stability. These responsible and moderate Afghanis are worried that the various Resistance factions will turn on one another as they manoeuvre for power. A complex civil war was the most likely outcome of the Soviet departure.

The Ultimate Refuge

According to diplomatic sources in Kabul, the government proposes to create a northern province by dividing the mountainous southern parts of Balkh and Juzjan provinces from their flat northern regions, which border the Soviet Union. These would then be merged to form a new province, Sari Pul. Balkh and Juzjan would thus have a defensible border and make it easier for the Soviet Union to annex part of Afghanistan's north.

The Gorbachev regime feels obliged to provide a sanctuary and homeland for the 75,000 dedicated Communists who could be in danger of their lives when the Soviet withdrawal is completed. Mazir-i-Sharif will be the capital of the Communist enclave. The Marxist Afghan government, say the diplomats in Kabul, will retreat there, should the Mujahideen take over the country.

Mujahideen Transitional Government Plans

The Mujahideen have become increasingly successful in co-ordinating their military efforts. They are also beginning to develop a common political strategy. In May 1987 it was reported that the Alliance might set up an elected *shura* or council with some 300 members as the nucleus of a new political system. In January 1988, the Alliance leaders announced plans to form a transitional government. In a communiqué issued on 23 February, the Alliance spelled out some of their ideas, proposing the creation of a 28-member Cabinet composed of fourteen ministers from among the Resistance leaders, seven representatives of the refugees and seven Muslims 'presently living within Afghanistan'. On 25 February, the Alliance further announced that it had nominated Ahmad Shah Massood as deputy leader of *Ittehad-i-Islami*, to be head of state and government in a transitional government. Shah, an Ahmadzai Pushtun from the Kabul area, trained as an engineer in the United States and later taught at the King Faisal University in Saudia Arabia. Senior members of all seven resistance parties were put forward for Cabinet rank.[9]

According to international relief representatives and observers with experience inside Afghanistan, the best chance for restoring peace lies with proven regional commanders of the 'Resistance of the Interior', rather than with leaders of the seven-party political alliance in Peshawar.

An estimated 850 local and regional commanders are believed to control over 80 per cent of the country. They are closer to the needs of civilians than the Alliance leaders. By contrast, the Alliance has no base inside Afghanistan, although its leaders were proposing to establish a provisional government across the border, possibly at Jagi in Paktia Province.

Return of the Monarchy?

The former King Zahir of Afghanistan, deposed by a Communist coup while visiting Italy in 1973, is widely regarded as the one Afghan leader capable of uniting the many factions and of forming a stable government. Aged seventy-three and living in a heavily-guarded villa near Rome, he would return not as a king but as head of a 'neutral' cabinet. Later he might become a constitutional monarch, with prestige but no political power.

The idea of King Zahir's return was that of the former US Secretary of State, Henry Kissinger, who suggested it to Dr. Armand Hammer, a man close to the Soviet leadership. He is also a friend of Zahir. In turn, Hammer sought approval from President Zia of Pakistan, Anatoli Dobrynin, Chief Foreign Policy Adviser in Moscow and US Secretary of State Shultz. Indirectly, the British Prime Minister was asked for her approval.

King Zahir's terms are: a free hand to form a neutral but national, independent government; withdrawal of the entire Soviet army; exile to Russia of Dr. Najib and his closest collaborators, probably 3,000 of them. A year later Zahir would hold free, democratic elections. Three years later a general amnesty would permit all collaborators of the Russians to return, even Dr. Najib.

Lessons from Afghanistan

Both the Soviet Union and NATO countries are studying the lessons of the Afghan War, now that Soviet involvement is being scaled down. Despite the political impasse—for the Soviet Union has achieved little—the army leaders are satisfied with the Afghan war experience. For eight years the armed forces have been repeatedly tested and the High Command has used the hundreds of clashes to assess concepts far beyond the needs in Afghanistan.

Many commanders have been tried in combat and given real responsibilities for the first time. After decades of peace, the High Command was anxious to give the army professionals battle experience and they are pleased with those survivors who have shown themselves to be genuine leaders. Senior officers have shown flexibility in learning and absorbing the lessons of combat experience. Their self-discipline in not committing their units at the expense of their designated missions has been noteworthy. Yet, when pursuit of the enemy was essential, they have done so vigorously.

Younger commanders, up to the rank of major, have become self-confident and their combat experience gives them an excellent foundation for promotion to more senior rank. The High Command is specially pleased by the performance of small-unit combined operations in hostile terrain and climate. The Russians now know more than anybody else about the use of combat helicopters as an integral part of tactical formations.

The seizing of key objectives has been shown to be the crucial factor in controlling a Third World country. Only a few highly-trained and strongly-motivated soldiers are necessary to take these objectives.

It will not have escaped the notice of those NATO officers assigned to study the Afghan war that the Soviet army relies on the cumulative impact of firepower, including that from aircraft and helicopters, to make the initial impact on the enemy. Ground troops then exploit the advantage. Such tactics require a finely adjusted system of command and control and the army has demonstrated this to a degree which NATO observers had not thought possible.

In the series of tactical engagements which made up the war, Soviet dominance was never seriously challenged. The Stinger and Blowpipe missiles shortened Soviet involvement in the war but they did not inflict a defeat on the Soviet armed forces. The Soviet leaders practised deep offensive operations in Afghanistan and then further experimented with them in the KAVKAS exercises of 1985, 1986 and 1987. These took place in the Transcaucasus Military District when the army rehearsed an invasion of Iran and eastern Turkey.

Special forces were honed to a fine pitch in Afghanistan operations. As the war progressed the High Command reduced the numerical strength of its special units and found ways of assessing the suitability of candidates for such units. By means not yet clear, the élite troops have been psychologically well prepared for their operations. The stamina of the men has been impressive, as has been their sense of self-sacrifice when this would lead to the success of a mission. Soviet soldiers in Afghanistan were taught that 'exhibitionist heroism' is a self-indulgence. The real heroism is that which saves the lives of a commander and comrades in order to complete a mission successfully.

Based on high mobility, the army experimented with use of artillery under the command of battalion commanders and tank squadrons. This has been successful. In one action, an officer commanding ten tanks called for an artillery barrage to be laid down just ahead of his rapid advance, thus depriving the guerrillas of any opportunity to aim at his tanks.

The Russians tested incendiary munitions, new, lethal, quick-acting nerve agents and other incapacitating chemicals. It was realized that such an opportunity to try out such weapons without the knowledge of the rest of the world might not occur again for many years. But the Soviet High Command had another motive in deploying chemical agents. The men who actually used them against the guerrillas became conditioned to think of them as legitimate. According to one report,[10] no soldier experienced a psychological barrier to the use of chemical warfare after his second experience of it.

In just one respect a big gap occurred between Soviet doctrine and its execution. The theory was that local leadership had to be destroyed and if it survived then its ability to achieve unity was to be destroyed. In addition, local social and economic infrastructure was to be destroyed and the area itself was to be militarily isolated. The Russians never did succeed in destroying local leadership. On the rare occasions when they killed or captured a leader, another equally effective leader rose in his place. The Russians had no real chance to test their ability to destroy unity since unity has never existed among the various Resistance groups. The Russians certainly destroyed the social and economic infrastructure of certain areas but this failed to wipe out the popular bases needed for successful guerrilla activity.

The Soviet withdrawal from Afghanistan has no parallel whatsoever with the US withdrawal from Vietnam. The Soviet army was not defeated and, as a senior official said, 'we are not withdrawing clinging to the skids of helicopters'. This was a sneering reference to the American departure from Vietnam.

Two points must be made about Afghanistan. The first is that the Soviet withdrawal did not come about because of the new leadership in Moscow, or because the Russians have suddenly been overtaken by remorse or a wave of reforming liberalism. It is coming about because the Soviet army has failed to break the guerrilla resistance. They were in a military mess and it was time to cut their losses.

The second point is that Afghanistan, after the Soviet army's departure, is not going to be a land of tranquillity and democracy. The transition from Communist dictatorship to democracy cannot come overnight. A struggle for power is underway. In addition, Afghanistan is unlikely to be non-aligned, as the West would wish it to be. It is a country on the border of the Soviet Union and it is inconceivable that the Russians will not try to retain influence there. Even after the entire Soviet army has withdrawn, 9,000 'advisers' are to remain to help the government.

The withdrawal in no way affects the Soviet government's determination to support the Afghan army. It is receiving vast quantities of arms and ammunition while Najib's administration is being given great sums of money with which to buy up tribal loyalties for the regime.

Women in the War

Sayed Majruh, a Pakistani who is well known to Amnesty International and other human rights organizations, says that he would rather 'a thousands times be a mujahid, with the likelihood of being killed or wounded, than a woman in one of the terrible refugee camps'.

'They live cramped together, and these are mountain women used to space', Majruh told the English novelist, Doris Lessing. 'Occasionally visited by their men who come out of Afghanistan for a brief rest from fighting, they are virtually prisoners, with their children. Many of them are severely depressed with no medicines or psychotherapy of the kind Westerners take for granted. Their children die, because they cannot feed or clothe them properly. There is no education.'

A woman doctor working in a clinic run by an American organization told Miss Lessing: 'An Afghan refugee woman is like a bundle of dirty washing, and when you unwrap that, inside is a sick body. They live with dust, flies, heat, often with no sanitation, and they are most of them ill.'[11]

The 400 refugee camps, some of which hold 40,000 people, have a total of only 200 hospital beds. One out of three children in the camps dies before the age of five. Apart from the five or six million Afghans in exile, another two million are 'internal refugees'. They have fled from very dangerous areas to the 'Liberated Areas', where the Soviet and DRA troops do not go. Women there are better off than in the camps outside, provided that the villages in which they find refuge are not bombed.

Resistance leaders give women little credit for their help, but Resistance activity in the towns would be impossible without them. They hide people on the run from the Russians and KHAD, carry messages, conceal arms and ammunition. Some groups of younger women, trained by women, have been fighting in Afghanistan for years and, according to reliable rumour, there are women commanders with men fighting under their command.

Human Rights in Afghanistan

On 7 December 1987 the UN General Assembly adopted by a large majority a Resolution on human rights in Afghanistan submitted to it by the Third Committee for Social, Humanitarian and Cultural questions.

As in the last two years, the Resolution was based on a report prepared by the UN's Special Rapporteur on Human Rights in Afghanistan, Dr. Felix Ermacora. In assembling the latest report, Dr. Ermacora had for the first time been allowed to enter Afghanistan. His visit was spent in Kabul, with a day each in Herat and Mazar-e-Sharif. He was accompanied throughout by regime officials, but was able to see certain prisons and hospitals at first hand. He reported that while he had observed no direct evidence of torture, he remained sceptical. The conditions of detention of persons under investigation in Sadarat prison, for example, showed that 'anything can happen to the prisoner without the knowledge of the outside world'.

Moreover, violations of human rights were occurring 'on an unacceptable scale' and were caused or exacerbated by the war. Dr. Ermacora also investigated the problems of Afghan refugees in Pakistan and refuted allegations that they were hindered from returning to Afghanistan—not least because of the ease of movement on the borders between Pakistan and Afghanistan. The report noted that only 82,000 Afghan refugees had returned, though their overall total had declined slightly to 5.5 million which still represents more than a third of the pre-invasion population. 'Their return, and the exercise of the right to self-determination', Ermacora concluded, 'are contingent upon the end of military confrontation and the withdrawal of Soviet troops.'[12]

The Mujahideen Resistance

Fundamentalists

Jamiat-i-Islami, led by Barhannudin Rabbani, formerly a Professor of Islamic Law. Rabbani's men are probably the best fighters but his organization gets only the third largest weapons allocation from the West.

Hezb-i-Islami, led by Younis Khalis, an elderly mullah unable to compromise with other leaders. His group is the second largest and gets the second biggest share of weapons.

Hezb-i-Islami 'reactionaries', led by Gulbuddin Heckmatyar, who is anti-Western and tricky even by Afghanistan standards. He gets the most arms but has only the third best fighting force.

Ittehad-i-Islami, led by Rasul Sayyef, a Wahhabi Muslim with Saudi connexions. Because of these religious links he receives vast amounts of Saudi money but has little local support.

Traditionalists

National Islamic Front of Afghanistan, led by Pir Sayyed Ahmed Gailani, a Westernised Pathan. As an hereditary Sufi saint, Gailani has a large following.

National Front for the Rescue of Afghanistan, led by Sigbatullah Mojadedi, a

Westernised Professor and monarchist. He gets the least foreign aid and wastes much of it.

The alliance of these seven groups was led by Younis Khalia. The present leader is Gulbuddin Hekmatyar.

Main Guerrilla Captains

Ahmad Shah Massood; 'Lion of Panjshir'.' Affiliated with *Jamiat-i-Islami*, Massood controls much of the north-east.

Abdul Haq; Efficient and thorough, Haq has specialized in attacks on Kabul and economic targets. He is affiliated with Khalis' *Hezb-i-Islami*.

Ismael Khan, a ruthless and persistent leader, operates around Herat. He is affiliated with *Jamiat-i-Islami*.

Other Anti-Communists

Shia Muslim groups function in the area indicated and were increasingly effective in 1988 but are not respected as fighters by the other guerrillas.

Various other groups, some of which are independent. Others have loose alliances with the Fundamentalists or Traditionalists and sometimes with both.

The Communists

The Russians and the Democratic Republic of Afghanistan. Despite the title, there is nothing remotely democratic about the government of the DRA. The People's Democratic party, which provides the government, was formed in 1965 but split a few years later into factions which hate each other. They are the Parcham city-based faction and the Khalq rural faction. Najib is Parchamite while his Interior Minister, Muhammad Gulabzoi, is Khalqite.

War As a 'Way of Life'

Under increasing pressure from the Resistance groups, the Soviet command adopted a more aggressive stand in mid-September 1988. For instance, Afghan or Soviet jet fighters bombed deeper into Pakistan, up to 30 miles in the case of the town of Bogay. Also, Moscow announced yet again that under the Geneva accords it was free to move its remaining troops wherever it wanted to inside Afghanistan. The Western powers believed that the Russians were trying to weaken Pakistani support for the Afghan resistance by increasing pressure on Pakistan in the wake of the death of President Zia al-Huq in a mysterious plane crash.

In September the focus of Afghan resistance activity moved from the southern city of Kandahar to Jalalabad, across the border from Peshawar, following tension among the different guerrilla movements in the south. The shift was connected with the issue of a *Loya Jirga*, a gathering of all the Afghan tribes, which was being proposed by Mujahideen moderates. It was called for by the UN envoy and negotiator Diego Cordovez, who suggested 1 March 1989 as the date for the *Loya Jirga*.

Cordovez compiled a list of 30 'impartial, respected Afghans' from inside the country and among the refugees, who could help to prepare the *Loya Jirga* and possibly form an interim government. The proposal appealed to the Soviet leaders, who were anxious for a face-saving compromise.

Following the withdrawal of 55,000 Soviet soldiers by mid-August 1988, the guerrilla groups became even more militarily active, not only against the Russians and Afghan government troops but against one another. They agreed only on the need to take Kandahar, the second city of Afghanistan. The government was unlikely to retreat from Kandahar as its loss would be a serious psychological blow. At the end of September another 2,000 troops reinforced the garrison.

The guerrillas captured the town of Spin Buldak, seven miles from the Pakistan border on the road from Quetta to Kandahar. Successful, but not successful enough, the Resistance turned to outright terrorism in September. Car and truck bombs were exploded in busy streets of Kabul and other cities and rockets were fired at government installations and public places. Kabul airport came under fire. A rocket attack on 28 September killed 35 people.

It could be confidently predicted, at the end of 1988, that when the Soviet troops had finally gone—by spring 1989 according to the schedule—the Resistance would war against the government and then among themselves. 'Everything is up for grabs', a diplomat in Kabul said. 'When the Soviet Army invaded Afghanistan in 1979 it set in motion a course of events which now has no apparent end and war will be a way of life for many years.'

References

1. In a conversation with the author.
2. Askold Krushelnycky, *Sunday Times*, 17 January 1988.
3. *Asiaweek*, a Hong Kong-based weekly, 1 January 1988.
4. Massood was speaking to Anthony Davies, *Washington Post*.
5. Ian Kemp, *Jane's Defence Weekly*, 5 March 1988.
6. Arthur Kent, *The Observer*, 17 January 1988.
7. 3 April 1988.
8. Diplomatic sources in New Delhi, where Najib made this statement on 6 May 1988.
9. British Foreign and Commonwealth Office briefing.
10. Diplomatic sources in Kabul.
11. Miss Lessing was writing in *Amnesty*, October-November 1987.
12. British Foreign and Commonwealth Office briefing.

Angola - Namibia Campaign Areas

Guerrilla—Civil War in Angola

Background Summary

The war began before Angola's independence from Portugal in 1975 and became more violent after it. The Popular Liberation Movement of Angola (MPLA) formed the government while the National Union for the Total Liberation of Angola (UNITA) was in opposition. Cuba sent 13,000 troops in 1975 to help the MPLA while South Africa helped UNITA. South African involvement was the consequence of fighters from the South-West African People's Organization (SWAPO) using Angola as a base for war against South Africa. Angola is strategically important because it lies close to the oil tanker routes linking the Middle East to Europe and the United States. This attracted superpower interest.

Dr. Jonas Savimbi, leader of UNITA, controlled a third of Angola in the east and engaged in conventional warfare as well as guerrilla warfare. He had some significant successes, such as the victory at Mavinga, 1985, and the holding of Jamba, his main base, against Cuban-MPLA attack in August 1985.

Summary of the War in 1986-87

Savimbi widened still further his sphere of operations. As a result, the refugee flow from the fighting zones to Luanda, the capital, increased. Many civilians became victims of landmines planted by both sides.

In March 1986 the Pentagon and the CIA increased the flow of American arms, notably Stinger missiles. UNITA troops fired them from camouflaged tree-top platforms and in one four-week period claimed to have shot down ten Soviet-built fighters, bombers and transports.

Also in March 1986, UNITA carried out its fifth mass kidnap of foreign civilians working in MPLA territory. These acts were part of Savimbi's concept of economic warfare against the government. On this occasion he hit the north-eastern mining town of Andrada, where the guerrillas blew up machinery and wrecked equipment. They also raided the farming village of Camabatela, which they destroyed; more than 100 civilians were killed or wounded.

With the help of the government in neighbouring Zaire, Savimbi began operations in the north. Using some of his best troops, Savimbi blew up Soyo airport's terminal building and threatened the oilfields of Cabinda province. In hit-and-run raids, UNITA caused immense damage to dams and power stations. The guerrillas also won pitched battles at Kangamba, Kuete and Mazombo. By late 1986 military activities were so frequent that UNITA's Chief-of-Staff, in Jamba, issued daily communiqués in the manner of a regular army at war.

Both sides intensified their radio propaganda. In January 1987 the government

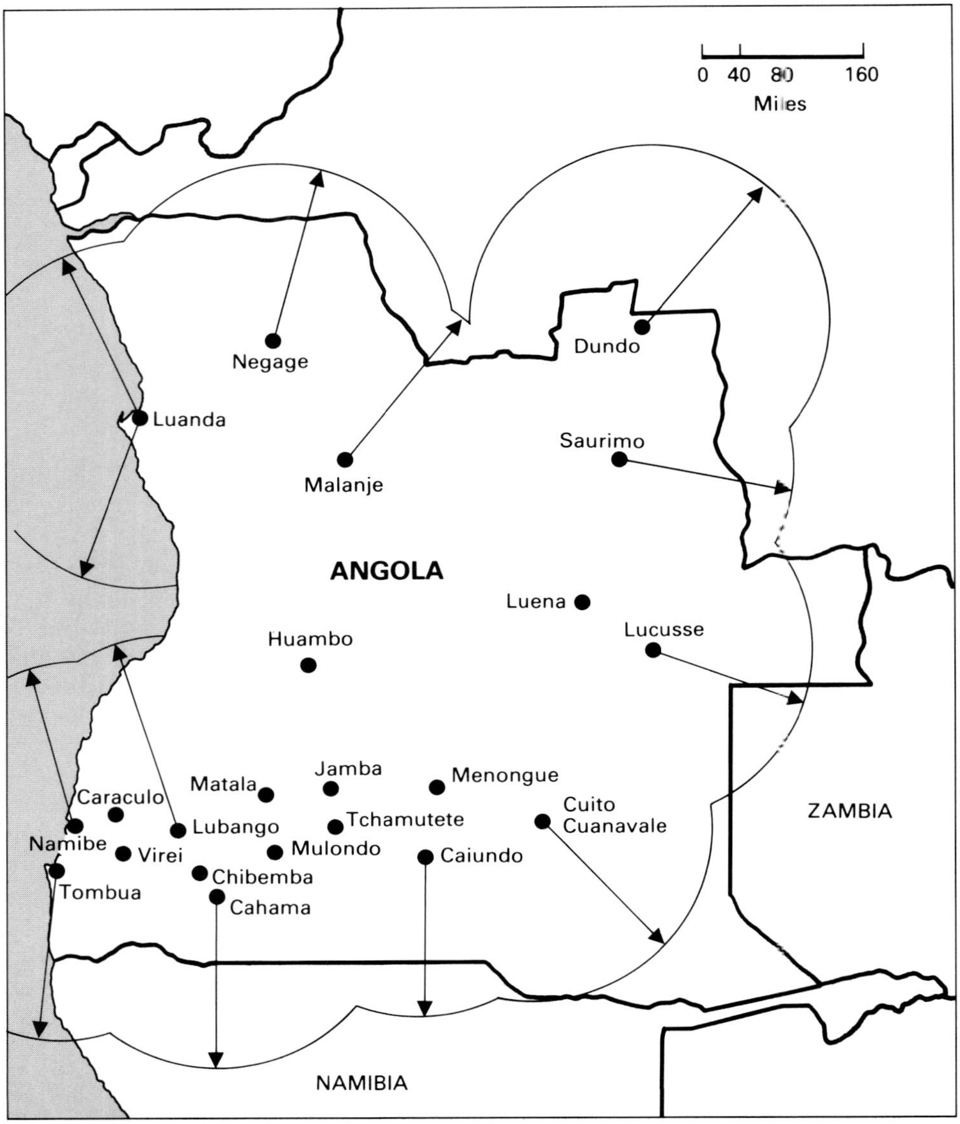
0 40 80 160
Miles
ANGOLA
Negage
Dundo
Luanda
Saurimo
Malanje
Luena
Lucusse
Huambo
Jamba
Matala
Menongue
Caraculo
Cuito
Cuanavale
Lubango
Tchamutete
Namibe
Virei
Mulondo
Caiundo
Chibemba
Tombua
Cahama
ZAMBIA
NAMIBIA

Angola's Air Defence Systems

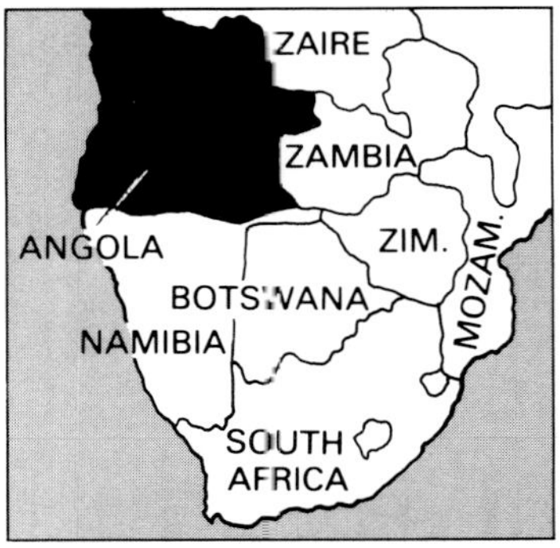
ZAIRE
ZAMBIA
ANGOLA
ZIM.
MOZAM.
BOTSWANA
NAMIBIA
SOUTH
AFRICA

scored a significant propaganda victory by winning to its cause a former prominent enemy, Daniel Chipenda, a leader of the pro-US National Front for the Liberation of Angola (FNLA), which is close to UNITA.

In 1987 the war reached stalemate. The MPLA government could not be overthrown for as long as the Soviet and Cuban leaderships were so deeply committed to its preservation. Similarly, Savimbi could not be beaten while he was backed by the US and South Africa.[1]

The War in 1988

Early in 1988 all the main parties involved in the Angola conflict, without any concerted agreement, stated or re-stated their political objectives and requirements.

The Marxist government of President Dos Santos announced that it would remain in supreme power and would 'reduce UNITA to impotency'. It demanded that the US should stop supplying UNITA and that the South African forces should withdraw.

Savimbi offered to negotiate power-sharing with the MPLA, requested formal recognition by black African states and demanded the removal from Angola of Cuban, SWAPO and African National Congress (ANC) troops and terrorists.

The US urged UNITA to form a coalition with the MPLA and to allow the Benguela railway to open. This would strengthen the economy of some black states and reduce their reliance on South Africa. The US threatened no penalty against UNITA should Savimbi refuse helpful American suggestions. On the contrary, the US administration announced that it would match Soviet and Cuban aid to MPLA with aid to UNITA.[2] Covert US aid has run to $15 m. for each of the last two years. Washington is considering boosting aid to $40 m. in 1989 to raise the pressure for reconciliation and increase UNITA's economy.

South Africa has made no public announcements but is content to go on backing UNITA in the hope that it will eventually oust the MPLA government. This would mean the removal of SWAPO and ANC activists from Angola.

The Soviet Union, through its proxy, Cuba, retains its foothold in Angola. Russian supplies to the Cuban and MPLA forces increased steadily throughout 1988. For President Castro of Cuba the situation is satisfactory since the war costs him little other than casualties—10,000 dead since 1976. He hires out Cuban soldiers on a mercenary basis. Unconfirmed reports say that Cuba makes more money from this source than from any other part of its economy.[3]

South Africa's Campaign

The South African government ordered the Chief of the South African Defence Force (SADF), General Johan Geldenhuys, to intervene in the Angola war in mid-1987 when it became clear that the MPLA forces were preparing for a major offensive against UNITA bases. South African Intelligence reported that scores of Soviet air transports were arriving in Angola to assist with the transfer of troops, supplies and equipment to the forming up areas.

The plan was to tie down UNITA forces by making a southward thrust from Lucusse against Cassamba and Cangamba. Simultaneously an attack would be

Soviet-made tanks in good condition captured by UNITA from the Angolan Army. (John Laffin.)

An MPLA amphibious assault light tank armed with missiles and cannon. UNITA troops captured it during an offensive in MPLA territory. (John Laffin.)

A SA-8 launching pad. (John Laffin.)

A SA-8 system destroyed by UNITA gunfire. (John Laffin.)

A Soviet-made Flat-Face system connected to its radar. It was captured in a joint UNITA-SADF operation. (John Laffin.)

The interior of a SA-8 radar control vehicle. UNITA has been trying to find ways of using such war booty against the Angolan forces. (John Laffin.)

made from Cuito Cuanavale towards Mavinga, and finally Jamba, the greatest prize of all. The northern part of the operation was planned to restrict UNITA's movement of reinforcements and supplies into central Angola.

UNITA did not allow the full plan to develop. Savimbi's men broke the communications and supply network of the Angolan forces. Other units harassed the leading Angolan units with light guns and rocket launchers. Two brigades, 3rd and 39th, were nearly trapped and suffered casualties.

The Angolan forces launched their southern offensive on 14 August 1987, with five brigades, the 16th, 17th, 25th, 47th and 59th. While the SADF was not involved in this fighting, which it called *Operation Modular*, South African officers had helped Savimbi's staff to evolve a plan to deal with the strong tank and AFV force deployed by the MPLA. The SADF brought in G-5 155 mm howitzers and its engineers laid protective minefields. SADF transport moved UNITA forces from the north to the Lomba River, along which the UNITA forces made ready.

The MPLA columns moved steadily and efficiently. The 47th and 59th Brigades approached from the region of the sources of the Hube, Vimpulu and Mianei rivers to the source of the Cuzizi river. The bush is thick here and the troops moved only three miles a day before digging in at 4 pm. The 16th and 21st brigades moved equally slowly from Chabinga to the source of the Cunzumbia river as they headed for the confluence of the Lomba river.

UNITA and SADF scouts brought in a flow of intelligence which led to the decision by SADF to block the MPLA advance. When the Angolans tried to establish bridgeheads across the Lomba River, UNITA and South African units stopped them. However, on 13-14 September, an MPLA force did get across the Lomba and overran a UNITA post. UNITA lost forty men killed, the South Africans six; they also lost several armoured personnel carriers. MPLA casualties were heavier, with 382 killed and six tanks lost.

On 3 October 1987, combined UNITA and SADF troops defeated the Angolan 47th Brigade, which lost 250 men killed and virtually all its guns, armour and transport. In detail: eighteen tanks, sixteen APCs, three IPCs, five armoured cars, three SA-8 Keco and two SA-9 Gaskin vehicles, six 122 mm guns, anti-aircraft batteries and more than 120 trucks. Pursuing the defeated Angolans, UNITA captured even more equipment.

Meanwhile six or seven other MPLA brigades, about 25,000 men in all, were deployed east of Cuito Cuanavale. New South African G-5 155 mm guns had already pounded MPLA positions; now they forced the MPLA to close the air base at Cuito Cuanavale.

In the period 9-16 November 1987 SADF heavily supported UNITA in the region of the source of the Hube River where MPLA lost 525 men killed, as well as thirty-three tanks, three SA Gopher rocket launcher vehicles, fourteen APCs and 111 trucks. By mid-December *Operation Modular* had ended decisively in favour of UNITA/SADF. South African casualties were sixteen.

On 15 December *Operation Hooper* began but did not get into its stride until 13 January 1988 when SADF units attacked the MPLA 21st Brigade and in a two-hour battle killed 250 Angolans and Cubans, destroyed seven tanks, 1 BTR-60, two APC's, two Multiple Rocket Systems and seven trucks. They captured five tanks, two m-46 130 mm guns and three trucks. According to the SADF, no South Africans were killed or wounded.

On 14 February MPLA suffered a further severe defeat at the hands of the SADF, and on 25 February yet another. During Operations *Modular* and *Hooper* the South Africans lost thirty-one men killed and ninety wounded out of a total force of 3,000; its equipment losses were two aircraft and a number of vehicles damaged. The allied UNITA forces moved into areas cleared of Angolan troops and consolidated on the SADF victories. MPLA lost 4,768 men killed and suffered a serious military reverse; foreign diplomats in Luanda say that MPLA officials regard it as a disaster.

Operations *Modular* and *Hooper* ended South Africa's attempt to show that its military aid for UNITA was marginal and merely supportive in logistics. South African troops were operating 400 miles deep in Angola and they had used tanks for the first time. In the middle of 1988 the SADF had 9,000 soldiers, 600 guns and 500 tanks and armoured cars in Angola. One of the SADF units prominent in the fighting was the 32nd 'Buffalo' battalion. This unit was raised in 1976 from Angolans fleeing from the Marxist MPLA takeover in Luanda. Dubbed South Africa's Foreign Legion, it is noted for its toughness and high morale.

In March, the battle for Cuito Cuanavale was one of the biggest anywhere in Africa this century, both in the number of troops involved and in firepower. The South African-led force totalled 8,000 and the defending Angolan army numbered 10,000, supported by thousands of Cuban soldiers and advisers, including crack Cuban Ranger special forces.

South African shelling was sustained for three hours at a time, but caused little trouble to the Angolans, who lived in deep bunkers. SADF and UNITA began their siege of Cuito Cuanavale late in 1987 but the battle deteriorated into a stalemate by January 1988 when Angolan-Cuban fighter aircraft stopped an SADF drive. The defenders, stiffened by the Cuban Rangers, held on. Foreign observers who went to the battle area reported that the South Africans seemed embarrassed by their inability to push the Angolans and Cubans out of Cuito Cuanavale.

Angola was running a risk in concentrating its forces there because it left in the rear wide open tracts of land which could be exploited by UNITA guerrilla raids, and UNITA did succeed in capturing a number of small towns. South Africa faced a dilemma. Even if the SADF captured the town, the Angolans and Cubans could withdraw and begin a counter-attack. Should the SADF decide to pull out, the retreating army would be an easy target for strafing runs launched from the Angolan airbase at Memonque. Nevertheless, South Africa's assault on Cuito Cuanavale strengthened its position both as a protector of UNITA and as a regional power to be taken into account in any peace talks.

Angola's Air Defence Systems

Angola is believed to have the most sophisticated air defence system outside the Warsaw Pact countries—more than seventy-five mobile radar units at twenty-three sites. Seven types known to NATO are used—the Barlock, Spoon Rest A, Flat Face, Side Net, Odd Pair, Squat Eye and Thin Skin. Several are linked to missile systems, notably Gecko, Goa, Guideline, Gainful and Gopher.[4]

In addition there are several varieties of anti-aircraft guns, notably the 37 mm M1939, 57 mm S-60, 23 mm ZU-23 and 14.5 mm KPV. Grail SA-7, Gremlin SA-14 and Grail SA-16 shoulder-launched missiles are also used.

The flying arm of the complex defences consists of three types of jet fighters. There are forty MiG-21 Fishbed aircraft, forty MiG-23 Flogger and about thirty Su-22 fighter planes.

The system's radar bases are so interlinked that it is difficult for aircraft of the South African Air Force (SAAF) to fly into Angola from any direction without being detected. Eight operations sector commands receive information from fifteen reporting posts. Deliberate duplication in the most likely places for aircraft to cross the border is an additional safeguard. South African sources concede that the air defence systems are formidable and thorough. It is these sources that claim that the entire radar system is manned by specialist East German military personnel. Angolan sources say that the East Germans are responsible only for electronic maintenance.

Air War

In the earlier years of the Angolan civil war it was not thought likely that air attack or defence against air attack would ever be a decisive factor in the fighting. While it is not yet decisive, it is nevertheless more important than before. South Africa's ageing air force of French Mirage attack aircraft is being depleted, while the Cubans and Angolans are flying the more modern MiG-23s.

During the later months of 1987 and well into 1988 MPLA anti-aircraft gunners, using sophisticated SA-8 missile batteries, were steadily shooting down Mirages, though Luanda's figure of forty SADF aircraft shot down between September 1987 and March 1988 is probably an exaggeration.

Despite the growing strength of Angola's air defence, raids on the strategic south-western town of Lubango have demonstrated that South African pilots are able to exploit the few holes in the defence system.

The main role of the SAAF in supporting Savimbi, apart from transport, was to isolate Angolan infantry and armour from their support units. On many occasions the SAAF has prevented reinforcements, ammunition supplies and bridging equipment from getting through to the fighting zone. After the MPLA offensive had been stopped Savimbi said that the ground fighting would have been much more severe had the SAAF not given so much support.

Angolan planes curtailed their combat sorties after the Americans supplied Stinger missiles to UNITA. To counter this advantage, the Soviet Union has given Angola Frog ground-to-ground missiles. They are useless against aircraft but Soviet advisers in Angola believe that with a range of forty miles they are more than a match for the excellent South African artillery.

Testing of Equipment

Under field combat conditions, South African equipment performed well, the G-5 155 mm howitzer being particularly effective. It played the main role in breaking up and then stopping the MPLA offensive. Its fire control system impressed even its crews, who knew its capabilities well. On one occasion an SADF reconnaissance patrol spotted several MPLA armoured personnel carriers (APCs) and reported their position by radio. After a single ranging round, a battery of G-5s destroyed the APCs.

The South African-built Seeker RPV proved as effective at picking up targets in action as it had been in trials. So as not to risk losses of their aircraft, the South African generals used artillery for tasks which might normally have been undertaken by close support aircraft.

The Olifant Main Battle Tank was first used in Angola. A modified Centurion, the Olifant outclassed MPLA's T-55 and T-62 tanks. Similarly, the RATEL-90 Fire Support Vehicle, designed for tank attacks, performed well. The RATEL-81 self-propelled 81 mm mortar and the Ysterval self-propelled 20 mm anti-aircraft gun were also used operationally for the first time. South African arms manufacturers have received many inquiries from potential foreign buyers following the success of the new equipment.[5]

Cubans in Angola: The Aids Factor

The exact number of Cubans based in Angola has long been unclear. An answer may have been provided by a member of the Cuban Ministry of Defence on a visit to Maputo, Mozambique, during January 1988. He admitted to a total of 40,000, the highest figure anybody has mentioned. The Cuban official said that this number included another 9,400 Cuban troops airlifted from Havana by Soviet aircraft following the setback in south-east Angola at the end of 1987.

Angolans do not like the Cuban troops and sometimes spit at them in the streets of Luanda. Open abuse is common. Angolans accuse the Cubans of further disrupting the country's appalling economic situation and of prolonging the conflict.

Cubans on active service in Angola are not allowed to move about alone in any of the towns and cities in which they are stationed. Because of a severe Aids problem which surfaced in Luanda, Huambo and other centres during the last year, the Cubans have been ordered not to fraternize with Angolans. Even more seriously, Angolan blood has not been given to wounded Cuban soldiers. Much of it was found to be HIV sero-positive. All blood supplies for Cuban and Warsaw Pact personnel comes from East Europe, principally East Germany, Czechoslovakia and Poland.[6]

Tension between Cuban forces and the Angolan army is acute. The Angolans resent Cuban control over their units; most Angolan commanders are under a Cuban regional commander. They are angry that the Cubans have better living conditions and food than their own men. They are even more angry that Cuban contingents are segregated; they see this as a form of apartheid. The Cubans also have better military equipment. Captured MPLA officers claimed that Cuban officers always call for evacuation helicopters as soon as real battle danger shows. If defeat seems imminent, the Angolans said, the Cuban officers fly out, taking with them as many Cuban soldiers as the helicopters can carry.

Cuban/Angolan Use of Nerve Gas

In March 1986 Jonas Savimbi first claimed that Soviet-supplied chemical weapons were being used against his men. There was no proof that this was happening until specialists from the toxicology department of Ghent University, Belgium, studied the matter. The inquiry team, led by Professor Aubain

Heyndrickx, funded by the University, examined patients in a Mavinga hospital and carried out other tests in Ghent.

In a report submitted to the UN,[7] the Ghent team said that from the condition of the soldiers examined and from toxicology tests, there was a 'high probability' that the men were nerve gas victims. Using a blood test capable of detecting nerve gas exposure long after an attack, the Belgians found positive results in two of eight patients examined. Clinical examination of the other six suggested that, although the nerve gas was no longer present, they too were victims.

Kits for the detection of gas have been found on Cuban soldiers taken prisoner by UNITA. They are of Soviet origin and carry instructions in Russian and Spanish. Identical kits have been found on Russian soldiers captured in Afghanistan.

Professor Heyndrickx reported that the very severely affected UNITA soldiers were practically completely paralysed and were incontinent. 'In my opinion it would be better if they were dead', he said. The details the men gave of their exposure to the gas were revealing. One group was resting in the bush near enemy positions south of Luanda when a shell exploded fifteen metres away. No flying metal resulted from this explosion but 'dark smoke' drifted over the men. The victims suffered from pains in the chest, difficulty in breathing and severe vomiting before they became unconscious.

The Ghent team's findings confirmed those of a previous medical mission to Angola, which found indications of nerve gas exposure in blinded soldier patients.

The Geneva-based *International Defence Review* reports that survivors of chemical attacks were examined by US army doctors. Some were paralysed and all were in a serious condition. According to South African sources, Soviet Hind helicopter gunships dropped chemical agents on UNITA troops during the fighting around Cuito Cuanavale. UNITA spokesmen say that many men died from gas poisoning before they could be taken to a hospital.

Soviet Interest in South Africa

The Soviet administration's interest in white South Africa became evident in 1987 when Soviet diplomats began to contact their South African counterparts in Europe. South African Intelligence found out that fifty-three Russians were employed fulltime on studying all aspects of South Africa. Responding to this, the South African Ministry of Foreign Affairs established, for the first time, a strong Soviet Department.

Early in 1988 Soviet leader Mikhail Gorbachev told Kenneth Kaunda, Zambia's President, that the settlement formula being pursued in Afghanistan could be applied to southern Africa. In March, South Africa's Defence Minister, General Magnus Malan, issued a direct invitation to the Russians to take up the analogy. If the Soviet Union were prepared to give up its insistence on a pro-Soviet regime in Luanda, South Africa would 'respond appropriately', Malan said. Since Malan is a hawk and because he made the offer with the approval of President Botha, the suggestion must be seen as a serious one.

Malan asked the Russians to help set up in Angola the sort of regime which the South Africans want—a 'non-aligned' governing coalition within which the Marxist ruling party, the MPLA, would receive UNITA. The Russians said that they would be ready to negotiate, but if South Africa wants Cuban troops and Soviet advisers out of Angola then South Africa must pull its own soldiers out of Namibia. The South Africans refuse to do this.

Talks Provide No Solution

On 28-29 January 1988 US Assistant Secretary of State, Chester Crocker, met high-level Angolan and Cuban delegations in an attempt to negotiate an approach to peace. Angola was reported to agree to a total withdrawal of the 40,000 Cuban servicemen. In previous talks the Angolans had offered only a part withdrawal. This changed position resulted from the failure of the much-heralded Angolan offensive in September 1987.

All parties to the conflict were shifting ground in 1988. The Angolan government wants to stop fighting and try to run its economy more rationally. The Russians want to stop wasting money supporting the MPLA's unworkable objectives. The Cubans would like to take their troops home. South African public opinion wants its soldiers out of the Angolan morass. In any case, many senior South Africans, including some generals, think that their national territory would be better defended from its own borders rather than Namibia's. The Americans want to keep their distance from Jonas Savimbi because supporting him makes them look like allies of unpopular South Africa. Only UNITA has a constant objective—to be part of a coalition with MPLA.

Statements made at the London talks in May 1988 showed the inflexibility of the parties concerned in the Angolan war. Alfonso Van-Dunem, the Angolan Foreign Minister and leader of the Angolan delegation, said that the Cubans would leave Angola only on condition that Namibia became independent according to UN Resolution 435, and that South Africa stopped aid to UNITA rebels, withdrew its troops from Angola and ceased all interference in Angolan affairs.

Jorge Risquet, a member of the Cuban Politburo who represented his country at the talks, announced that Cuba had increased its forces in Angola to 35,000. About 20,000 had been moved close to the Namibian border to help repel a South African incursion, while 15,000 were in the north. (The total figure was actually 40,000).

Glen Babb, Deputy Director-General of the South African Foreign Affairs Ministry, claimed that the Cubans had moved in strength to the south purely as a negotiating ploy. They could then offer to withdraw large numbers to the north without in any way reducing their normal strength in the south.

A UNITA spokesman's statement that he was encouraged by the talks was probably the result of repeated US assurances of continued support. The meeting was chaired by Chester Crocker, the US Assistant Secretary of State for African Affairs, who said that US backing for UNITA was not a bargaining chip. 'We have no intention of ending our relationship with UNITA', he said.

UNITA controls a greater area than it occupies. For instance, it is in control of the entire region bordering on Zambia. Also a mobile force operates only 100 miles from Luanda. Savimbi's men seized several villages along the Benguela railway. With UNITA holding the initiative it is unlikely that the war can end on terms put forward by Angola.

UNITA alone cannot defeat the MPLA. Nor can MPLA defeat UNITA, even without SADF help. Were South Africa to withdraw, Savimbi's men would merely revert to operating as a wholly guerrilla force. The Russians, Cubans and Angolans understand that even a massive military effort cannot be guaranteed to get rid of Savimbi. The alternative is to negotiate a peace with him, hence the talks which began in London on 3 May 1988. Savimbi was interested in what his enemies might propose, but in any case was glad of the respite to restock, regroup and reposition his supply dumps.

For all outside parties the Angolan war is expensive; for Angola it is ruinous. Angola earns between $1.3 bn. and $1.8 bn. a year from oil, now almost the sole foreign exchange earner. About ninety per cent of this is spent on the war. By mid-1988 the war had cost $12 bn., 60,000 dead, 150,000 refugees, 600,000 people displaced and probably the world's largest population of amputees.

Organisation and Equipment

Angolan Armed Forces

About 54,000 men, of which 50,000 are in the army, half of them conscripts: 10,000 men are designated guerrilla forces, but operate more like irregulars. The army has ten motorized infantry brigades and nineteen ordinary infantry brigades, with ten tank battalions and six artillery battalions. Tanks total 600, the bulk of them Soviet T-54s and T-55s. There are 475 armoured fighting vehicles, 260 of which are armoured personnel carriers. With 500 guns and howitzers and 500 heavy mortars, the army has ample artillery. It is even better off with recoil-less anti-tank weapons—900 of them up to 107 mm.

The air force, with 2,200 personnel, has 150 combat aircraft and about thirty armed helicopters. The teeth of the air force are four squadrons specially trained in ground-attack roles. They have 100 of the total number of aircraft, mostly MiG-23s, MiG-21s and Su-22s. The navy has 1,200 personnel but many of its forty craft are old. Its role is mostly coast-watching for possibly South African commando landings.

In addition to the army, the Angolan paramilitary forces are numerically quite strong, with 50,000 militia and a border guard of 7,500. Part of the militia is always on service with the army.

Apart from the 40,000 Cubans, Angola has the help of 500 East Germans, 950 Soviet advisers and technicians and up to 4,000 North Koreans, many of whom are engaged on garrison duty to free Angolans for fighting. Angola provides bases for 9,000 SWAPO fighters, about a quarter of whom actively fight against UNITA in return for Angolan help in Namibia. The African National Congress (ANC) has 1,200 members in Angola, most of them undergoing training in sabotage.

UNITA has a strength of 26,000 regulars and 34,000 militia. Apart from their small arms, which are either US-made or South African-made, UNITA has a good supply of captured tanks, guns, mortars and heavy machine-guns. Some UNITA raids have the sole objective of capturing more weapons and ammunition.

UNITA is backed by two small rebel groups—the National Front for the Liberation of Angola (NFLA) and the Front for the Liberation of the Cabinda Enclave (FLEC). The NFLA has 500 men in the field and the FLEC 300. Savimbi uses the Bakongo tribesmen of the NFLA for scouting duties.[8]

The Meaningless Cease-fire

On 8 August 1988 Angola reached a cease-fire agreement with South Africa but since UNITA took no part in the talks the arrangement was tactically insignificant. Follow-up peace talks were planned between Angola, South Africa and Cuba but again UNITA was not to be represented. As South African troops withdrew from Angola, the Luanda government took the opportunity to attack UNITA.

Angolan troops captured five important points on the 'Savimbi Trail' in the central region—Cangumbe, Munhango, Cangonga, Sautar and Luando. After a month of fighting, ending in mid-September 1988, the government announced that it 'totally controlled' the Cangumbe region. Since the towns captured are all on the route which UNITA used to move men and weapons from south to north their loss was a blow to the rebels. However, UNITA had established a large new base near Quimbele, close to the border with Zaire, from where US aid reaches Savimbi's forces.

Soviet Change of Policy

Towards the end of 1988 it was clear that the Soviet was taking a more pragmatic view of the racial conflict in southern Africa and its own role in the region. The Russians have abandoned their long-held assumption that the white minority in South Africa would be overthrown in a classic socialist revolution. Instead, they had concluded that a widely destructive and insoluble race war would take place. According to a source in the African Studies Department of the Soviet Academy of Sciences, the Soviet government had spent the equivalent of billions of dollars in Angola. There was no apparent gain for this expenditure and with acute economic difficulties within the Soviet Union Russian leaders were strongly inclined to pull out of their involvement in Angola. This is not an easy task, if only because the Cubans are not so keen to leave. Cuban generals believe that their military prestige is high as a result of the army's performance in Angola and Namibia and that anything other than a long, slow withdrawal would be damaging in terms of international reputation. The Cubans were engaged in much troop movement in Africa at the end of 1988, probably to conceal the increase in the number of Cuban troops, in direct contradiction to their stated intention to reduce their forces. South Africa wants all Cubans out by the end of 1989. The Cubans want four years while the Angola government said that it might induce its Cuban allies to leave within three years.

References

1. See *War Annual* 1 and 2.
2. US State Department 2 January 1988.
3. Diplomatic source in Havana.
4. *Jane's Defence Weekly* 19 March 1988.
5. Diplomatic source in Pretoria.
6. World Health Organization.
7. Confirmed by UN Secretary-General's office.
8. Statistics from diplomats in Luanda. They are close to those given in *The Military Balance 1987-1988*, published by the International Institute for Strategic Studies.

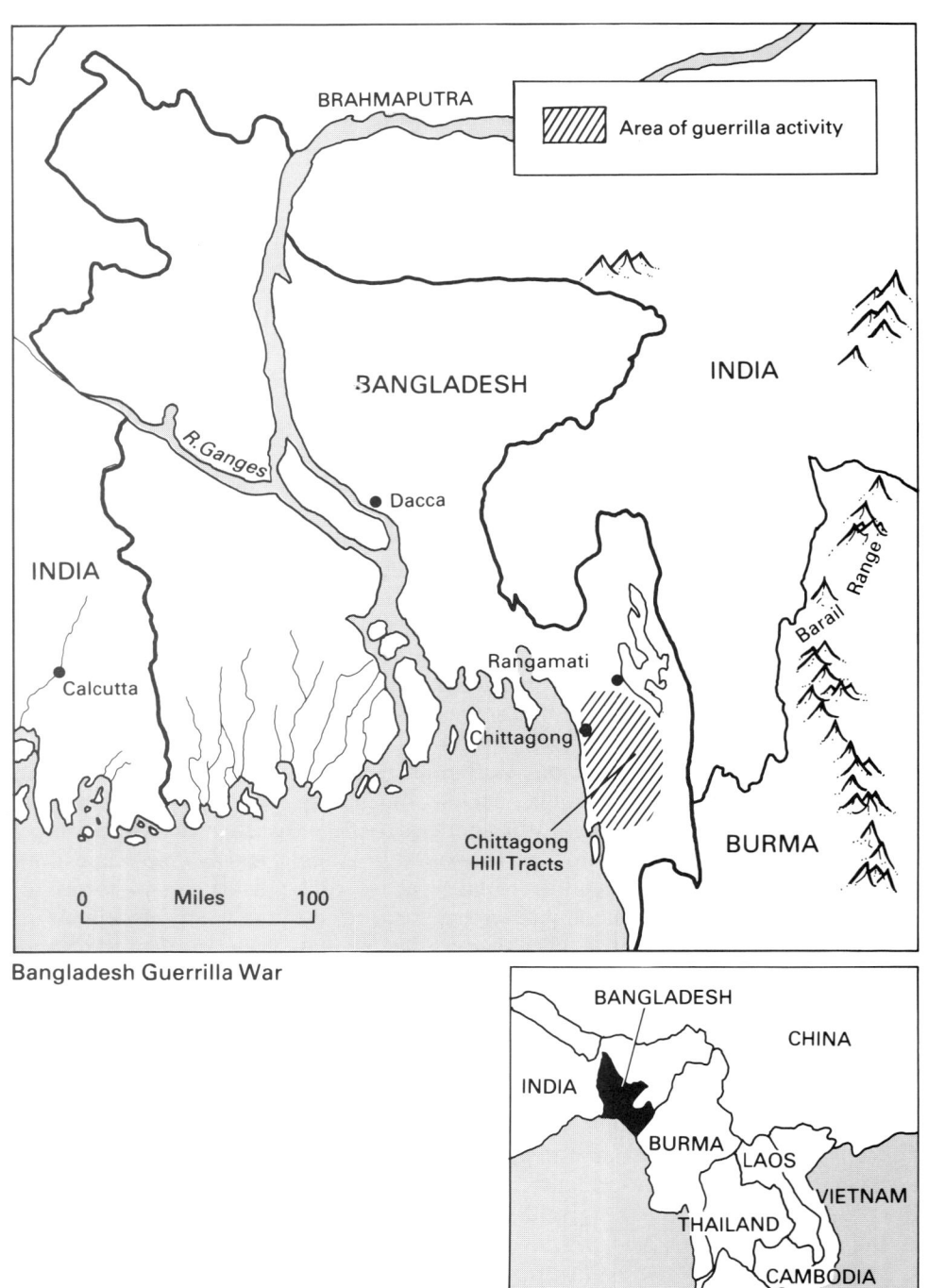

Bangladesh Guerrilla War

Bangladesh Guerrilla War

CREEPING GENOCIDE

Background Summary

The Chittagong Hill Tracts of Bangladesh is the most sparsely inhabited region of one of the world's most densely populated countries—more than 104 million people in an area of 55,598 square miles. The Hill Tracts covers 10,000 square miles of valleys and forested hills and its population is mainly tribal, divided into 32 tribes with a total of 600,000 people. The Chakma tribe is the largest, accounting for more than half the total.

Under British rule, the Chittagong Hill Tract people enjoyed autonomy for many years. When India and Pakistan became independent in 1947 the chiefs sought recognition of the Tracts as a native state or as part of a confederation with the mainly tribal parts of north-east India. Instead the area became part of the Muslim-majority East Pakistan.

In 1971 East Pakistan became Bangladesh after nine months of bloody civil war. Within a month it was clear that the new government of Bangladesh proposed to drive out the tribal peoples to make way for Muslim Bengali settlers. The Buddhist tribes, in self-defence, formed a solidarity association, the *Jana Sanghati Samity* (JSS). The Chakmas, who as a peace-loving Buddhist people had no martial tradition, nevertheless created a JSS military wing, the *Shanti Bahini*.

These guerrillas resisted Bangladeshi harassment and massacre and, to the surprise of everybody, became a proficient and ruthless fighting force. They were armed by India and the Soviet Union. In 1984 the Bangladeshi government sent the 24th Division, known as the Bengal Tigers, into the Hill Tracts. The commander, Major General Noor Uddin Khan, was ordered to find a 'permanent solution to the Hills Tracts problem'.

In mid-July 1986 President Ersham estimated the number of non-combatant villagers killed by the army at roughly 1,000. A report by Reuters at the same time said the true figure was more like 6,500 in twelve years.

The *Shanti Bahini* went on the attack, ambushing enemy patrols in the jungle and raiding army outposts. Despite coming from at least thirty-two tribes, the Chakma fighters appear to be able to collaborate against the common enemy without inner feuds and mistrust. When Indian military advisers arrived in the Hill Tracts to help the *Shanti Bahini* guerrillas it was clear that the Bangladeshis still had some way to go before cowing the Chakmas.

Many fleeing Chakmas found refuge in India, which did not want them. In December 1986 it was announced that 24,500 tribal people would be returned to Bangladesh. The tribal elders objected on the grounds that the returnees would be massacred. Under international pressure, the repatriation did not go ahead and remains suspended.

Summary of the War in 1987

Unable to trap the guerrillas, General Uddin Khan sent messages to their leaders that they could stay in the Hill Tracts if they converted to Islam. To the Buddhists this was a naked threat of forced conversion to a hated religion and tens of thousands fled to India. Building on this success, Uddin Khan ordered his soldiers to begin a campaign of rape to drive out still more Buddhists. Many Chakma girls were forcibly married to Bangladeshi Muslim soldiers.

The guerrillas were indirectly helped by political opposition in Bangladesh towards the President, Muhammad Ershad. The greater part of the army was engaged in putting down urban riots and the drive to get rid of the Chakmas was given low priority.

The War in 1988

The Shanti Bahini guerrillas, numbering about 5,000 men in 1988, faced an occupation army of more than 40,000, as well as paramilitary forces and police numbering 85,000. Their only advantage is that they know every trail in the swamps and jungles. The Bangladeshi army has tried to neutralize this advantage by building small forts in the key villages, as well as at the junctions of much used trails, river crossings and valley entrances.

General Uddin Khan, who remains the general in charge of the region, has abandoned any idea of trying to round up the guerrillas and massacre them. His tactics now are to wear them down and cut them off from the support in the villages on which they depend. Brutality is itself a military tactic in the General's hands. By systematic torture, rape and execution in a particular village he has tried to bring his quarry out of the jungle as anxious *Shanti Bahini* fighting men come to their village to find out what has happened to their families. Soldiers lie in wait for them. However, Uddin Khan has caught very few guerrillas by this ploy because the *Shanti Bahini* men, masters of night movement, easily infiltrate the waiting lines of soldiers and then creep away again.

The *Shanti Bahini* and the Chakmas generally hope that a change of government might bring better times to the Hill Tracts. General Ershad's regime is fragile. During local elections on 10 February 1988 at least 200 people were killed and 8,000 injured during anti-government riots. The country's seventeen years of independence have been a history of coups and counter-coups. In mid-1988 there were twenty-eight main opposition parties and seventy-two others. Some of them hate each other more than they hate the government.

The two largest opposition parties are run by women. Sheikh Hasina Wazed, leader of the Awami League, is the daughter of Sheikh Mujibur Rahman, the country's first president. He was killed in a coup. Begum Khaleda Zia, of the Bangladesh National Party, is the widow of another murdered president. Both have called for 'bloody revenge' against Ershad.

One of Ershad's more popular and shrewd policies has been the promotion of Islam. The dispirited *Shanti Bahini* know that the president calls for action against 'infidels and unbelievers' as a way of directing attention away from his pressing problems. As Buddhists they are infidels and therefore to be killed. They pin their hopes on one of the women party leaders being more tolerant and allowing them to live unmolested in their tribal lands, should either of them become president.

In the meantime, they kill careless Bangladeshi sentries, blow up forts on jungle trails and steal from army dumps. All this activity is classic guerrilla warfare. The Bengal Tigers Division has no answer to it. However, the guerrillas can only slow down the process of deforestation which is the government's policy. More and more cleared land is necessary for the Muslim Bengalis who are brought in to farm the cleared land in the Tracts. In a few years the *Shanti Bahini* may have nowhere to hide.

Despite the efforts of Amnesty International and the Anti-Slavery Association to alert the world to the dangers, creeping genocide may finish off the Chakmas.

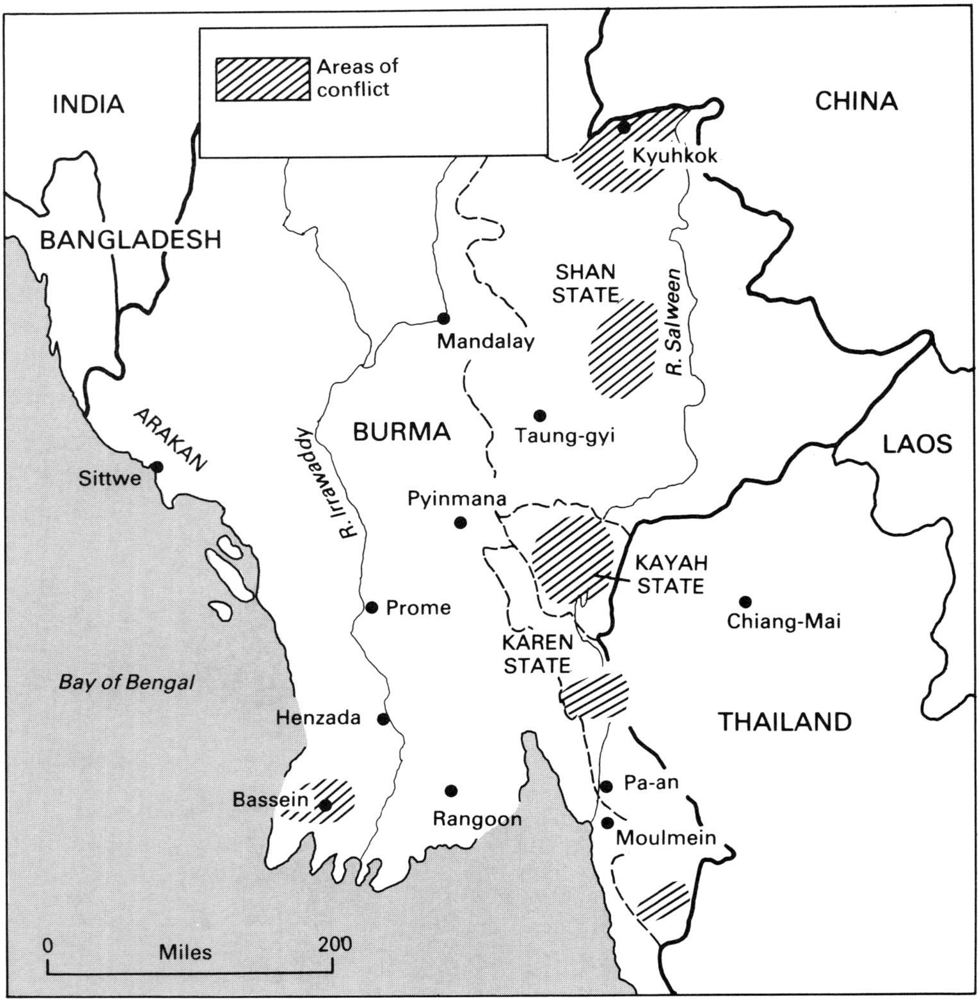

INDIA

CHINA

BANGLADESH

Areas of conflict

Kyuhkok

SHAN STATE

R. Salween

Mandalay

BURMA

Taung-gyi

LAOS

ARAKAN

Sittwe

R. Irrawaddy

Pyinmana

KAYAH STATE

Prome

Chiang-Mai

KAREN STATE

Bay of Bengal

THAILAND

Henzada

Bassein

Pa-an

Rangoon

Moulmein

0   Miles   200

Burma Guerrilla War

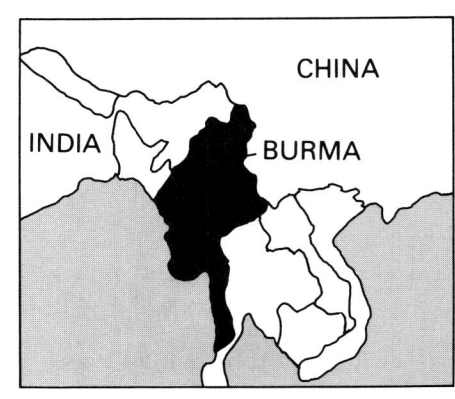

CHINA

INDIA

BURMA

Burma Guerrilla War

THE FORTY-YEAR WAR

Background Summary

The war between the Burmese Army and the Karen people has been in progress since 1949. The Karen National Liberation Army (KNLA) of 4,500 is fighting for an independent homeland for the four million Karens which, they say, the British promised them when they fought with the British army against the invading Japanese in 1941-45. Loosely linked with KNLA are guerrillas from the Kachin, Kayan, Shan, Arakan, Mon, Naga, Kerreni and other tribes. Collectively they make up about a quarter of the 41 million people in Burma.

Opposing the guerrillas are the Burmese armed forces of 186,000; the army alone has a strength of 170,000. In addition, there are the People's Police Force of 38,000 and the People's Militia of 35,000. For the Karen people the battlefield is the hill and jungle region of eastern Burma, hard against the Thailand border. Other groups oppose the state's forces in the Irrawaddy delta and in the mountainous north. Commander of the KNLA, as well as President of the National Democratic Front Alliance, is General By Mya, who fought with the British in World War II.

Summary of the War in 1987

With the Burmese Army preoccupied against the Karens in the south, the anti-government Burmese Communist Party People's Army (BCPPA) attacked government posts in the north and enlarged the area under its control. Elite light infantry was sent in to crush the BCPPA. The counter-offensive succeeded but 20,000 guerrillas escaped.

The KNLA still caused the government the greatest amount of trouble because By Mya is by far the most experienced and clever general. He induced some of the smaller groups to act as decoys and position themselves in such a way as to invite attack by the army. Meanwhile, he prepared an ambush with his well-trained and highly-disciplined KNLA fighters. The army suffered heavy casualties and retaliated by attacking Klerdy, a KNLA stronghold. About 1,000 Karen civilians fled across the Thai border. The army had another success against the 100-men army of the Kayan people.

Of the ninety-one infantry battalions in the Burmese Army, twenty-five were reconstituted as 'independent battalions'. On active service against the rebels, the commanding officer of each of these units was told to make all decisions without reference to higher authority. This was to give battalion commanders greater flexibility and speed of manoeuvre.

The Burmese Army is probably the best in South-east Asia, partly because it is a totally regular force. Conscription does not exist in Burma. Despite its professionalism, in 1987 its resources were stretched to the limit because of the incessant conflict with the numerous guerrilla groups.

The government, sensing that General By Mya is the key to the 'Resistance problem', promised rapid promotion to those soldiers who could kill or capture him. A large reward was offered to any civilian providing information leading to his capture. By Mya is not popular with some of the guerrilla factions but they know that to betray him would bring the wrath of the Karens on their heads. In Marniplaw, the Karen capital, By Mya is a godlike figure.

The Karen state has a formal infrastructure, with schools, a health service and a judiciary. The economy is built on teak, which is cut in the forests and smuggled down the river. The other major source of currency is a toll on smugglers entering Burma through Karen territory. The Karens also impose a tax of £2 on each cow going out of Burma to Thailand.

The War in 1988

No fewer than twenty-seven resistance fighting groups were identified in 1988.[1] Four are Communist, the largest being the Communist Party of Burma People's Army. Fourteen are non-Communist, the Kachin and Karen armies being the strongest. Four smaller groups, fighting for the Mon, Naga and Lahu states, have no permanent affiliation. The Kawthoolei Muslim Liberation Front is a grouping of Islamic armed factions. Finally, there are at least four private armies, all of them in effect organized bandits.

The Karen fighting men are no longer guerrillas but regular soldiers. In Marniplaw they have an established headquarters with most of the branches that a European army would have—transport, supply, medical and even a legal department. New recruits are given sixteen weeks training in weapons and warfare and fitted with uniforms. In 1988 young women became liable for service as fighting soldiers for the first time, to the dismay of some Karen elders who consider that women should remain in their traditional role. Men and women soldiers are strictly segregated. Soldiers are forbidden to marry until they are thirty-five and premarital sex, when discovered, is punished by ten years in prison. Women have already been in action and appear to have been successful. Men and women serve seven years without pay.

Probably seventy per cent of the fighting is from static trench lines. The front line is twelve miles from Marniplaw and a bare eighty yards separates the opposing Karen and Burmese forces. The Karen soldiers tie down 30,000 Burmese. Spasmodic mortar and artillery fire goes on day after day. When the Karens run short of ammunition for their mortars they raid the Burmese lines to get some more. In this way they also replenish their stock of small arms, which are always in short supply. Recruits do much of their training with wooden rifles.

The Karen send their signals mostly by Morse code over landlines, while the Burmese use radio. As frequently as the Burmese change their code, the Karen break it. They are particularly interested in the enemy's casualty reports, for then they know that their mortars are on target.

During 1988 the Burmese called their military operations 'The Campaign of the Four Cuts'. They propose to cut the Karens' trade routes; to cut off outside aid; to cut off one rebel group from another; and to cut off rebels' heads.[2]

To demoralize the Burmese troops, the Karen soldiers make periodic elephant patrols behind the enemy lines. The wet season is the favoured time for this activity. The Karens fix machine-guns to the backs of elephants which slosh along the muddy trails and shallow creeks. They rarely take prisoners alive but those Burmese who do reach Karen lines are put to work strengthening the defences.

Other patrols operate in motor boats on the rivers. They run the constant risk of ambush but the rivers must be kept open for the rafts of teak floating down to the Bay of Bengal.

The Karens' resistance continues to be a slow stubborn rearguard action against overwhelming odds. Their will to resist is stiffened by the many Burmese Army atrocities against civilians. More than 17,000 Karen people have fled to Thailand, where they lead a precarious existence away from the main streams of international humanitarian aid.

In an interview with a British television crew, Karen spokesmen expressed bitterness about their 'abandonment' by Britain.[3] At least 10,000 Karens fought for the British against the Japanese but the Burma Independence Army backed the Japanese. When the Burmese saw that the Japanese would be beaten they switched alliances just before the war ended, thus winning British favour. The Karens says that they were then cast aside.

The Karens are the best organized and most proficient resistance fighting force but only the second largest. Further north, along the Chinese border, are the Kachin, who have more than 8,000 soldiers. Together, Karens and Kachins are the backbone of the National Democratic Front Alliance (NDFA). Increased pressure from the Burmese Army in 1988 forced the NDFA to co-ordinate their operations. In this way they can take pressure off a group which needs respite.

The NDFA is trying to gain some sympathy from abroad. Brang Seng, the Kachin leader, spent three months in the West, arguing the rebels' case. In particular he tried to induce West Germany and Japan to stop aid to the Ne Win administration. Because the resistance groups are said to be involved in the opium trade, Western donors are reluctant to help them. In fact, among the strict and moralistic Karen and Kachin people opium trafficking is punishable by death.[4]

The Shan people do cultivate opium and will continue to do so until outside aid enables them to substitute some other crop. The notorious Golden Triangle opium area is located in Shan state.

Pressure from the West and from Japan would probably force Ne Win to the negotiating table. Otherwise there is no sign that the resistance war will end.

Meanwhile, the Burmese Army continues its atrocities. Amnesty International alleges that the security forces are killing and torturing villagers as part of operations to eliminate ethnic rebels. Amnesty's report publishes statements by refugees in Thailand detailing sixty cases of 'extra-judicial execution', rape and other abuses.[5]

War of the Cities

In the face of fierce opposition from student groups in Rangoon and in other dissident organizations, President Ne Win resigned in the middle of August 1988 and was replaced by Sein Lwin, reputedly a political hardliner, so much a hardliner that he is called 'the Butcher'. Sein Lwin is the man most identified with the repression of the Ne Win years. The link went back to 1962 when Sein Lwin, then an army captain and a fellow plotter in Ne Win's group, commanded a company of soldiers that massacred students at Rangoon University. He became Ne Win's chief enforcer and, as commander of the riot police, was responsible for brutal oppression of demonstrators in March 1988. His appointment as President angered the public and violence engulfed Burma. Sein Lwin broadcast commands by walkie-talkie. To riot police deployed in the capital, he said, 'I order you to *yike that, pyit that.*' ('Beat, kill; shoot, kill.')

In Sagaing, population 70,000, security forces opened up with shotguns on a crowd of 5,000 that had surrounded a police station and thirty-one people were killed. In the suburbs of Rangoon three policemen were beheaded by mobs. In various parts of the country military units either mutinied or were on the verge of mutiny.

In five days security forces killed several hundred rioters and wounded thousands. In Rangoon the situation was made worse by the recall of the 22nd Light Infantry Division that had been fighting the Karens and their allies. Only half an hour after this tough unit took over from the less forceful 77th Brigade the riots turned into a war. Soldiers surged into Rangoon General Hospital in search of wounded demonstrators. When doctors and nurses refused to hand them over they were shot, along with their patients.

Some guerrilla leaders of the National Democratic Front announced that the tribal armies would join forces with their allies, 'the urban resistance fighters'. Brang Seng, head of Kachin Independence Organization, called for an offensive to drive government troops out of the cities. After only 17 days in office, Sein Lwin was removed by the Burma Socialist Programme Party, the only lawful political force, and replaced by General Saw Maung.

The great mass of Burmese people demand democracy in the Western tradition. In the absence of a strong class of businessmen or a highly organized church—both of which existed in the Philippines when President Marcos was deposed—the party and the 163,000-man army it controls have a monopoly on political power.

The fighting in the city and the army's need to protect vital installations against sabotage, reduced pressure on the Karens, Kachins and other guerrillas. All the guerrilla leaders sent patrols to the riot-torn cities to steal weapons, ammunition and military equipment from army stores and barracks. They judged—correctly, as it turned out—that there would be rich pickings during the period that the defence forces were stretched.

Until real democracy returns to Burma the army is likely to be stretched even further. At the end of 1988 guerrillas from the jungles were teaching the urban resistance fighters how to use explosives. Burma's once-beloved army, the Tatmadaw, had become an army of occupation in its own country.

References

1. Diplomatic sources in Rangoon.
2. Army communiqué, dated 3 January 1988, smuggled out of Rangoon.
3. Produced by Twenty-Twenty Television, broadcast on ITV, London, 23 May 1988.
4. Author's interview with Brang Seng.
5. Amnesty International report, 10 May 1988.

Central America

When Nicaragua's Sandinist-led revolutionaries overthrew the dictator Somoza and seized power in 1979 it was feared that the Marxist insurgents would also take over El Salvador and Guatemala. By 1982 President Reagan was actively supporting the anti-Sandinist Contra guerrillas. The US trebled its aid to friends in the region. Now the trend is moving rapidly the other way. In 1988 America's friends received twenty-six per cent less US aid than in 1987 and Congress stopped the Contras' military aid. The Salvadoran and Guatemalan guerrillas, though not defeated, were much weakened.

The fresh uncertainties were depressing because of the hopes raised when President Arias of Costa Rica put forward new proposals in January 1987 in an effort to relaunch the peace process. An agreement based on this plan was signed in Guatemala City on 7 August 1987 by the Presidents of Costa Rica, El Salvador, Guatemala, Honduras and Nicaragua. It provided for the simultaneous implementation of a series of measures designed to establish peace and democracy throughout Central America. The Guatemala Peace Agreement won considerable international support and President Arias was awarded the 1987 Nobel Peace Prize for his initiative.

One of the most significant clauses in the agreement read: 'The Governments of the five Central American states request Governments of the region and Governments from outside the region, which are providing either overt or covert military, logistical, financial or propaganda support, in the form of men, weapons, munitions and equipment, to irregular forces or insurrectionist movements, to terminate such aid. This is vital if a stable and lasting peace is to be attained in the region.'

This urgent request was taken to be directed mainly at the Soviet Union, the United States, Cuba and Spain.

Despite the 'Arias Accords', peace was still a long way off. The Contras had not given up and on 18 April 1988 a group of their leaders ended four days of talks with the Sandinistas about details of the ceasefire they had signed in March. No deal was reached. The Contras complain that the ceasefire zones into which the guerrillas were supposed to move were too small. Also, they wanted to be able to continue their training in those zones.

Throughout Central America, those who once put their faith in the United States were thinking again, according to several observers on the spot.[1] There were fears in Washington that Nicaragua's Sandinistas, freed from the threat to their own regime, would increase their efforts to destabilize their neighbours. By US predictions, those neighbours would react violently, reversing the region's recent move towards democracy.

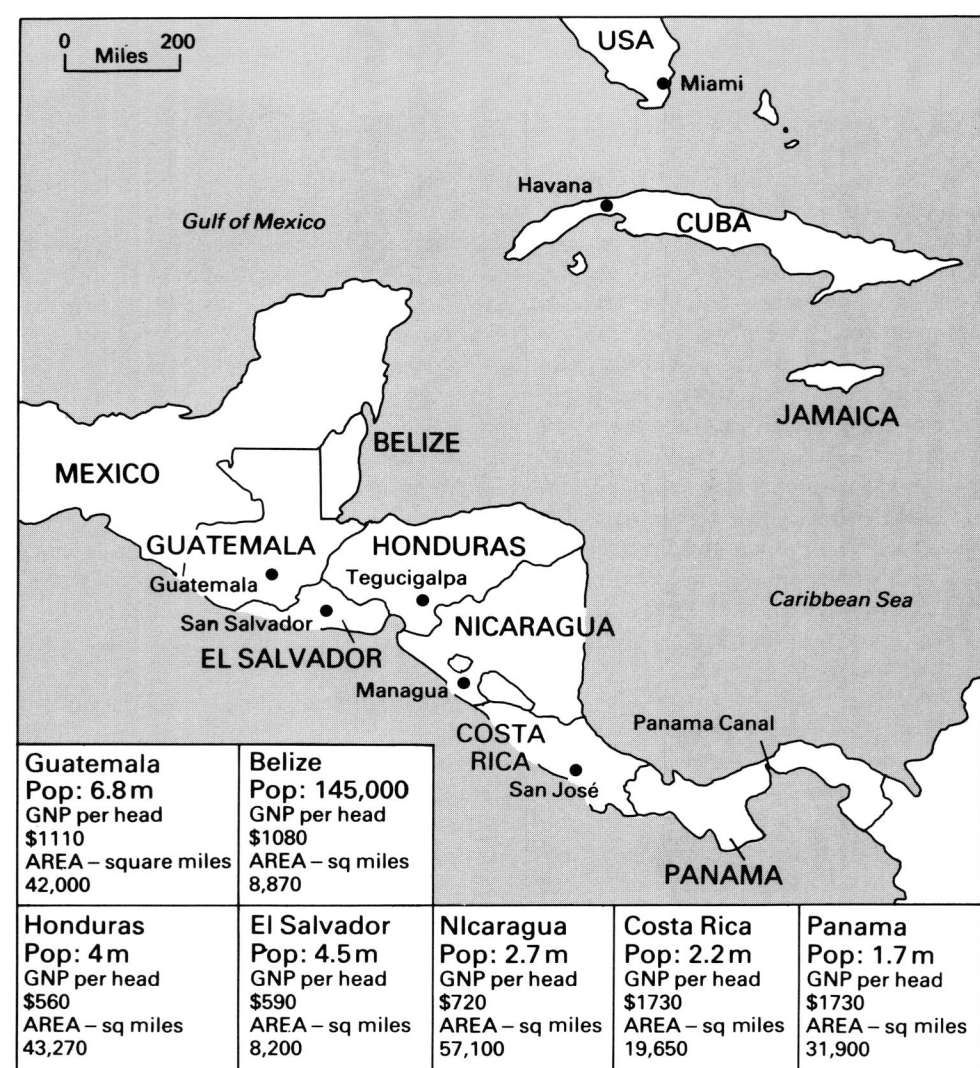

Guatemala Pop: 6.8 m GNP per head $1110 AREA – square miles 42,000	Belize Pop: 145,000 GNP per head $1080 AREA – sq miles 8,870			
Honduras Pop: 4 m GNP per head $560 AREA – sq miles 43,270	El Salvador Pop: 4.5 m GNP per head $590 AREA – sq miles 8,200	Nicaragua Pop: 2.7 m GNP per head $720 AREA – sq miles 57,100	Costa Rica Pop: 2.2 m GNP per head $1730 AREA – sq miles 19,650	Panama Pop: 1.7 m GNP per head $1730 AREA – sq miles 31,900

Central America

The prospects were most dangerous in El Salvador where American encouragement had seemed to yield the most promising developments. In 1984, at the time of a presidential election, José Napoleon Duarte accepted American aid and American advice in favour of cleaner counter-insurgency tactics. As a consequence, the ferocious Right-wing death squads reduced their killings. At the same time land reforms reduced rural support for the guerrillas, who found their numbers down to 6,000.

In 1988 the insurgents demonstrated that they were still potent. In February they imposed a transport strike on most of El Salvador. On the eve of the March election for a new National Assembly they exploded fifteen bombs in the capital. On polling day they sabotaged the electricity supply. The army and the middle class began to lose their patience.

A hardliner, General Reinaldo Golcher, took over from the milder General Reynaldo Lopez as deputy defence minister and, no surprise, Right-wing officers did well in the army's annual promotions list. The death squads have emerged again and tough counter-insurgency methods are again in operation. Half the voters backed the Arena Party, which has links with the death squads.

President Duarte did not comply with the Arias plan's demand for an amnesty. Instead of releasing only prisoners associated with the Left-wing rebels, Duarte also released those accused of involvement in the death squads which operated with the approval of parts of the military establishment. Duarte's opponents regard those killers as common criminals to whom the amnesty should not apply. They accused Duarte of lacking the courage to bring the killers to trial for fear of army anger.

The US still has great influence in the El Salvador army because it gives the country $86.5 million a year in military aid. However, the army and the rebels point to American 'failure' to keep propping up the Contras in Nicaragua and say that this is clear proof that the US is not to be relied upon. The result is that in El Salvador the rebels have become more daring and government repression is harsher.

Guatemala's democracy is only a little less likely to be shaken by what is happening in Nicaragua. The Guatemalan Army received no US aid between 1977 and 1986 but in that period reduced the number of Left-wing rebels to a mere 2,000. The army then handed over government to the civilians, who elected a President, Vinicio Cerezo.

Cerezo gets on well with his Defence Minister, General Hector Gramajo. Not all the generals approve of peace talks with the guerrillas but Gramajo keeps his subordinates under control. Should the Nicaraguan Sandinistas start to help the Guatemalan rebels the Guatemalan Army might well throw out its civilian government and take a tough line with the Sandinistas.

The image of Washington's closest ally in Central America, Honduras, has been tarnished. A critical Amnesty International report,[2] suggested that death squads linked to secret military units might be emerging in Honduras, a country that has long lent territory and troops for the US government's programme of aiding the Contra rebels of Nicaragua.

Honduran officials, denying the army's complicity in killings or torture, say that army officers have been disciplined for human rights abuses. Amnesty International asked the government to explain what it sees as a campaign of intimidation against peasants and Left-leaning trade union organizers.

Honduras has become the first nation to stand trial before the Inter-American Court on Human Rights. In this case, the army was accused of harbouring death squads and causing the disappearance of civilians. The most disturbing development to both diplomats and human rights activists was the murder of two prominent witnesses in the international court case.

Amnesty International, besides asking the Honduran government to clarify the fate of 100 people reported to have disappeared between 1980 and 1984, sought an investigation into the murder of the two witnesses, Miguel Angel Pavon and José Isais Vilorio, head of the Human Rights Commission, Pavon was machine-gunned in the street; Vilorio, a former army sergeant and reputed death squad member was killed a few days earlier.

At times during 1988 Honduras came close to civil war. Bayardo Arce, one of the Sandinista revolutionary committee, told President José Azcona de Hoyo, the Honduran leader: 'If you don't get the Contras out of Honduras fast, the Central American wars will descend upon your country'. Chief-of-Staff General Humberto Regelado announced that the army was launching a major counter-insurgency campaign against large forces of pro-Communist guerrillas operating in the eastern provinces.

The powerful Catholic Church blamed the armed forces for a long string of assassinations—at least twenty—of human rights activists and union leaders. The Prior of the Jesuit Order, José Ferrero, issued a statement on behalf of the Catholic Episcopate threatening General Regelado with excommunication unless the assassinations stopped. It seemed likely, in mid-1988, that a full-scale guerrilla campaign could begin within months.

According to a *Time* analysis,[3] Hondurans resent 'high-handed' treatment. For years Honduras has been a reluctant party to Reagan's war on Nicaragua's Marxist Sandinistas. While acting as host to the Contras in exchange for extensive military aid, Honduran leaders have repeatedly issued embarrassed denials that rebel bases exist within their borders. But more than once Honduras was force to give the lie to its own claims. In March 1988 the Hondurans were compelled by Washington to halt a Sandinista cross-border attack aimed at Contra camps, then watched dismally as 3,200 US troops rushed into the country.'

The armed forces of most Central American countries increased in strength in 1988. In manpower, Nicaragua's army rose from 69,000 to 77,000; Guatemala's from 30,000 to 33,000; El Salvador's from 39,000 to 44,000. Only in Honduras did the number of soldiers fall, from 19,000 to 14,600, though the paramilitary Public Security Forces have probably increased from 5,000 to 7,000. The Nicaraguan military strength increased significantly in several ways. (For details see *Nicaragua-Contra War*).

President Reagan's personal goals for Central America have not been fulfilled but the State Department professionals' more realistic long-term aim of a stable *pax Americana* is progressing step by step. The Sandinistas have been reined in, the Salvadoran warlords have chosen ballots to bullets, at least temporarily. The US attempt to drive President Noriega from Panama failed but it showed that the Americans were determined to clean up Central America. Panama is not strictly part of Central America, as defined by the countries themselves, but it became a test case of America's ability to help the new political middle class into power in the region.

References

1. *The Economist*, 23 April 1988.
2. Amnesty Report on El Salvador, 24 February 1988.
3. *Time* Magazine, 25 April 1988.
4. International Institute for Strategic Studies.

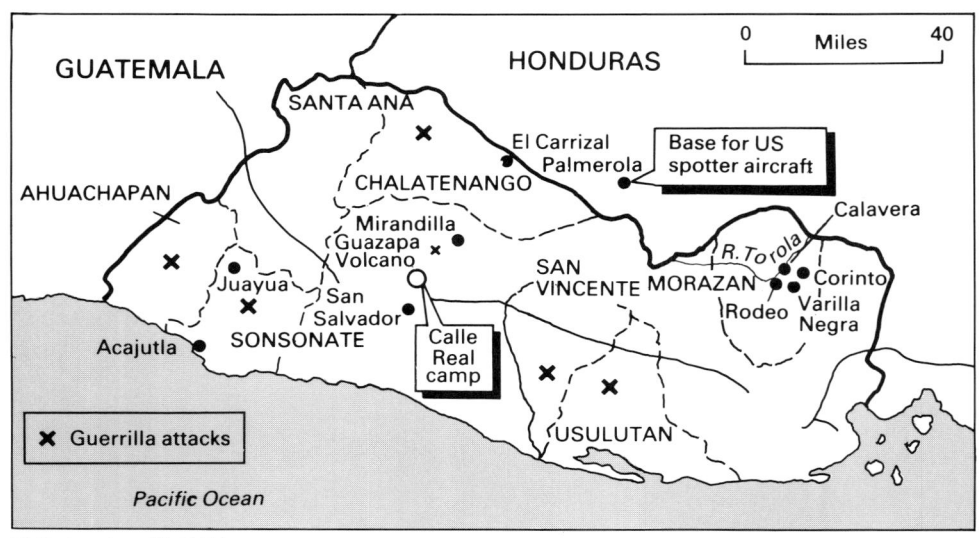

El Salvador Civil War

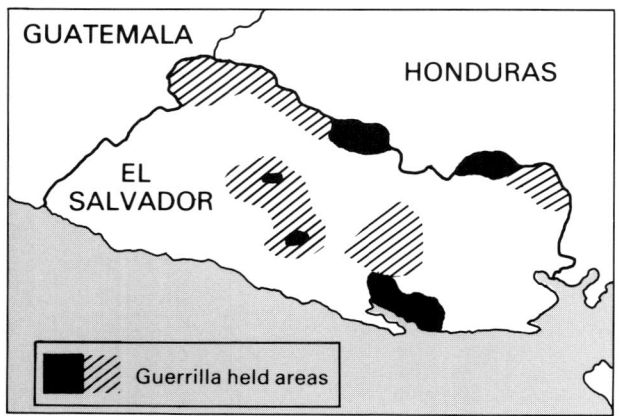

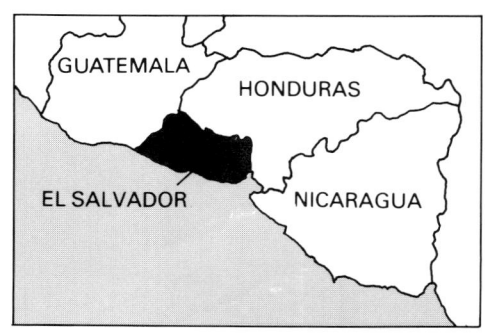

El Salvador Civil War

'THE MILITARY HAVE NO HOPE'

Background Summary

This conflict, which began in 1980, is commonly called a civil war but it is more of a guerrilla war, with several organizations fighting the army. The guerrillas, all avowed Communists, oppose the Right-wing government of Jose Napoleon Duarte, of the Christian Democratic Party (CDP), whom many foreign observers describe as a fascist. In 1983 Fidel Castro of Cuba persuaded the anti-government bodies to amalgamate. The three bodies which resulted are:

1. The Democratic Revolutionary Front (FDR), an amalgum of revolutionaries and representatives of the Left-wing parties.
2. The Unified Revolutionary Directorate (URD) a 15-member war council of top guerrilla *commandantes*.
3. The Farabundo Marti National Liberation Front (FMLN), a co-ordinating, organizational body.

Joaquin Villabos of the People's Revolutionary Army (ERP) became the key guerrilla leader in 1983. Other important figures are Shafik Jorge Handal, General Secretary of the Salvadorean Communist Party, Eduardo Sancho Cantaneda (alias Ferman Cienfeugos) leader of the Armed Forces of National Resistance (FARN) and Roberto Roca, of the Central Americas Workers' Revolutionary Party.

President Duarte used death squads as early as 1978 and in the period 1978-84 the murder toll was 14,629 peasants, 2,255 industrial workers, 1,783 students and 25,789 others.[1] The army of 46,000 steadily eroded FMLN resistance but the army suffered a reverse when Colonel Domingo Monterrosa, a brilliant officer, was killed in a helicopter crash.

United States financial aid enabled the army to increase its strength to 50,000 in 1985. Joaquin Villalobos stepped up the guerrilla campaign of economic sabotage and FMLN and its constituent parts remained the most potent insurgent army in Latin America. ERP was said to be responsible for 80% of army casualties in 1985-86, largely through mines and booby traps.

Duarte, running short of manpower for the armed forces, brought in a new law, on 2 October 1986, making military service obligatory for all men and women over the age of eighteen. Colonel Sigifredo Ochoa, regarded as El Salvador's most effective combat commander, established twelve free-fire zones in Chalatenango Province, where the army regards everybody as a guerrilla fighter. In free-fire zones troops destroy all human habitation, burn crops and kill animals.

Summary of the War in 1987

The Roman Catholic church's two offices, *Tutela Legal* and *Socorro Juridico*, reported that the war had displaced about 600,000 people of the total population of ten million, and that another 500,000 had fled to neighbouring countries, mainly Honduras. *Tutela Legal* is the Catholic Church's respected human rights office and *Socorro Juridico* provides legal aid.

Peasants began to return to their homes in the remote mountain hamlets of Morazan Province, despite army efforts to keep them away. Local army commanders suspected that the return of the villagers would help the guerrillas to operate north of the Tortola River. Intensified army attempts to trap guerrilla parties failed. El Salvador covers an area of 125,000 square miles, about the size of the British Isles, and the guerrillas could readily hide in mountains and forests.

President Duarte gave the military greater authority in the running of the war after two attempts at a dialogue between the FDR-FMLN and the government had ended inconclusively. With American help, the army became stronger and stronger in terms of matériel, and its tactics became more ruthless. The guerrillas, supplied by Cuba, probably numbered no more than 8,000 but they were operating in twelve of El Salvador's fourteen provinces. At the end of 1987 both sides seemed confident of victory—in the long run.

The War in 1988

President Duarte began the year by arousing great anger in Washington and throughout the United States by including, in a blanket political amnesty, the three Left-wing guerrillas who, in June 1985, had massacred thirteen people at a roadside cafe in San Salvador. The dead included four off-duty US Marines. Duarte introduced his general amnesty for all political prisoners to demonstrate to the world that he, more than anyone, was complying with the Central American (Arias) peace agreement. For the US government, the killers of June 1985 were terrorist murderers, not political prisoners, and for a time it seemed that President Reagan would reduce American aid.

The year began with fewer killings than in the worst years of the violence, when up to thirty tortured bodies were found each day on San Salvador's streets. However, in February violence was on the increase. *Tutela Legal* and foreign diplomats attributed the killings to the armed forces' frustration with lack of progress against the insurgents in the civil war.

The army has an increasingly powerful, conservative army group of officers in the Military Academy's 1966 graduating class, nicknamed the *Tandona*. The *Tandona* wants to crush the rebels at any price. Other matters which concern the *Tandona* include:

- The return from abroad of moderate rebel leaders who refused to renounce their alliance with the guerrillas.
- The Central American (Arias) peace plan: the Right-wing military fears that the peace plan would allow the continued existence of the Leftist Nicaraguan government, which the military views as the source and support for El Salvador's insurgency.
- Indications that the guerrillas intend to go on the offensive in 1988-89.

They were certainly becoming active in new areas, including the cities where they were forming urban units.

Three international revolutionary groups were known to be operating in support of FMLN. They were *Alfaro Vive Carajo* from Ecuador, *Tupac Amaru* from Peru and *Bandera Roja* (Red Banner) from Venezuela.[2]

These foreign groups have contingents in El Salvador to show revolutionary solidarity and FMLN welcomed them. Already trained and experienced, they were given further training to acclimatize them to fighting conditions in El Salvador. Some are sent into San Salvador and other cities on spying missions. However much FMLN welcomed the moral support of the foreign units, it hardly needed military reinforcements. Villalobos's ERP fighters may well be the most efficient and elusive guerrilla force in the whole of Central and Latin America, and the other groups are almost as competent.

The guerrillas compensate for lack of numbers by speed of movement. The security forces have descriptions and details of very few of the guerrillas, apart from the leaders. The few who have been killed, such as Salvador Carpio of the Popular Liberation Forces, died at the hands of his ERP colleagues because they suspected that he wanted to take over as senior guerrilla leader.

Elections for the National Assembly were scheduled for 20 March and the FMLN groups stepped up their campaign to disrupt them. In effect, they were giving notice to whichever party might win the elections that they could not ignore the FMLN. On 17 February guerrillas attacked the HQ of the 6th Army Brigade in Usulutan Province and, taking the garrison by surprise, caused much damage and stole weapons. They also blew up a nearby cotton-processing plant, destroying 20% of the nation's cotton harvest.

In March, the guerrillas for the first time exploded car bombs in fashionable parts of San Salvador. They also exploded 'propaganda bombs' in the centre of the capital, releasing anti-election leaflets.

In the elections, Duarte's Christian Democratic Party lost to the ultra-Rightist Arena party. Foreign observers said that the shock result was a result of disillusion with Duarte's failure to fulfil his 1984 campaign promises of peace and economic prosperity. Under El Salvador's constitution, the vote did not mean the end of CDP power but Duarte must govern with a minority until the presidential elections in March 1989.

Arena's victory did not bring peace closer. The party was likely to present unacceptable peace proposals to the rebels and, when they were rejected, call for even greater military pressure. Arena's triumph might well prove to be ominous, given the party's links to rampant death-squad activity in the early 1980s. At that time it was headed by Major Roberto D'Aubuisson, who was responsible for the assassination, in 1980, of Roman Catholic Archbishop Oscar Romero. While D'Aubuisson continues to be Arena's only charismatic speaker, the balance of power has moved to Alfredo Cristiani, the new leader of the party, a soft-spoken, US-educated, wealthy coffee-grower.

A few months after the defeat of his party, Duarte flew to the US for treatment for a malignant stomach cancer.

The Villalobos Interview

In April 1988 Joaquin Villalobos revealed that ERP had been buying weapons from the Nicaraguan Contras.[3] He did not specify the type of weapons but his second-in-command, Commander 'Jonas', said that they were mostly M-16 rifles, M-60 machine-guns and hand-grenades. 'Guns intended for the Contras and paid for with US tax dollars are reaching us', another guerrilla commander, Roberto Roca, said.

These claims were politically damaging to the US administration and a State Department spokesman, Greg Lagana, denied them, as did Contra spokesman Jorge Rosales. The reporters who interviewed Villalobos questioned him on several important points. For instance, Villalobos said that if FMLN came to power it would seek American economic assistance, though it would not align itself to either superpower bloc. However, he said, 'we feel closer to the US culturally than we do to Western or Eastern Europe'.

Villalobos also said that the economic, social and political circumstances in El Salvador were much worse than in 1980 and that daily life for the people was more difficult. Nevertheless, the guerrillas' links with the people were better than ever and therefore the likelihood of an FMLN victory was high. The years 1988 and 1989 would be critical.

Villalobos was asked if he could maintain armed opposition indefinitely considering that there was no indication that US aid levels ($618m. in 1987) to the Salvadorean government would be cut.

He replied: 'Just because the two major US parties agree to continue the war does not mean that they will be successful. What are they going to do? Send the government some more helicopters? Send in the Marines at the very time when the Americans have realized that the Contras are not a viable force? The war policies in Washington are in decline. I doubt whether the war here will last another four years.'

The reporters commented that this sounded over-confident for a guerrilla force facing one of the region's modern and best equipped armies, including US-supplied helicopter gunships and bombers. Villalobos retorted:

'It is true that the air war is the cornerstone of Salvadorean military strategy. Our first response to this was to disperse our forces and also to extend our influence throughout the country. Remember that our strategy is essentially insurrectional. And what good is an air war against an insurgent population, unless you are willing to commit genocide? The air war is no problem for us. Our only problem is political—how to link up with the population. And we have done that very well. The military have no hope, no future. The game is already lost for them.

American Role in El Salvador

The US has consistently supported the El Salvador government, largely because the guerrilla opposition is Communist or Marxist and receives aid from Communist Cuba and, through Cuba, from the Soviet bloc. To counter this the US administration gave the El Salvador armed forces $454m. in 1985. More than 100 US military advisers were in the country in 1987-88, twice the number which the

US administration had officially undertaken not to exceed. The advisers have been responsible for counter-insurgency strategy and tactics, though they are not necessarily responsible for all the operations. *Operation Phoenix* of early 1986—the attempt to drive all civilians from the Guazapa volcano region—was carried out on American advice. The object was to deprive the guerrillas of support in one of their favourite areas.

US technology made the operations of the Salvadorean air force more effective, by supplying 300-lb and 500-lb fragmentation bombs. The transport helicopter fleet of about seventy was used to ferry troops into guerrilla territory for rapid attacks. In 1987 a number of Douglas C-47 aircraft, armed for airborne fire-support, were added to the air force, as well as seven UH-1M gunships to add to the twenty-three already in service. With eleven Cessna 337 aircraft for reconnaissance, the air force felt able to cover the regions where guerrillas were most active.

US involvement in the war intensified in 1987, with American specialists training and equipping units of the El Salvador National Police, a paramilitary force of 6,000, and the National Guard of 3,600. As urban terrorism increased in 1988, so the training was extended to army units. This programme was said to be costing $10m. Military aid in 1987 was more than $600m., making a total of $3bn, in the period 1980-88.[4]

Return to the Killing Fields

September 1988 brought a return to open warfare between the army and guerrillas and with it a resumption of wholesale atrocity. First of all guerrillas attacked the El Paraiso base in Chalatenango province, one of the most important of all army bases, and inflicted many casualties. Then they decreed a three-day boycott of public transport which paralyzed San Salvador. On 22 September the guerrillas destroyed an army communications centre near Corinto in Morazan province, killing an officer and fourteen soliders.

After a pause of several years, the Salvadoran army again resorted to mass executions. On 21 September it killed 10 peasants near the village of San Sebastian, 30 miles east of San Salvador. The bodies of seven men and three women, all poor peasants getting ready to work in their fields, were found riddled with bullets. All had been accused of giving food to the guerrillas. The army public relations department published a communiqué about the incident.

> The Jibao Battalion of the Fifth Infantry Brigade in San Vicente surprised a group of extremists as they were moving near San Sebastian and killed ten of the Farabundo Marti National Liberation Front (FMLN) fighters. The soldiers recovered two M-16 rifles, 300 rounds of ammunition, five anti-personnel mines and two haversacks.

No diplomats, foreign journalists or church organizations in San Salvador give the report any credence. 'It was not even a clever communiqué', one diplomat said. 'If the soldiers killed ten extremists in an ambush why did they recover only two rifles? These victims were undoubtedly peasant farmers.'

These and other incidents took place as President Duarte's health became worse day by day from cancer of the stomach and liver.

References

1. The statistics are those of *Tutela Legal*, an internationally respected office of the Roman Catholic Church in El Salvador.
2. El Salvador Military Intelligence put their total number in July 1988 at 'no more than twenty-five'. Other intelligence sources within the country estimated that the number 'exceeds 500'.
3. In an interview with Marc Cooper and George Noll of *The Christian Science Monitor*. The CSM published it on 4 April 1988 and broadcast it on 101 US television stations.
4. All of the information about the American role was obtained from independent sources and verified by diplomats in San Salvador. The US State Department makes no secret of the total amount spent in military aid.

Guerrilla War in Guatemala

'THE DIRTIEST WAR'

Background Summary

Guatemala has known nothing but upheaval since 1954. Problems were at their worst in 1982-83 during the regime of President Rios Montt. The army massacred 10,000 unarmed civilians, part of the 110,000 which Amnesty International estimates have been killed since 1960. Another General, Mejia Victores, succeeded Montt as President and continued the oppression. Roman Catholic priests, journalists, academics and labour leaders were the main targets. In 1985 the four guerrilla groups formed a coalition known as the Guatemalan National Revolutionary Unity. Its membership was no more than 3,000 but they were well led and well armed. Rodrigo Asturias, leader of the *Organizacion del Pueblo en Armas* or Organization of the People in Arms (ORPA) stepped up attacks on army bases and supply depots. The army, built up to 33,000, responded by increased death squad activity.

Summary of the War in 1986-87

Vinicio Cerezo became the first civilian President for thirty-two years but General Victores remained as head of the armed forces. Victores believed that the peasants could easily become guerrilla supporters if left in their original hamlets so he created the 'model villages' scheme. Villages were clustered in what the army called 'development poles' and are part of the counter-insurgency campaign. Overlooking each village is a fortified army outpost.

The new villages were attractive but the peasants had no option about moving to them as their original homes were burnt, and their crops and stock destroyed. All males between the ages of fifteen and fifty-five were required to take part in civil defence patrols. This meant that more than one million men did a 24-hour shift each week under the orders of the local army commander. The concept was to induce the peasants to believe that the guerrillas were their enemy.

The guerrillas remained active in 1987 and were well able to hide in the mountains, jungles and valleys of Guatemala's 108,889 square miles. The ORPA fighters frequently attacked the army posts guarding the villages. Well armed with Soviet-made equipment which reaches them from El Salvador, Honduras and Mexico, the ORPA fighters often attacked at night, a tactic which is unusual among Central American guerrillas.

The guerrillas had a remarkable success in sinking a Zodiac-type patrol boat at Puerto Quetzal naval base and another success when they destroyed a Bell helicopter at an air force station at Coban.

Human rights violations continued. Amnesty International reported that 200

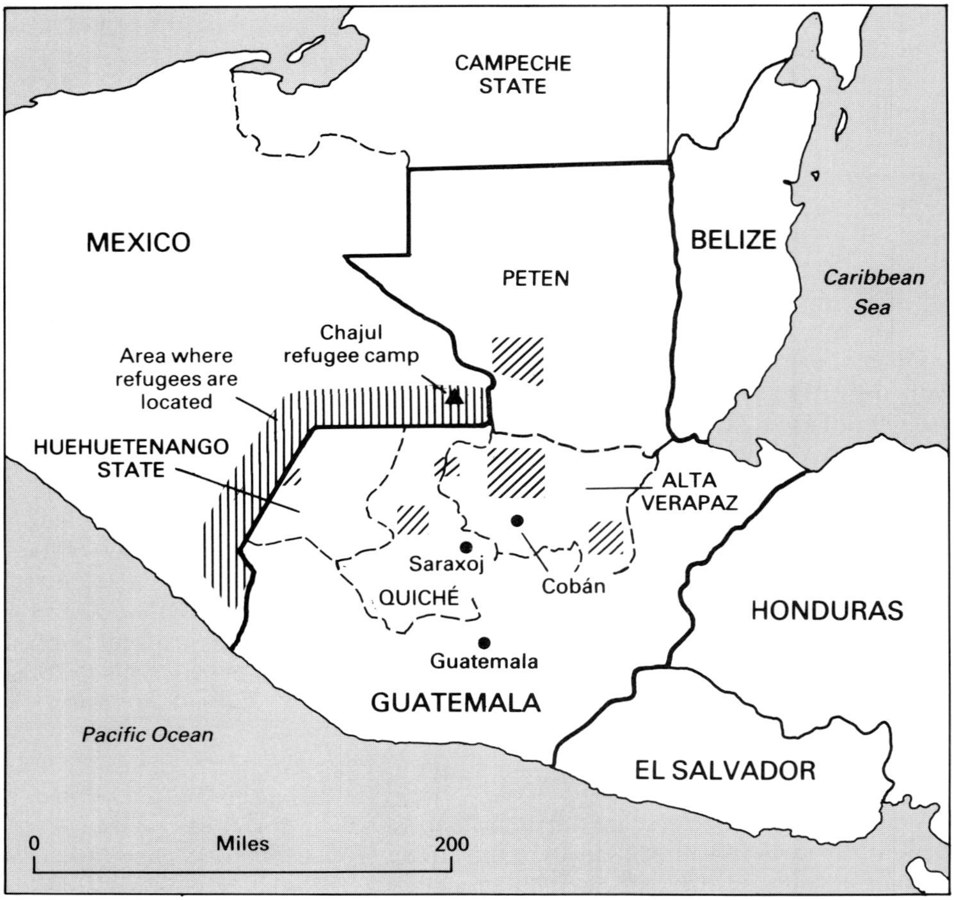

Guerrilla War in Guatemala

Development poles
(Areas to which Army has
moved sections of the peasant
population in efforts to erode
support for guerrillas)

massacres had taken place between 1980 and 1987, in addition to countless individual murders and 'disappearances'. Army patrols went so far as to cross the Mexican border to attack Guatemalans in refugee camps. The Inter-American Commission for Human Rights reported that 'the Guatemalan Army has been principally responsible for the most grievous violations of human rights, including destruction, burning and sacking of entire towns and the deaths of non-combatant populations in those towns'. The description of the conflict as 'the dirtiest war' seems appropriate.

The War in 1988

Early in 1988 it became clear that the model villages scheme did not involve as many peasants as the army had originally claimed. Foreign travellers in the interior reported that about 75,000 people were in the villages, all of which are in areas which the army considers strategic.

Each path to a village passes a patrol post, where a record of all community activity is kept and where unknown travellers are kept until the local military chief is contacted. Each village has between 40-50 heavily-armed men on patrol at any time. The system closely resembles that first used by the British in Malaya in the 1950s and then by US forces in Vietnam in the 1960s.

The villagers are prohibited from selling goods in the nearby markets. Their resulting lack of cash forces them to be dependent on the army for almost all household requirements. The two government-appointed teachers in each camp repeatedly tell the people that any inconvenience they suffer is the fault of the guerrillas. Every day all villagers must take part in classes to 'raise their consciousness', as the army puts it. In effect, it is an indoctrination programme. According to the UN Human Rights Commission, the process is 'vicious brainwashing'.

The church's role in Guatemala as a whole, and in the model villages in particular, is ambiguous. The government sees Catholicism as 'tainted' by liberation theology and Catholic priests are therefore prevented from working in the villages. However, the doctrines of fundamentalist Protestant sects from the US are heavily promoted by the army. One in three Guatemalans is affiliated to one of 200 Protestant denominations, many of which encourage docility.

The Guatemalan Press rarely mentions the model villages. However, the refugees in the camps in Mexico understand the system very well and they refuse to return unless the government guarantees that they will not be resettled in the villages. All want to return to their Indian ancestral lands, which mean much to them, psychologically as well as agriculturally.

In 1987 President Cerezo promised to dismantle the model villages when 'circumstances permitted'. He did nothing to keep his promise because the army prevented him.

However, on 11 May 1988, when Right-wing extremists tried to overthrow him in a coup, Cerezo acted decisively against them. He had advance information about the coup and troops loyal to him intercepted at dawn several truckloads of rebel soldiers approaching the capital from outlying military bases. Order was so quickly restored that morning rush-hour traffic was barely disrupted.

The President announced that eleven military officers, including three Colonels, would be court-martialled for their role as instigators of the plot. Seven civilians, two of them former presidential candidates, were also implicated. The decision to prosecute the conspirators rather than send them into exile or arrange for their 'disappearance', reflected Cerezo's increasing boldness in office. Hard-liners in the military were unhappy with what they perceived as Cerezo's 'tilt' to the Left. They specifically referred to his decisions to establish diplomatic relations with Yugoslavia and permit the Soviet news agency TASS to open a bureau in Guatemala City.

Army Strength

In 1988 the armed forces had a total strength of 40,500, all conscripts, of whom 38,000 were in the army. This was a great increase on the previous year. Now there were nineteen infantry battalions instead of the twelve for 1987, and seven reconnaissance squadrons instead of four.

The government has tried to give vast numbers of men some sort of military or police role, so that the 'territorial militia' comprises 725,000 men, a vast force from a total population of 8,850,000. The National Police, in effect a secret police, totals 9,500 and the Treasury Police 2,100. In addition, there is an army reserve of another 35,000 men. This vast apparatus is controlled by a headquarters in Guatemala City and nineteen regional commands.

According to government estimates, no more than 2,000 guerrillas were active in 1988, but the great size of the armed forces would seem to indicate otherwise. The various commands make periodic sweeps for guerrillas but they are rarely fruitful. Despite the government's attempts to isolate them, the guerrillas still operate an effective intelligence system which keeps their leaders informed of army operations.

The Guatemalan guerrilla war is the least reported in Central and Latin America. It is difficult for journalists and other observers to travel in rural Guatemala and extremely difficult for them to make contact with the guerrilla leaders. Guerrilla tactics are to pick off isolated army posts and to ambush patrols. Diplomatic sources in Guatemala City say that they are much more successful than the government admits.

Nicaragua—the Contra War

NO APPETITE FOR PEACE

Background Summary

The Sandinistas, the ruling party in Nicaragua, take their name from Augusto Sandino, an army general who rebelled against the corrupt Somoza family which ruled Nicaragua for decades. Sandino was assassinated in 1933. After a war in which 45,000 people died, Anastasio Somoza fled the country in 1979 and was later murdered.

The junta which gained control was led by radical Left-wingers Daniel Ortega, his brother Humberto and Thomas Borge. Their Sandinista National Liberation Front (FSLN) is Marxist-Leninist and élitist. It has a nine-man Directorate, an eighty-member Committee and party membership is pegged at 5,000.

Three days after taking office in 1981, President Reagan cut off US aid to Nicaragua on the grounds that Nicaraguan arms were reaching Communist insurgents in El Salvador. The CIA began a covert war against Nicaragua, which was itself strengthened by Soviet-bloc weapons. The US gave money and arms to the Contras, the name given to the Right-wingers opposing the Sandinistas. The Contras, 15,000-strong in 1984, were in several groups. The largest, the Nicaraguan Democratic Force (NDF) operated in the north and was led by Colonel Enrique Bermudez, a former Somoza officer. In the south the Democratic Revolutionary Alliance (ARDE) with 3,000 fighters was led by Eden Pastora Gomez, 'Commander Zero'.

In 1985 the Nicaraguan Army, under Humberto Ortega as Defence Minister and nominal commander-in-chief, had 60,000 regulars and 120,000 reservists. This large, well-armed army was able to restrict the Contras to the mountains, river valleys and coastal swamps. As the Contras could make no territorial gains, the US put pressure on the Sandinist regime with a show of sea, air and land power.

Soviet-bloc activity increased and the number of Cuban advisers grew to 7,000. On Soviet advice, in 1985 Ortega moved 50,000 peasants from the northern provinces to deprive the Contras of village support. Nevertheless, on 1 August that year the Contras made their biggest raid—on the town of La Trinidad. Frequently the army chased the Contras across the Honduran border back to their refugees.

The Contras' political and financial capital was in Miami, Florida. Money was never a serious problem for them since Saudi Arabia, the Gulf states and Portugal added to the cash supplied by the US. The Contras spent some of it, in 1986, on a public relations campaign to present themselves as crusaders rescuing Nicaragua from Communism and Cuban-type dictatorship.

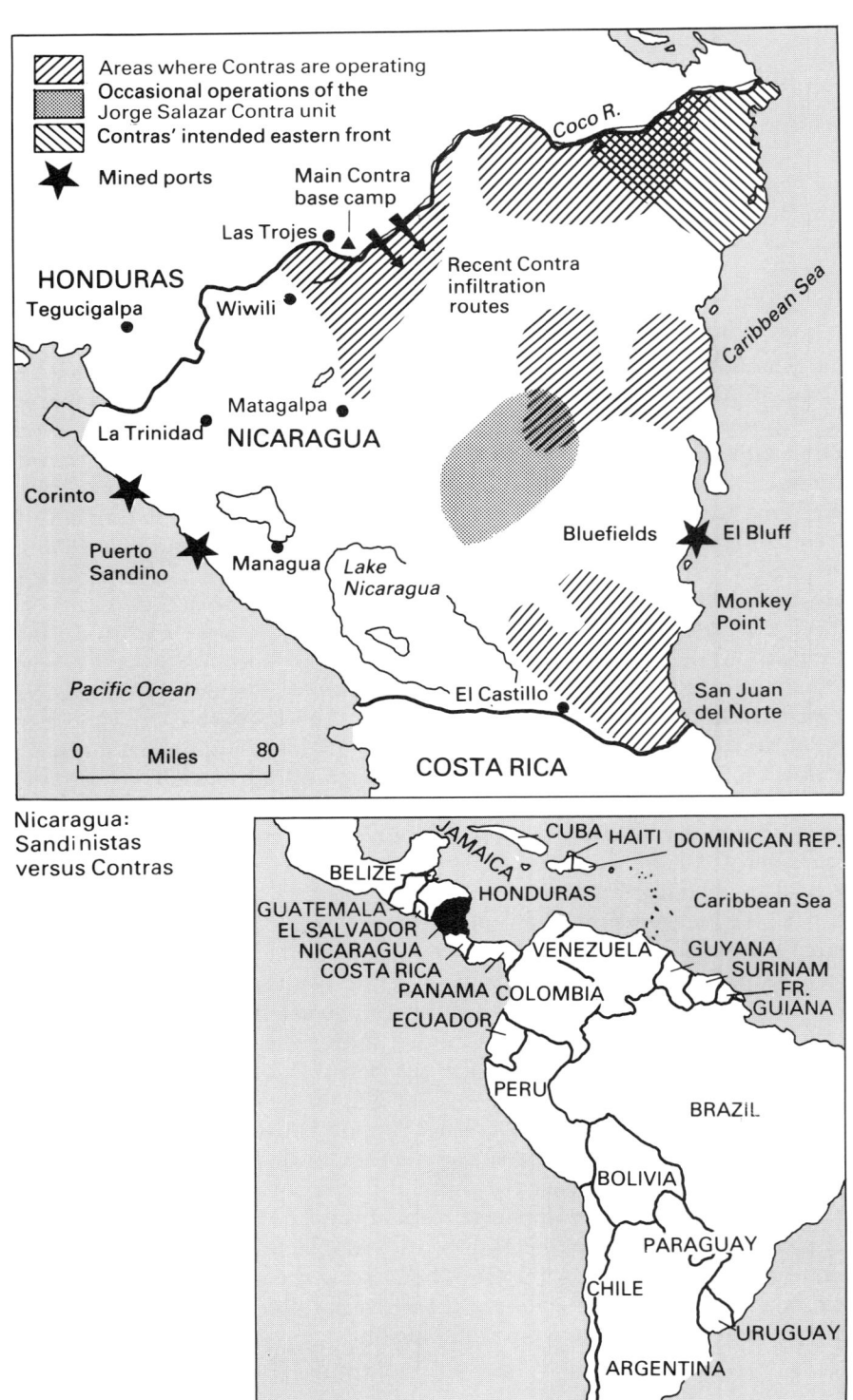

Nicaragua:
Sandinistas
versus Contras

Summary of the War in 1987

In January 1987 the Contras helped President Reagan to convince the US Congress and others that theirs was not a lost cause by increasing their activities in the centre of Nicaragua. More than 1,000 guerrillas made a 45-day trek across the mountain ranges to the cattle lands, where many ranch owners are anti-Sandinist. Their presence here forced the army to withdraw some of its units from the northern border. In March, Contra guerrillas killed eight forestry workers and in the village of Aguas Calientes they killed ten co-operative farmers to dissuade others from participating in the Sandinistas' rural programme.

The Nicaraguan Army showed that it, too, could mount surprise offensives with an expedition into Honduras to drive the Contras further back into that country. The Honduran President, José Azcona Hoyo, having ignored sixty Sandinista incursions during 1986, now hit back with cross-border howitzer fire, followed by raids by Super Mystère fighter-bombers against the Sandinista 'project town' of Wiwili. Since Honduras is heavily backed by the US, President Azcona knew that the Sandinistas would not dare to attack Honduras directly.

Late in December 1987 the Contras mounted their biggest offensive in six years and succeeded in showing that they were still militarily strong. About 4,000 guerrillas crept for days through thick jungle to launch an attack against three towns in the gold and silver mining region, Siuna, Bonanza and Rosita. The Nicaraguan government depends on gold and silver exports for earning hard currency.

In Siuna, the rebels overran and destroyed the headquarters of the Sandinist 366th Brigade, routing 800 soldiers in the process. They also destroyed the offices of several Eastern bloc advisers and captured enough weapons to arm 1,000 fighters. In Bonanza, the Contras destroyed fuel storage tanks and two electric power-stations while in Rosita they routed another army brigade, cut two bridges and captured an airfield on which they destroyed some aircraft.

The Nicaraguan Army command rushed reinforcements to the towns aboard Soviet Mi-17 helicopters. They regained control of the three towns without further fighting, as the guerrillas had vanished. Each side had more than 100 casualties. The Nicaraguan chief of intelligence, Major Ricardo Wheelock, played down the Contra attack in which, he said, only 1,000 men took part, not the 4,000 claimed. Government losses of all kinds, he said, were 'trivial'.[1]

The official Sandinista newspaper *Barricada* declared the attack was a Contra publicity stunt to impress the US Congress, which had just decided to give the Contras $8m in non-military assistance. The White House said that the Contras' claims were 'very encouraging' and that their new offensive had shown that they were a force to be reckoned with. Spokesman Marlin Fitzwater said that the attacks on 'several installations of military significance would keep military pressure on the Sandinistas and hopefully will lead to a negotiated ceasefire'.[2]

At the same time the Contras reported that during 1987 they had shot down twenty-four Sandinista helicopters with US shoulder-fired Redeye missiles. The Sandinistas admitted to the loss of only eight helicopters, but even this figure was impressive. In January 1988, Contras in the south of the country brought down a Nicaraguan commercial airliner over Costa Rica. The DC-6 was flying at 12,500ft. when hit and the pilot crash-landed it on a river.

The 'Ejercito Popular Sandinista' (EPS) troops of the 'Batalion General Miguel Angel Ortez'—3rd Company. This BLI (Batalion de Luchar Irregular) battalion is on patrol in the jungles of central Zelaya.

Despite Contra successes, at the end of 1987 the balance of power rested firmly with the Sandinista government. The rebels' southern front was in disarray and 'Commander Zero' had no more than a few hundred effective guerrillas. Miskito Indian guerrillas on the east coast were observing a ceasefire and the Contras' political leadership had collapsed. Adolfo Calero resigned from the triumvirate directorate which controls the United Nicaraguan Opposition (UNO), though as leader of the FDN, he was still the most influential Contra. Then Arturo Cruz, the leader most popular with the Americans, resigned. The third triumvirate member, Alfonso Robelo, who wanted the activities of all fighting groups to be co-ordinated by UNO, clashed with Calero who demanded independence for FDN. The Contras were no closer to winning popular appeal in Nicaragua than at the beginning of the war. They meant nothing to young Nicaraguans and they had no appeal to anyone old enough to remember the bloody Somoza days.

Following the collapse of the triumvirate, a five-man Directorate became dominant in the Contra movement. One of the new leaders in Alfredo Cesar, a young and intelligent man who is respected by the Sandinista commanders in Managua.[3] Another new director is Aristides Sanchez, also young, who is liked by the Contra rank-and-file. Calero is still influential because of his large following among the fighting men and because he remains the CIA 'favourite'.

The Nicaraguan government went further and faster than its neighbours in complying with the Guatemala (or Arias) Accord. (*See Central America*). It allowed the opposition daily, *La Prensa*, to publish without censorship after more than a year of closure; banished priests were allowed to return; the radio station of the Catholic Bishops' Conference, *Radio Catholica*, was returned to the Bishops; a National Reconciliation Commission was set up; and 253 local reconciliation commissions were established throughout the country.

On 5 November 1987 President Ortega announced that he had asked Cardinal Obando to act as intermediary in indirect negotiations with the Contras. This decision was a major shift in policy since the government had previously refused to negotiate with the Contras on the grounds that they were a proxy army with no support or legitimacy in Nicaragua which would not exist but for US support. The policy change caused consternation among the Sandinista supporters, especially those who had suffered most from the Contras' activities.

The War in 1988

In the early part of 1988 the Contras appeared to be doing well in the mountainous coffee-growing region 120 miles north of Managua and ninety miles south of the Honduran borders. They had been able to develop an intricate network of civilian support and as a result their patrols were able to penetrate further than ever before. Their operations in the Salvador Perez regional command were sophisticated, with provision for food, accommodation, medical treatment and a courier information network. The 700 fighters were not trying to hide, as they were accustomed to doing, but were picking the place and time to fight. One such place was Rama Road, in the Central Province of Chontales where, according to diplomatic sources, 200 Sandinista soldiers died and 300 were wounded.

In 1987 the Contras had instituted a Special Operations Commando of ninety-five men and this became operational in 1988. Small groups several times parachuted into Nicaragua to blow up bridges, electricity stations and fuel dumps.

Following the Guatemala (Arias) Accord, it was necessary for the Contras to negotiate with the Sandinistas, a process which caused great strain among the Contra leaders. This was largely due to two flaws in the rebels' organization. In the first place, they had developed a dependence on US officials to hold the movement together. Secondly, the Contras had never built up a unified political-military leadership; they merely had a political bureaucracy with an office in Miami, with the military commanders separated from it in the Honduran capital, Tegucigalpa, and in Nicaragua.

In March the rebel leaders signed a truce with the government and agreed in principle to move their men into ceasefire zones inside Nicaragua by 30 May. Instead, during the three weeks prior to this deadline many were leaving Nicaragua for Honduras. Some of the troops were mutinous and the political leaders were divided on how to proceed with the truce talks.

A journalist, Maria Laura Avignola, who toured the northern battle zones in April-May, reported:[4]

> Neither side really wants peace. Hundreds of Contras made it plain to me that they regard the ceasefire as a frustration, a waste of fighting time. They recognize that they have no choice but to hold their fire because they have no military aid from the US. They are hoping for either a Sandinista mistake or a successful deal between President Reagan and Congress to set the money and arms flowing again. But the idea of disarming or simply returning to civilian life is unthinkable. Blind loyalty explains why the Sandinista propagandists have been unable to win over the Contras during their fraternal encounters. There is too much hatred and suspicion in the rebel ranks for them to be seduced by toothbrush and paste—two treasures which the Sandinistas are distributing to these lost young men.

Some leaders had lost credibility and none more so than Colonel Enrique Bermudez, the field commander. In April, Adolfo Calero attempted a coup to seize this job. In May, Colonel Bermudez' troops became disaffected, many being forced by hunger out of Nicaragua and into their camps in Honduras. Dissident officers collected signatures from more than fifty of the seventy field commanders for a petition requesting the Colonel's resignation. This was mutiny and about 2,000 of the rank-and-file guerrillas of the 12,000 total were ready to join in.

Bermudez met the mutiny head on by sacking eight ringleaders and sending them to Miami. Most of the other dissident officers now signed another document, this time professing loyalty to Bermudez. However, the charges against him were serious. Walter Calderon Lopez, the most senior mutineer, accused him of failing to devise any serious strategy, of tolerating corruption among his assistants and of collaborating with the Americans in plans to resettle Contra troops outside Nicaragua. This would, in effect, be an admission of Contra defeat. Many Contras were frightened by the idea of peace because this would leave them open to vendettas from the families of people whom they had killed.

Operation Golden Pheasant

On 18 March 1988 the US Army flew 3,126 soldiers of the 82nd Airborne Division into Honduras. This controversial move was the result of a vigorous Sandinista offensive by 2,000 soldiers across the Honduran border to attack Contra bases. In twelve days they penetrated five miles and briefly occupied forty square miles of the strategically-important Bocay region of Honduras while overrunning some Contra positions.

The Sandinista offensive was designed to capture the Swan Island base just inside Honduras, where half of all the rebels' military supplies were stored and where 4,000 members of the guerrillas' families live. Had the plan succeeded the Contras would have been all but finished as a fighting force. The Contras held their main positions and each side lost about 100 men killed before the Sandinista withdrawal.

The Reagan administration had three objectives in dropping paras into Honduras in what was known as *Operation Golden Pheasant*.

- To scare the Nicaraguan into calling off an offensive.
- To spur the Hondurans into taking firm action themselves against the Nicaraguans.
- To jolt Congress into approving further military aid to the Contras.

The administration was concerned that the Nicaraguan army offensive would seriously undermine the Contras' ability to continue their guerrilla war unless they were given fresh supplies.[5]

Aircraft from the Honduran air force bombed along the border. The bombs caused neither damage nor casualties but the attack was seen in Washington as a boost for the administration's wish to goad Honduras into action.

The Bocay region has re-emerged as a strategic supply and information corridor for the Contras since the CIA was barred by Congress, in February, from continuing its serial re-supply operation, crucial to maintaining rebel units inside Nicaragua.

Inflation at 10,000 Per Cent

The desperate state of the Nicaraguan economy became a major factor in the Sandinistas' ability to wage war efficiently. Under Sandinista rule the country's foreign debt rose from $1.6bn. to $7bn. while real wages had fallen by ninety per cent. In 1987 inflation was estimated at 1,800 per cent and some economists predicted that in 1988 it would be 10,000 per cent.

Throughout the country, horse-drawn, hand-pushed and pedal-powered vehicles reappeared, together with paraffin lamps, candles and firewood stoves. Many amenities such as electricity, petrol, running water and postal services had declined or vanished.

In February the regime replaced the existing currency, the *cordoba*, which was officially valued at 20,000 to the US dollar, with a 'new *cordoba*' pegged at ten to the dollar.

President Ortega attributed the national hardships to US sanctions and the Contra insurgency. However, during 1988, increasing numbers of Nicaraguans were blaming their predicament not on outside aggression but on the Sandinistas.

Carlos Huembes, president of a coalition of anti-Sandinista groups known as the Democratic Co-ordinator, told a foreign Press conference: 'People are losing their patience and people are losing their fear.'

Many areas seethed with resentment over the government's decision to maintain the conscription law, which stipulates two years of military service by all men over seventeen years of age. In Masaya, in February, army recruiters dragged 300 teenagers from their homes, handcuffed them and after checking their identities pressed about fifty into the army. Over the next three nights relatives and friends of the young men set fire to official cars and street barricades and fought the riot police.

The social unrest did not necessarily indicate support for the Contras but the Sandinistas' grip on the country suddenly seemed much less secure. Public expressions of discontent grew rapidly after the government lifted a five-year state of emergency in January.

Divisions in the Contra Command

In July 1988, Enrique Bermudez was elected to the seven-man directorate, the highest decision-making body in the rebel movement. Officials acknowledged that the election placed him in complete control of the guerrillas. His ties to the Somoza dictatorship, as well as charges against him of corruption and authoritarianism, led almost at once to the resignation of all southern front commanders and their troops from the Contra coalition.

A group of moderate Contra political leaders, led by Alfredo Cesar, another member of the directorate, presented an ultimatum to the Bermudez group. The Cesar faction leaders resented having no say in future strategy, following Bermudez's consolidation of control. The moderates also saw Bermudez as uninterested in negotiating with the Nicaraguan government. They issued three main demands:

- That the Contra high command be staffed with rebel commanders from all three fronts—northern, southern and Atlantic coast—in accordance with the agreement which unified the various factions into the Nicaraguan Resistance in May 1987.
- That a new 'balance of power' be struck that would give more influence to Cesar-type moderates on the directorate.
- That the Contras restructure their relations with the United States. This would mean more co-operation with the US Democrats in seeking a diplomatic end to the war.

The hard-liners are based in Honduras, the more liberal Contras in Costa Rica. The Costa-Rican based leaders, who represent a wide array of key Contra officials and members of moderate parties, seemed likely to form an alliance with Cesar and the southern commanders. Cesar was joined, in September, by Alfonso Robelo Callejas and Pedro Joaquin Chamorro, former rebel directors who oppose Bermudez, as well as Brooklyn Rivera, a Miskito Indian leader. Rivera waged a solitary battle against the Sandinista government long after most other Nicaraguan Indian leaders had given up the fight or had joined forces with Bermudez.

References

1. Western diplomatic sources in Managua say that heightened government activity indicated serious concern over the Contra attack.
2. White House briefing. 23 December 1988.
3. A Honduran source reports that President Azcona regards Cesar as the future Contra political leader.
4. *Sunday Times*, London, 8 May 1988.
5. By US State Department assessment, all objectives were achieved. This seems to have been the case, despite the derision shown by some newspapers of international repute. *The Observer*, London, carried the headline *War That Borders on Farce*, 20 March 1988.

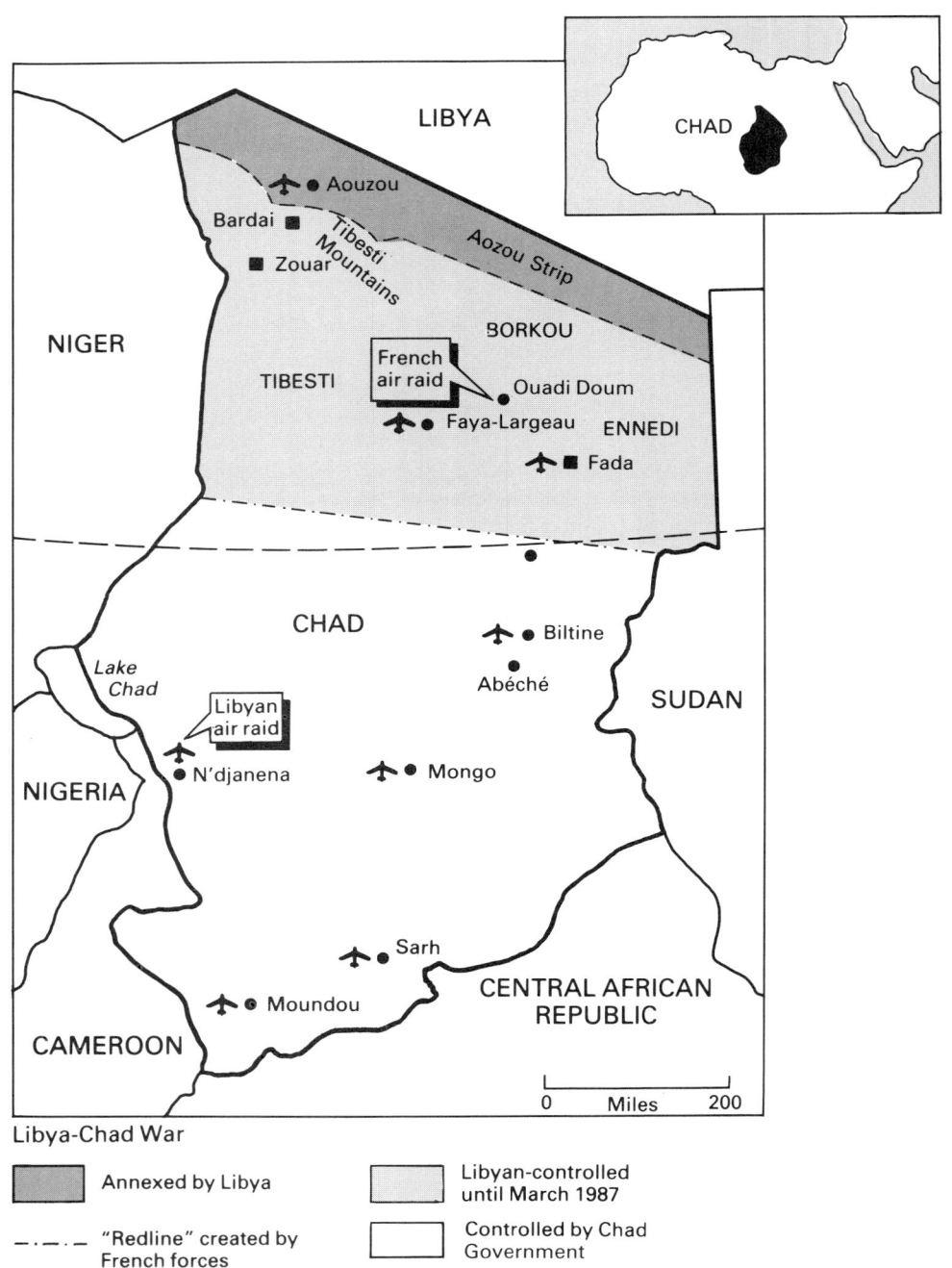

Libya-Chad War

▨ Annexed by Libya		▨	Libyan-controlled until March 1987
–·–·– "Redline" created by French forces		☐	Controlled by Chad Government
▨ Routed Libyans			

War in Chad

UNEASY TRUCE

Background Summary

From the time of his coup in Libya in 1969, Colonel Gaddafi has interfered in the affairs of his neighbour, Chad. This compounded the problems caused by the civil war between Hisseine Habré and his *Forces Armées du Nord* (FAN) and Goukouni Oueddei and his *Forces Armées Populaires* (FAP). Libya occupied the 60-mile wide Aouzou Strip in 1973 and backed Habré. When Oueddei formed the Government *d'Union Nationale de Transition* (GUNT), Gaddafi abandoned Habré and backed Oueddei, sending 15,000 troops to fight against FAN.

FAN troops captured the capital, N'djamena, in June 1982, Oueddei fled and Habré formed a government. Gaddafi was determined to control the country and in May 1983 his army helped GUNT to capture Faya-Largeau and other towns. France, as the former colonial power in Chad, sent troops and aircraft to support Habré's FAN, which already had the support of Egypt, Sudan and the United States.

Gaddafi established six bases in Chad. FAN troops defeated Libyan-supported Chadians in two battles while the French threatened action against the Libyans if they crossed the 16th parallel.

Summary of the War in 1986-87

On 12 December 1986 a Libyan offensive was launched to capture the oasis towns of Fada and Zouar, while Chadian forces routed the Libyans at Bardai. The French dropped arms and supplies to the Chad troops and encouraged Habré in his attempt to recapture Libyan-occupied territory. Habré now commanded the new Chadian National Armed Forces (FANT).

In January 1987 the Chadians decisively defeated the Libyans at Fada and recaptured Zouar. When Libyan MiGs bombed Chadian positions south of the 16th parallel, French Mirage and Jaguar fighter-bombers destroyed Libyan radar installations at Ouadi Doum. Gaddafi's next step was to bomb Chadian troops at Kouba Olanga.

Habré, despite his successes, failed to capitalize politically on his military victories. Gaddafi sent envoys to Harare, Algiers, Khartoum, Accra and Lagos to canvas support for his own 'peace conference'. Simultaneously he sent 8,000 more Libyan troops into northern Chad, a move which the French countered by airlifting another 1,000 soldiers to southern Chad.

Oueddei's GUNT disintegrated and Oueddei himself, completely discredited, left Libya for Algiers. The conflict was now not a civil war but a war between Libya and Chad, and Chad was much the more successful. During 1987 the Chad soldiers knocked out about a tenth of the Libyan Army.

The War in 1988

In November 1987 the commanding officer of Chad's victorious military forces, Hassan Djammous, strengthened the already firm ties between France and Chad by visiting Paris. The visit coincided with the formation of a Committee for a Free Chad. The committee's 'board of honour' includes some famous and influential figures and is led by General Massu. The Committee supported the French government's case for Chad's sovereignty over Aouzou.

Gaddafi was planning a fresh offensive. It was to be launched from Sudan and Libya's southern military bases of Toumo, Maaten es Sara and Sebha. The offensive was all the more predictable because of renewed unrest in the Libyan Army and anti-government demonstrations in Tripoli and in the southern bases. Gaddafi hoped that renewed military action in Chad would deflect the opposition away from him. In addition to ending the humiliation he had suffered in Chad, Gaddafi expected to divert attention in the Arab world from his support for non-Arab Iran in the Iran-Iraq War. His new offensive would be under the banner of 'Arabism'.[1]

However, he faced a major tactical problem. The Chadians now had US Stinger missiles. This led Syrian pilots, on loan to Gaddafi, to decline to operate against Chad.[2]

Part of Gaddafi's preparation for the Chad offensive was an attempt to acquire chemical weapons and to develop Libya's own capability to produce them. Mahamat Ali Adoum, Chad's ambassador to the US, claimed that Gaddafi was actually building chemical plants to produce war gases and chemicals.[3] During the summer of 1987 Chadian soldiers had suffered skin burns during a Libyan gas attack. The gases then used had come from Iran but most of the released gas missed the Chadians and floated over the Libyan forces.

A number of suspicious facilities were spotted by satellite surveillance of Libya in the earlier part of 1988. US specialists say that these could include chemical-weapons manufacturing plants. One is located at Maaten es Sara base, sixty miles north of the Chadian-Libyan border, which was overrun by the Chadian army in September 1987, then recaptured and rebuilt by Libya.

It is known that Libya could produce nerve agents with relative ease using technology related to insecticides.[4] The technology, materials and equipment needed for producing a range of chemical weapons are readily available on the international market.

In the summer of 1987 the US State Department publicized a secret exchange in which Libya sent Soviet-built mines to Iran in exchange for chemical weapons. US officials say the evidence is so conclusive that 2,000 American gas masks were sent to Chad.

On 13 September 1987 a cease-fire negotiated by the Organization of African Unity came into effect but nobody expected Gaddafi to respect it fully. Libya continued to carry out almost daily overflights of Chad, often aggressively approaching Chad's forces before turning away. Elements of Libya's Islamic Legion several times tried to enter Chad.

According to Egyptian military intelligence, Libya employs about 2,000 mercenaries in the Darfur region, organized as the Islamic Legion under Libyan officers and purporting to be farm specialists. This force confuses Sudan's civil war, apart from being ready to mount a diversionary raid into Chad.

In January 1988 several Libyans were taken prisoner by Chadian units in the Sudanese region of Darfur. To offset this 'defeat', Gaddafi announced that there were Chadian prisoners in Libya. He displayed them to various human rights organizations which reported that they were being well treated. However, there were no Chadian POWs in Libya. Gaddafi merely used men who might reasonably be taken to be Chadians.

Throughout the latter part of 1987 and into 1988 Gaddafi strengthened his hold on the Aouzou Strip, digging fortifications and bringing in more tanks and anti-aircraft batteries.

On the whole, Gaddafi has been reducing Libya's targets. He has been unusually conciliatory towards his North African neighbours, especially Egypt, which had often incurred his hatred in the past. On 28 March 1988 he finished a month of friendly gestures by announcing that he was withdrawing Libyan troops from the border with Egypt. Earlier, Egypt had released four Libyan MiG-23 aircraft which had landed in Egypt's western desert during a sandstorm. On 24 March Libya repatriated thirty-six Egyptian political prisoners long held in Libya, including some alleged spies. Egypt sent back five Libyan air force personnel who arrived in Egypt inadvertently in 1987 when their superior officers defected in Libyan aircraft. As another friendly gesture the Libyans are studying the financial claims from Egyptians who were among the thousands of guest-workers sent home in 1985.

The Egyptians, Tunisian, Algerian, Chadian, French and American governments have no doubt that Gaddafi plans further attacks against Chad. Also, should Chad seek to regain the Aouzou Strip, which Gaddafi claims is now annexed to Libya, Gaddafi would fight to retain it.

In 1988 Libya's armed forces were impressively strong for a country with a population of only 3.8 million. The army, with a strength of 60,000 men, has thirty tank battalions, fifty mechanized infantry battalions, forty-one artillery battalions and fourteen paratroop and commando battalions. There are 2,300 tanks, of which 200 are the advanced T-72s. The others are T-54s, 6-55s and T-62s. Armoured fighting vehicles total 2,200, including 700 armoured personnel carriers. Gaddafi's artillery strength is massive, with at least 1,500 guns other than mortars. For air defence he has 600 guns as well as SA-7 missiles.

The air force, with only 10,000 personnel, has 544 combat aircraft and 52 armed helicopters. This is exactly the same aircraft strength as the Royal Air Force, which has 93,000 personnel. Libya has both French Mirage and Soviet MiG war planes. In mid-1988 another 120 aircraft were on order, including MiG-25s.

Chad's armed forces are pathetically weak compared with those of Libya. The army totals 17,000 men. It has one unit classified as armoured but in reality it uses armoured cars. The sixty or so captured Libyan tanks are not operational. Chad's infantry strength comprises three infantry battalions and sixteen independent companies. Artillery consists of only a few 122 mm howitzers and 73 mm anti-tank guns. For air defence, Chad depended on old guns and some SA-6 batteries until the arrival of the Stinger missiles.[5]

The enormous Libyan advantage in military manpower and matériel makes the

Chadian ability to hold off the Libyans and even defeat them all the more impressive. In close combat and in tactical manoeuvre the Chadians are greatly superior.

On 25 May 1988 Gaddafi stated that he was prepared to recognize Hisseine Habré's government and restore normal diplomatic relations. This seemed to suggest that Libya was ready to disentangle itself from the Chad civil war. No interested party could trust Gaddafi's offer and some observers suspected that he was simply planning a trade for Libyan prisoners of war held in Chad. Certainly Libyan disengagement would starve the Chadian opposition of support, and on 17 June Chadian opposition leaders in Libya were detained. At the end of July, 2,000 rebels crossed from Libya into western Sudan, saying that they had been ordered out of Libya. Because of Gaddafi's previous history of deceit and betrayal he was deemed capable of complex political and military machinations.

References

1. Diplomatic source in Tripoli.
2. According to Libyan pilots defecting to Egypt.
3. In communication with the US State Department, January 1988.
4. According to Robert Kupperman, specialist on chemical warfare, Center for Strategic and International Studies, Washington.
5. These statistics more or less conform with the figures given in the IISS *Military Balance* 1987-88, but it does not mention Stingers.

Colombia Civil War

PEACE IMPOSSIBLE

Background Summary

In 1948 Colombia plunged into a civil war from which it has never emerged. First of all a conflict between liberals and conservatives, it quickly involved the Colombian Revolutionary Armed Forces or *Fuerzas Armadas Revolucionarias Colombianes* (FARC), which is the military wing of the Colombian Communist Party. In 1960 the pro-Cuban Army of National Liberation (ELN) and the Maoist People's Liberation Army (EPL) were formed and joined in the war. In 1973 a Leftist-nationalist-Castroite group known as M-19 came into being and within a few years was the most powerful fighting force.

In 1982, the Workers' Self-Defence, known in Colombia as ADO, joined the guerrilla war. In that year a new President, Belisario Betancur, secured a ceasefire but it lasted only weeks before pitched battles occurred between the security forces and FARC and M-19. By the end of 1985 more than 20,000 people had died in the war.

Summary of the War in 1987

Virgilio Barco, a Liberal, had become president in 1986 and promised peace. He could not deliver it. Political assassinations, criminal murders, peasant massacres, daily acts of sabotage by guerrillas, attacks on army posts and executions by paramilitary groups continued unabated.

ELN, having amassed vast sums of money through robberies and blackmail, built its strength to 50,000 and displaced M-19 as the most dangerous group. It changed its name to National Guerrilla Co-ordination (CNG) and gave orders to M-19, EPL and other armed bands. CNG has close ties with El Salvador guerrilla groups. The Patriotic Union, a Right-wing organization of government officials and supporters, became CNG's target and 500 of its members were killed. FARC, under Manuel Marulanda, remained the most powerful organization outside the cities.

The immensely powerful drug barons possessed their own armies and President Barco used the armed forces against them. The army carried out 1,700 anti-drugs raids in 1987 and arrested 650 suspects. The government ordered that the import and export of chemicals used in making illegal narcotics was to be strictly controlled and the army, navy and air force collaborated closely to enforce the order. Nearly 3,000 Colombian companies were placed under surveillance to prevent the drug mafia from gaining access to the products of these firms.

As was noted in **WAR ANNUAL 2**, 'this was a remarkable display of military planning and precision but its very success invited retaliation'.

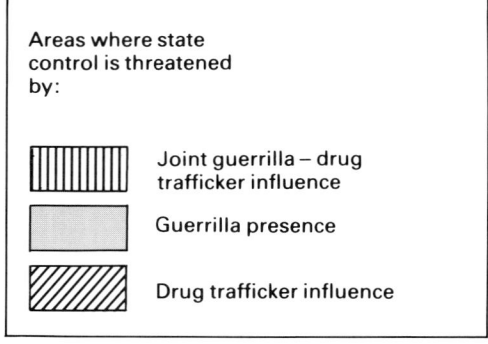

Colombia Guerrilla and Narcotics War

Areas where state control is threatened by:

Joint guerrilla – drug trafficker influence
Guerrilla presence
Drug trafficker influence

The War in 1988

At the end of 1987 Pablo Escobar Gaviria, the leading drug baron, declared total war on the President, government and armed forces of the Colombian state. Gaviria had prepared his ground carefully by winning popularity among the people. He did this by building huge housing estates and giving decent homes to thousands of desperate people living in shanty towns. In the city of Medellin, the 'drugs capital' of Colombia, a great housing estate was named after him. Pathetically grateful to Gaviria, these people were ready to support him in any way.

Simultaneously, Gaviria was selling drugs to the newly-housed people. The particular narcotic which he supplied was the potentially lethal *bazuko*, known as 'the poor man's cocaine'. The government claims that up to a million Colombians, out of a population of twenty-nine million, are already addicted to *bazuko*.

At Medellin airport, in January, Gaviria's thugs abducted the country's Attorney-General, Carlos Mauro Hoyos Jiminez, a dedicated democrat and courageous reforming politician. After a brief 'trial', in which he was accused of 'treason and selling out the homeland', Jiminez was murdered. Specifically, Jiminez had advocated that Gaviria and four other drug chiefs, known as the Medellin cartel, should be hunted down and extradited to the United States to stand trial. These five men control 80% of the world's cocaine trade. Three years earlier, Justice Minister Rodrigo Lara Bonilla had been murdered for having tried to bring the Medellin Cartel to justice. In January 1987, Bonilla's successor as Justice Minister, Enrique Parejo Gonzalaz, survived an assassination attempt in Budapest.

President Barco had always hesitated to attack the Medellin Cartel openly and forcefully, as various Justice Ministers had urged, though he often pointed out that Colombia was paying a heavy price in lives in the struggle against international drug trafficking.

Just before Jiminez was killed, the Medellin Cartel had organized the kidnapping of Andres Pastrana, son of a former President. By holding him and threatening to kill him, the drug chiefs intended to dominate the government. As it happened, while searching for the killers of Jiminez, the police stumbled on the hideaway where Pastrana was being held, and rescued him.

Returning to Bogota, Pastrana resumed his campaign as Social Conservative candidate to become mayor of the city. His major promise was to attack the capital's chronic drug-addiction problem.

During the early part of 1988 the rule of law virtually disappeared. Bernardo Jaramillo, president of the Patriotic Union, reported that in the run-up to the elections in March 1988, 600 party members, including seventeen candidates for major, had been killed by death squads. Jaramillo has a 14-man bodyguard provided by the government but one of these men was found to be in the pay of the Medellin Cartel.

In March 1988 twenty-three trade union members in Uraba, a region on the Caribbean coast under the army's control, were dragged from their beds in banana plantations in the early hours of the morning and shot. Their 'crime' was that they were members of the Patriotic Union and trade unions.

It is now practically impossible to disentangle guerrilla activity from the drug barons' operations. Some guerrilla groups are, in fact, financially supported by drug money. Others have the backing of either liberal or conservative groups.

A new group which came on the scene in 1988 is the 'America Battalion', whose members are not only Colombian but Bolivian, Ecuadorean, El Salvadoran, Nicaraguan Sandinistas, Panamanian and Peruvian. 'America Battalion' is said to be financed by North Korea and Cuba and it seems to have no affiliation within Colombia.

All problems are settled by the gun and so many murders occur that the police do not even try to solve them. A Bogota television station ran a programme about stress and interviewed a car driver who had been overseas. 'I have been to foreign countries', he said, 'and I can assure you that people there do not shoot other drivers if they have an argument'. Some Bogota people formed an Association of Non-Murderous Drivers but it was generally considered that they had a short life-expectancy.

The genuine guerrillas, as distinct from the death squads and private armies, are content to see Colombia torn apart by violence. Manuel Marulanda of FARC and Father Perez, the former Catholic priest who controls CNG, believe that when order has broken down completely, they will be able to mount a successful coup which will be accepted by the great mass of Colombian citizens.

Marulanda, in a statement in mid-1988, said that after such a coup the guerrillas 'may have to cleanse Colombian society by killing all the men of violence'. Apparently he saw no irony in his words.

Colombian Armed Forces

The security services had gained a grip on drug trafficking in 1986-87 but they lost it in 1988, largely because the Medellin Cartel and other drug barons had bribed key officers to provide information. Also, they infiltrated their own men into the forces. These agents then set about turning servicemen into drug addicts. This sabotage campaign has blunted the security forces' cutting edge.

However, the armed services are still strong and have even more personnel than in previous years. The total strength is 67,000, with reserves of 100,000 for the army, 15,000 for the navy and 2,000 for the air force. The army has a strength of more than 57,000, of which 26,000 are conscripts. It is among the conscripts that the drug saboteurs are most active.

The armed forces would achieve better results against the guerrillas if they had more specialist jungle and mountain warfare units. The establishment includes one ranger and one paratroop battalion but they are not of high standard. Some of the eleven infantry brigades are well trained but are only suitable for conventional warfare. The forty-three combat aircraft of the Colombian air force include sixteen armed helicopters. This is a small number to cover the large area of wild country in Colombia in which the guerrillas have their camps. The military Air Transport Command is strong, with fifty aircraft. The roads are so dangerous that most troop movement is by air.

East Timor Resistance War

'OPERASI KEAMANAN'—13 YEARS ON

Background Summary

The Portuguese abandoned their part of East Timor in 1975, after 500 years of colonialism, and several factions sought to gain control of the territory. The Indonesians already controlled another part of East Timor, known as Timor-Dili, and the western half had belonged to the Dutch. This passed to Indonesia. Civil war broke out in former Portuguese Timor on 11 August 1975 when the Unaio Democratica de Timor (UDT) seized key positions in Dili and Baucau. The most powerful group, Frente Revolucionara de Timor-Leste Independente (Fretilin) won the war and declared independence on 3 November 1975. The following week, in 'Operasi Keamanan'—Operation Security—Indonesia forcibly annexed East Timor. Within 10 years the Indonesians had massacred 200,000 of the population of 688,000. The Indonesian Army and Air Force sealed off the island to prevent news of the genocide seeping out but Roman Catholic priests escaped to alert the world.[1] Meanwhile, the East Timorese Resistance fought against occupation.

Summary of the War in 1986-87

The Indonesian government denied that 'criminal' resistance activities presented any problem to 'peaceful administration' but escapees gave convincing evidence that a vigorous resistance movement was worrying the Indonesian Army commanders. In May 1986 a batch of documents which reached friends of the East Timorese, in Lisbon, gave proof of an organized resistance.

Sent by the Fretilin commander, José Guamao Xanana, the documents included a map which showed Fretilin's forces organized into companies operating in ten military zones in the central and eastern highlands. The whole of the former colony covers 15,000 square miles and Fretilin appeared to be active in about half this area. Xanana explained that since the Indonesians knew Fretilin's operational areas he was not breaching his own security. In 1986 and again in 1987 reports reaching the West, through diplomatic and church routes, indicated that Indonesian soldiers dreaded posting to East Timor because of Fretilin activities. Appeals by friends of the East Timorese people for action by the UN—an official visit of inspection, for instance—were unsuccessful. Some reports, perhaps Indonesian-inspired, allege that Fretilin is a Marxist group but Roman Catholic priests who have left the country assert that Fretilin wants a democratic government.

The War in 1988

In the jungle-clad hills the ill-equipped Fretilin guerrillas nevertheless continued

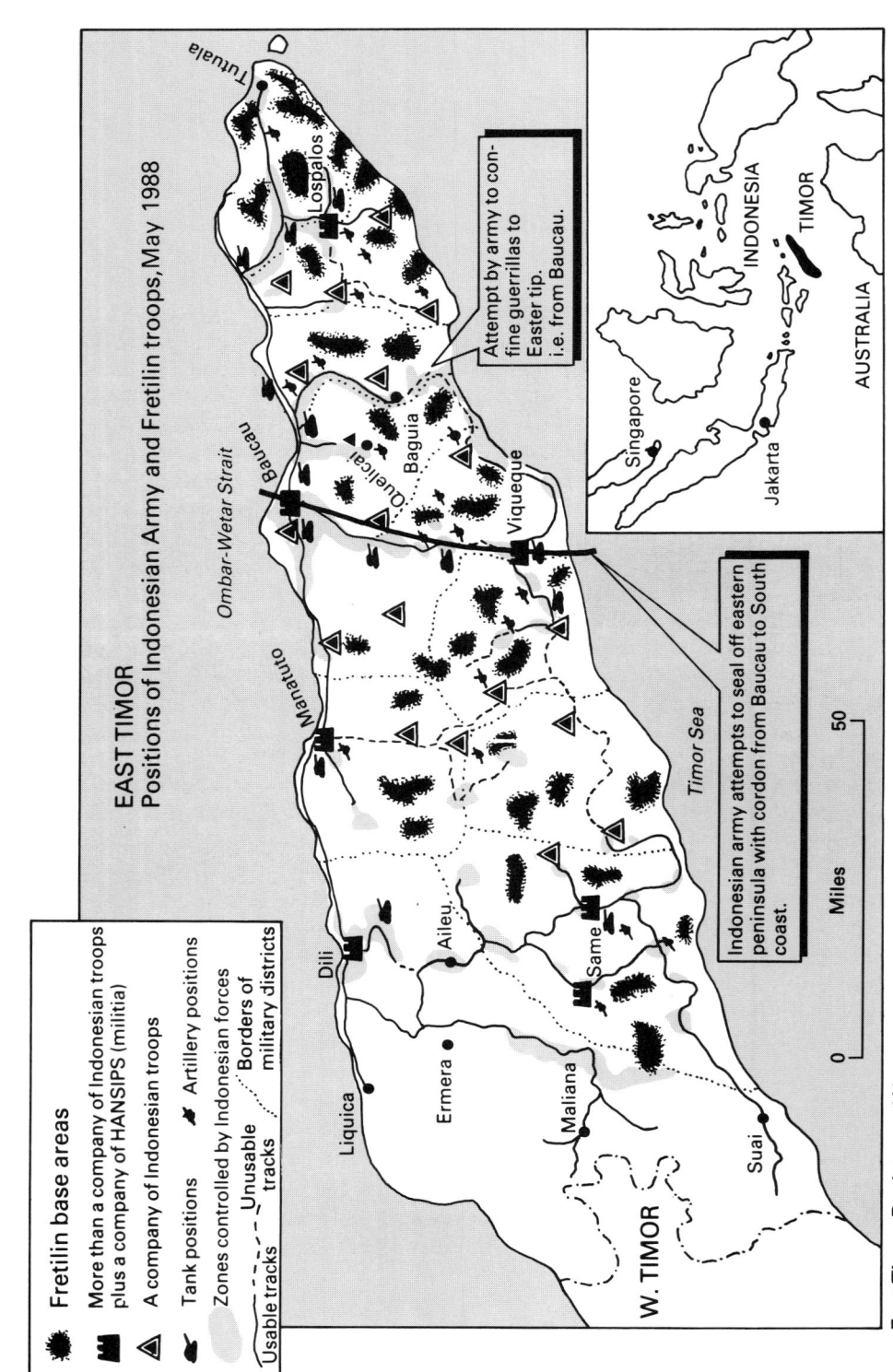

East Timor Resistance War

East Timorese villagers, under attack by the Indonesian Army since 1975, can still manage a show of resistance. (Courtesy CI/IR.)

to harass Indonesian patrols and to attack isolated posts. That these attacks are effective is shown by a government order to newspapers in Indonesia itself not to report military activities in East Timor. Diplomatic sources in Djakarta say that East Timor might not exist for all that is said about it in the information media.

During the year Fretilin apparently made a strategic policy change. Indonesian soldiers would be attacked when off duty in the towns. This move was partly in retaliation against army brutality to the civilian population and to political prisoners. A colonel is reported to have been killed in the southern town of Betana.

Fretilin operations, being selective, are not expensive in use of ammunition, but supplies have reached the guerrillas from supporters in Malaya. The manufacturing origin of these munitions is obscure. During 1987 Fretilin carried out few operations using explosives but in 1988 several Indonesian vehicles were blown up, indicating that fresh supplies had arrived. One source suggests that Soviet-made mines are being used. A raiding party blew up an army supply dump at Lospalos. This operation is significant because Lospalos is in the middle of the eastern tip of the island, into which the army has been fruitlessly trying to drive the guerrillas.

In August 1988 explosions occurred simultaneously in the widely separated towns of Dili, Manatuto, Beguia, Aileu and Same. They appeared to have caused little damage but the Fretilin message was clear: They could operate with impunity all over the island. Church sources say that no Fretilin commander was captured in the period September 1987-September 1988 and that only two guerrillas were caught. They were tortured and executed.

The Minority Rights Group (MRG) of London, says: 'East Timor has incurred, in percentage terms, greater suffering from the Indonesian invasion than almost any other victim of an invasion this century. The suffering shows no signs of easing. It seems very much that the government is seeking to starve East Timor into submission. Indonesia's invasion has been marked by a degree of barbarity which many people outside the area find difficult to comprehend.[2]

In fact, it is not so difficult to comprehend. Indonesia is an Islamic country—it has the largest Muslim population in the world—while about 200,000 East Timorese are Roman Catholics. According to confidential and reliable sources, Indonesian soldiers in East Timor have been told that they are engaged in a holy war or *jihad* against infidels, that is, non-Muslims. This would account for the barbarous nature of the occupation.

MRG points out that non-governmental organizations are doing more to help the East Timorese than the UN or any government. The main ones are the Australian Campaign for an Independent Timor and its equivalent organization overseas, and the New York-based International League for Human Rights. 'The foreign mass media have played a disgraceful part in reporting or non-reporting or misreporting East Timor', states an MRG report. 'There are certain exceptions, such as some small circulation left-wing newspapers and notable conservative newspapers in Australia—*Age*, Melbourne; *Sydney Morning Herald* and *National Times*, Sydney.'

References

1. The Roman Catholic Institute for International Relations has sought to bring the East Timorese tragedy before world opinion since 1975.
2. *East Timor and West Irian*, Report No. 42, published by the Minority Rights Group, London.

Ethiopia–Eritrea–Tigré–Somalia

Background Summary

The people of Eritrea have long regarded themselves as a separate people from the Ethiopians. Much of Eritrea's identity as a nation was imposed by the Italians, who ruled the area from 1880 until 1941. Having imposed their language on the people, they welded the Christian, Muslim and Animist peoples and the eight major nationalities into a political entity. The British threw out the Italians during World War II and the United Nations agreed, through Resolution 390A, that Eritrea would be an autonomous territory federated with Ethiopia. However, the Ethiopians would not permit autonomy to develop and the predominantly Muslim Eritreans claimed that they should have a separate state from the mainly Christian southerners who inhabit Ethiopia.

Ethiopia annexed Eritrea in 1961 and the Eritrean Liberation Front (ELF) fought for independence. With only 40,000 men, the ELF held off the 80,000 Ethiopians. In 1977 the Soviet Union, which had been arming neighbouring Somalia, dropped that country and backed Ethiopia. Russian support enabled the Ethiopians to expel the ELF guerrillas from the main towns.

Simultaneously, the Tigrean People's Liberation Army (TPLF) was fighting the Ethiopians for autonomy in the region adjoining Eritrea and in the south the Ogaden tribes fought to unite with their countrymen in Somalia. For its massive operations, the Ethiopian army of Colonel Mengistu was increased to 306,000. The ELF became the Eritrean People's Liberation Front (EPLF) and, as the main opposing force, inflicted several defeats on the Ethiopians.

By 1986 the EPLF was no longer a guerrilla force and was fighting as a regular army. They used British, French, US, Italian and West German equipment, though it reached them through Kuwait, Somalia and the United Arab Emirates. Much captured Soviet-made equipment, particularly tanks, vehicles, guns and armoured personnel carriers, added to their stocks.

The War in 1987

In 1987 the EPLF, with 26,000 fighting men and women, controlled northern Eritrea from the Red Sea to the Sudanese border, with a 340-mile line of trenches. However, they had lost ground during the Ethiopian Army's eighth general offensive which forced the Eritreans to retreat into the hills of Nakfa. The Ethiopians, despite air attacks with napalm and cluster bombs, could not dislodge them.

By then the EPLF held more than 10,000 Ethiopian prisoners, who survived only with Red Cross aid. The EPLF did not have the resources to feed them and Ethiopia disowned them.

0
Miles
150
SAUDI ARABIA
Red Sea
Nakfa
Halhal
ERITREA
Afabet
SUDAN
Keren
Massawa
Agordat
NORTH
YEMEN
Asmara
Eritrean
Highlands
Adigrat
Makale
TIGRE
GONDER
Assab
Maychew
Korem
Lake Tana
WELLO
DJIBOUTI
ETHIOPIA
GOJAM
SOMALIA
HARERGE
SHEWA
Dire Dawa
WELEGA
Addis
Ababa
ERITREA
ETHIOPIA

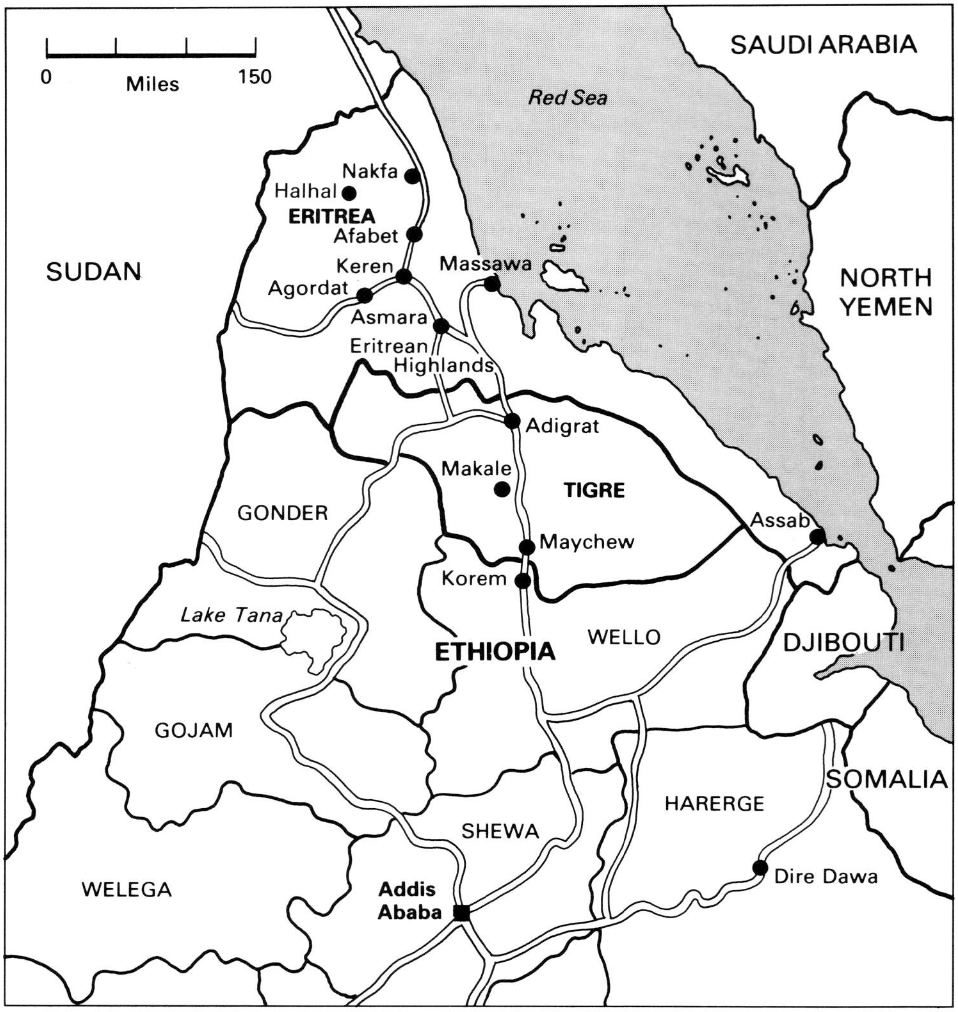

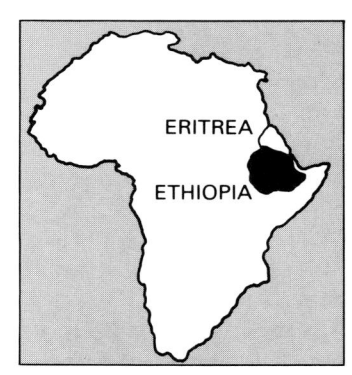

Because of the EPLF's socialist character, the West apparently saw it as a more serious long-term threat than that of the ruling Ethiopian Dergue. Some Western leaders were confident that Ethiopia, once it defeated the Eritreans, would turn away from the Soviet Union and side with the West.

While the EPLF was still struggling, it seemed that the TPLF appeared to have won its 12-year war against the Ethiopians. It claimed support in eighty per cent of Tigré and in 1986-87 brought 100,000 refugees back from Sudan. The Somali government continued to watch the war anxiously. They feared that if the Soviet Union could not gain Red Sea and Horn of Africa bases through Ethiopia-Eritrea, the Russian leaders would break through Somalia to achieve their objectives.

Capture of Maidama and Areza

On 24 December 1987 the EPLF began an offensive near the devastated town of Nakfa. They pushed twenty-five miles north against spasmodic opposition and then surrounded an Ethiopian brigade. The Eritreans took many prisoners and captured two T-55 tanks and much equipment.

Moving on, they overran the defended towns of Maidama and Areza, forty miles south of Asmara. Many inexperienced young Ethiopian conscripts were mown down in this fighting. Some survivors told foreign relief workers that they had been press-ganged from farms and villages to fight what President Mengistu calls 'the Eritrean bandits'.

In this offensive the EPLF said that it killed 710 government troops, wounded 230, captured 147 prisoners and seized artillery and ammunition. The figures could not be confirmed but foreign aid workers are constantly aware that the number of prisoners is growing.

The Battle of Afabet

The town of Afabet, forty-three miles to the south-east of Nakfa, had become the main Ethiopian command and head-quarters post on the Nakfa front in 1979. It was also the main military depot for the Ethiopian divisions deployed on the Nakfa front, the site of the strategic army reserve and the centre of the army's intelligence operations.

Having been victorious in an attack on the left flank of the Nakfa front in December 1987, the EPLF command planned an attack on Afabet itself. For an army totally without air cover and without adequate heavy artillery to soften the defences, the concept was ambitious. Afabet was held by more than 20,000 Ethiopians in long-established and strong positions. The three divisions protecting Nakfa were considered the best in the Ethiopian army, especially the *Nado* (Destroy) division, and reinforcements could readily reach them in an emergency.

Under the Secretary-General of the EPLF, Issayas Afewerki, and the Front's Chief of Intelligence, the Eritrean commanders evolved a plan that involved practically the whole of the EPLF's military strength. During the night of Thursday 17 March 1988 the attacking troops, roughly thirty per cent of them women, crept into positions in front of and on both flanks of the Afabet defences.

The first phase was to be an infantry attack to overrun the front Ethiopian positions. Simultaneously, hundreds of lightly-equipped Eritreans would move in

Aftermath of battle where EPLF ambushed Ethiopian convoy. (Jenny Matthews.)

Woman fighter, Afabet. (Jenny Matthews.)

columns to encircle the garrison and demoralize the Ethiopians by fire from flank and rear. With their infantry committed, the Eritrean artillery, including tank guns, would pound positions behind the Ethiopian infantry and machine-gun lines.

The Eritreans were counting on total surprise. The Ethiopian High Command had long assumed that Afabet was unassailable. Even should it be attacked it could not be captured. Three Soviet Army advisers stationed there, two of them colonels, had inspected the defences only a few days before the Eritrean attack and were impressed with their strength. But their assessment was based on the assumption that the Eritreans could not risk an attack in which they ran an enormous chance of being slaughtered in thousands. Both the Ethiopians and their Soviet advisers were still thinking of the Eritreans as guerrillas.

When the attack started at dawn on 17 March the Eritrean surprise was complete and the Ethiopian outposts were captured at once.

The Ethiopians had fifty tanks in Afabet as well as eighty guns, mainly 130 mm and 122 mm calibre. There was also a plentiful supply of BM-21 rocket launchers and twenty Zu-23 anti-aircraft guns which the Ethiopians used as ground attack weapons. Few of these weapons were any use to the defenders, since they could not find a target. The EPLF troops, intelligently using ground cover and advancing on a simple fire-and-movement principle, were rarely visible long enough for the defenders to bring their heavy weapons to bear.

Army reinforcements set in motion along the Keren-Afabet road were unable to get through the passes, now held by the EPLF. Air strikes against them achieved little and the MiG-21s and MiG-23s which strafed the Eritreans caused few casualties.

During the first day the Ethiopians in Afabet tried to regroup but to do this they needed to expose themselves. Eritrean snipers—who are probably the best trained in Africa—picked off many of them. This inhibited further movement. At dusk, when the risk from the strafing MiGs was less, the Eritreans continued their encircling movement.

In fact, numerous Eritreans had been in position in the rear, under cover, for some days. When the Ethiopians tried to move towards the rear they found their escape cut off. It seems that not one of the 200 or so transport vehicles in Afabet managed to get out. Many were hit by rocket-propelled grenades (RPGs) and burst into flames. Tanks and guns were hit by RPGs and by shells fired at longer range.

Within forty-eight hours the Ethiopian 14th, 19th and 21st divisions, the 29th Mechanized Brigade and nine battalions of artillery—the entire enemy force—had been killed or captured. The EPLF took 18,000 prisoners, including the three Soviet officers, fifty tanks, including some T-62s, a number of M-113 armoured personnel carriers, eighty guns and vast quantities of personal weapons and ammunition.

The capture of Afabet meant the collapse of the Ethiopian positions on the entire Nakfa front and a general retreat took place, though this was not authorized from Addis Ababa. The battle of Afabet, which some observers have already renamed the battle of Nakfa, was a major victory for the EPLF and a great blow to the Ethiopians, who moved quickly first to deny it and then to play it down. Ethiopian radio broadcast the result of a purported football match in Afabet several days after the town was captured.

Following their defeat at Afabet, the Ethiopians evacuated the towns of Tessenei,

Ali Ghidir and Haicota on 26 March and on 31 March abandoned Barentu after setting fire to the army depots.

Early on 1 April EPLF forces attacked on the Halhal front, the only remaining trench line. In a three-hour battle they inflicted an estimated 2,000 casualties and captured large quantities of arms and stores. The fall of the Halhal front forced the Ethiopians into a hurried withdrawal from the Eritrean town of Agordat, capital of Barka province.

The EPLF fighters then tightened their grip around Keren, the most important town after Asmara. In a series of engagements they pushed Ethiopian detachments from the strategic passes of Genfelom, Jengeren and Mesihalit, all within twelve miles of Keren. A few days later, Mount Lalmba, only four miles from Keren, fell to EPLF troops who had scaled the heights and attacked from the rear. Army garrisons in and around Keren became vulnerable to EPLF gunfire.

The EPLF leaders knew that their victory was not decisive and they also knew that they could not indefinitely hold Afabet. The Ethiopian Army has a strength of 313,000 and powerful reinforcements could be moved up. However, they would have to come from Tigré, where a separate war was in progress. The Tigreans had recently captured two important towns.

The EPLF success had three important effects. It demoralized the Ethiopian Army, whose men had been fed for years on the idea that the Eritreans were merely bandits, incapable of a sustained military action. Also, the victory brought badly needed worldwide recognition to the Eritreans. The third effect was that it started a line of thought in the Soviet High Command that perhaps they had backed the wrong side in the war.

Ethiopian Counter-Offensive

Goaded by the EPLF successes following the battle of Afabet, the Ethiopian Army planned a multipronged counter-offensive for 13 May 1988. EPLF Intelligence heard of this impending attack and on 11 May hit the Ethiopians with a pre-emptive operation around Keren. The EPLF claimed to have 'wiped out' 4,000 Ethiopian troops.

The army's counter-offensive went ahead and in three main directions. One force attempted to break through the northern edge of Keren; the second moved from Massawa along the eastern plains towards the Felket and Azahra passes, about eighteen miles east of Afabet; the third set out along the Mensae mountains.

The column that approached the passes included paratroop and commando units but, in the battles which ensued when the Ethiopians came up against the EPLF positions they suffered as much as the other units. Of the sixty-five Ethiopian tanks engaged, about twenty-one were destroyed, mostly by rocket-propelled grenades. The paratroops and commandos were encircled and only a handful of men escaped. The commander of Ethiopia's paratroop and commando forces, Brigadier Temesgen Gemechu, was killed. All three columns were repulsed.[1]

The Famine Fight

In 1988, as the country suffered its second food shortage in four years, the Ethiopian government and the EPLF waged yet another 'battle' over rights to feed the peasants. Part of the battle was operational—actually delivering food by aircraft, truck and camel. Another part is rhetorical, that is, propaganda attacks on the 'enemy' for playing politics with relief food.

It is recognized among relief workers that whoever controls food controls people. In 1988 the rebels were prepared to fight to win the food battle. The UN operation in Sudan feeds Ethiopians who cannot obtain food in their own country. In 1984-85 about 300,000 refugees, most from Tigré and Eritrea, walked west to the UN camps in Sudan to wait out the famine. Many of the peasants were escorted into Sudan by rebels, part of whose objective was to prevent the refugees from eating donated food delivered under the auspices of the Ethiopian government. In 1988 the EPLF and other groups increased their capacity to deliver their own donated food.

There appeared to be a good chance, late in 1987, of preventing families from abandoning their farms and congregating in the feeding centres where hundreds of thousands of people died in 1984-85, mostly from infectious diseases.

The Eritrean Relief Association, linked to the EPLF, is better equipped and organized to cope with famine than in 1984 and could reach 850,000 people. The 1984 famine found the world unprepared but in 1988 the agencies in Khartoum which co-ordinate aid programmes for Eritrea were well supplied with trucks and had greater expertise. They had also overcome their reluctance to assist in the rebel areas of Eritrea and Tigré for fear of upsetting the government in Addis Ababa.

The Eritrean Relief Association and the Relief Society of Tigré were given at least 80,000 tons of food during 1988. About half came from the US government and half from the European Community (EC). The US and EC are the largest suppliers of relief food for distribution in the government-controlled areas. The Eritrean Relief Association can move in 10,000 tons a month from Sudan. Tigré rebels have 170 trucks and the capacity to transport 7,000 tons of food a month.

Then a serious setback occurred. On a road outside the Eritrean capital of Asmara EPLF men attacked a convoy of twenty-three UN trucks carrying US-donated wheat to government-controlled distribution centres in Tigré. All the food, enough to feed 45,000 people for a month, was burned. Also burned were £2m worth of trucks donated by the US; they comprised one third of the UN's fleet of long-haul relief trucks.

The EPFL claimed that its men destroyed the UN aid convoy by mistake, then alleged that the convoy carried military supplies as well as food and finally reported that the local commander had attacked the wrong convoy.

The world's perception of the attack was a public relations disaster for the EPLF because it generated news coverage portraying the organization as callous and barbarous. The US threatened the rebels with a total cut-off in food assistance if they destroyed other food relief convoys. This forced the rebels to state that they 'would make every effort to select out and protect relief vehicles in future attacks on government-sanctioned convoys'. It also suggested that it would give advance warning to foreign relief agencies of attacks that might endanger their operations.[2]

Trucks, and the food they carry, save lives. However, Western agency workers say that trucks and food further the military aims of the government and of the rebels. Promise of food will take peasants to a government town, as desired by the Ethiopian regime. Supply of food on the spot will keep the people there to do what they can for the long war, as the EPLA wants. A friendly village will raise sons and daughters to become rebel fighters.

For years, Western relief agencies working in Eritrea have been accusing the Ethiopian government of systematically attacking rebel relief convoys and killing livestock to defeat the efforts of civilians in rebel areas to feed themselves. Farmers are often bombed while weeding their sorghum crops. Also, there is no doubt that the Ethiopian government often uses UN convoys for military movement in the rebel-held areas.[4]

It is true that the EPLF showed maximum restraint and allowed food convoys to pass even when their conditions had not been fully met. It is also true that the Ethiopian government on several occasions in 1988 mixed troop movements with relief convoys. Sometimes the army painted its military vehicles with the insignia of humanitarian organizations.[5]

The Ethiopian government has had to bend to world opinion and donor pressure. Addis Ababa does not like it but the US government has insisted that its donated food should not be handled or distributed by the Ethiopian government. Instead, it was to be distributed by such private relief agencies as Catholic Relief Services or the International Committee of the Red Cross.

However, donor pressure has lost out at times to military strategy. While private relief agencies hand out US-donated food in the north, it is the government which strictly limits the distribution sites. And the EPLF stated that, while it would try to avoid destroying food convoys, it had no intention of delaying an offensive that was likely to complicate the movement of food.

For its part, the TPLF insisted that it was only interested in the well-being of the people of Tigré but it threatened to begin seizing food convoys unless the government cancelled its population resettlement programme.

Given enough outside donations of food, the rebels have no doubt that they can meet the needs of their people. At night the rough and winding dirt roads are crowded with Mercedes trucks hauling in food from Sudan. The trucks travel only at night, when they are invisible to Ethiopian aircraft. At dawn, the drivers hide their trucks under giant acacia trees.

The EPLF bring in their own supplies 180 miles along the rough track from Port Sudan to their base area, high in the mountains near the Sudanese border, in a fleet of about 250 Mercedes trucks. The rebels also have a satellite telephone link with friends abroad. A fleet of yellow motor-bikes provides a postal service connecting the many camouflaged villages from which they run their war operations.

Westerners do not understand why suggestions for a 'food truce' have never been taken up in northern Ethiopia. The reason reveals the combatants' strategy. In Ethiopia's case, a formal agreement allowing unrestricted passage of humanitarian convoys would force the government to acknowledge officially that it is fighting a war that it cannot win. In the rebels' case, they would have to be convinced that the government was not using relief convoys as cover for military operations. The EPLF and TPLF leaders, at war for more than a generation, are too warwise to be so convinced.

In fact, a glut of relief food could upset war strategy for both sides. If relief food moved too freely they could lose loyalties carefully built up over many years.

Tigré Victories

For several years the Ethiopian Army has had strong garrisons in towns in Tigré province. The TPLF has tried several times to capture some of them but until 1988 had succeeded only in isolating some centres. At the end of February 1988 the TPLF embarked on a more ambitious and carefully planned offensive and in March captured four towns, Wukro, Abi Adi, Senkata and Debub.

Wukro and Abi Adi are food distribution centres and their loss threatened to cut off supplies to about 400,000 people. The rebels invited international agencies to continue sending emergency supplies but the agencies pointed out that the Ethiopian government did not allow them into rebel-held territory. The TPLF operated its own small-scale relief operation from Sudan but its resources could not match those of international Ethiopia-based organizations.

Senkata and Wukro lie on the main road south to Mekele, capital of Tigré, from Asmara, capital of Eritrea. Debub is twelve miles east of the road, and Abi Adi forty miles west of it. Debub and Abi Adi were occupied after government troops withdrew but the TPLF had to fight for Senkata and Wukro. Relief agency officials confirmed TPLF claims to have inflicted 'numerous casualties' on the Ethiopian defenders.

Mengistu's Desperation

Following the humiliating EPLF and TPLF victories in March-May 1988, the Ethiopian regime resorted to vengeance attacks. One of the most ruthless was made against the town of Shiib in eastern Eritrea, on 12 May. Fifteen tanks rumbled into the undefended town and the community fled before the tanks and soldiers who herded the people into a narrow valley. Here 320 were machine-gunned and eighty crushed by the tanks. More than 2,000 homes were burnt down.

The EPLF alleged similar atrocities in other towns but these remain unconfirmed. However, such attacks are in keeping with Mengistu's stated policy of forcing the Eritreans into submission.

In a series of massive airlifts, the army transferred several divisions from the Ogaden and frontiers with Somalia. The senior Soviet advisers were asked for replacement tanks, guns and other equipment, which, if supplied, would cost £1bn. By 1988 the Soviet had already given Ethiopia £4bn. worth of material.

Even before the army's worst defeats, Mengistu punished several senior officers for failing in their duties. Brigadier Tariku Taye, chief of the 'Nadew Command' on the Nakfa front, was executed on 15 February 1988. His front had been broken by the EPLF in December 1987. Major General Regass Jima, commander of the army in Eritrea and Lieutenant Colonel Shiwarega Bihonegm, the political commissar of the army in Eritrea, were sentenced to death but Mengistu could not summarily execute them as both were members of the Dergue's central committee.

Colonel Demeke Banjaw, chief medical officer of the army in Eritrea, was sentenced to twenty years in prison. General Taye Balcher, police chief commander in Eritrea, was severely reprimanded. Brigadier Kebede Bagshaw, commander of all troops behind the fixed fronts, was demoted. Colonel Girma Taferi, GOC 22nd Division, was dismissed.

After the major defeats of Afabet and Halhal other officers were reported to have been executed.[6]

Foreign Professional Assessments

Numerous foreigners, apart from relief workers, have visited Eritrea. Western journalists have written about the high degree of EPLF organization. Basil Davidson of *The Guardian*, London, reported on the 1,250 miles of new roadway carved through Eritrea's difficult terrain by engineers of the EPLF. 'No other movement of national resistance that I have known since 1943 has achieved anything like this', he wrote.[7]

Professor Fred Hollows, an Australian ophthalmic surgeon who worked for some time in the EPLF base hospital at Orotta, described the medical administrative area and a visit to the EPLF front line.[8] 'There are several valleys, all surrounded by steep rocky hills. On the sides of the valley floors there are trees, mostly the thorny acacias, and under these trees and partly dug into the valley sides are the different parts of the base area administration. Each institution, such as the operating theatres, maxilla facial unit, orthopaedic ward, pediatric ward and others are placed separately so that vulnerability to attack from the air is lessened.

> Sharp at 7am a sound of distant automatic gunfire startled me. It was a sort of rhythmical triple burst. The Eritreans were amused at my surprise. The rifle fire burst is the call theme of the thrice daily EPLF broadcast. This station operating from the highlands of Eritrea can be heard from Beirut to Kenya. I visited the front line. Young fighters were on sentry duty a few hundred yards from the Ethiopian positions. The narrow trenches, cramped conditions and proximity of danger made me happy to retreat to a dugout just behind the trenches.
>
> The dugout was filled with young fighters, women and men, engaged in an animated eyeball to eyeball debate. The vigour of the debate prompted me to ask my guide what the subject of the matter was. It was the hygiene of living conditions and was part of the daily programme of education and consciousness-raising that I saw everywhere Eritreans gathered.
>
> I know there are many different classes, ethnic groups, levels of education and religion that make up the amalgam that is Eritrea, but for me the factor that set Eritrea apart from other Third World situations that I have worked in is the high level of consciousness about the history, nature and direction of the Eritrean struggle for freedom and peace. To me it seemed that the Eritrean consciousness was not cluttered with dogma and religious bigotry, but firmly based on an understanding of their history yet sensitive to Eritrea's place in the Middle East. To me it seems that Eritrea is a leading model for a post colonial African state.

Somalia War Erupts Again

For several years the Somalia National Movement (SNM) and another rebel movement, the Somali Salvation Democratic Front (SSDF) has received strong but discreet support from Ethiopia, which has had a border dispute with Somalia since 1977. The rebel movements shared a radio station which broadcast from Ethiopia and the SNM had a rearguard base in the north-eastern town of Dire Dawa.

However, with Eritrean and Tigréan rebels giving Ethiopia enough problems, the Addis Ababa government agreed, on 3 April 1988, to 'normalize' ties with Somalia. The immediate effect of the agreement was a demilitarization of the

Ethiopia–Somali border and a commitment that both governments would refrain from supporting each other's guerrilla enemies. *Radio Halgan*, the Somali rebel radio station, fell silent.

Regional analysts thought that the agreement marked a downturn in the ability of the guerrillas to sustain their campaign against the nineteen-year rule of President Muhammad Siad Barre. Diplomats in Mogadishu, the Somali capital, say that the SNM, dominated by the north-western Issaq clan, resents domination of the government by Barre's immediate family and the Marehan clan from central Somalia.

The SNM has always denied that its guerrilla campaign, centred in the rugged mountains of north-western Somalia, is a tribal war. Until the beginning of June 1988 SNM offensives amounted to guerrilla attacks on military outposts and occasional propaganda exploits, such as the kidnapping of ten French aid workers from refugee camps near the Ethiopian frontier in January 1987. The hostages were released a few days later at Addis Ababa.

On 27 May 1988 the SNM launched a full scale attack on Burao, an administrative centre 120 miles east of Hargeisa. Four days later it attacked Hargeisa itself and fighting continued more-or-less constantly between the guerrillas and government troops.

By mid-June the SNM claimed to control the whole of Hargeisa town and its airport, as well as Burao and other towns in north-western Somalia. Government forces still held the port of Berbera where the United States has air and naval facilities.

Government forces, with superior firepower, forced the guerrillas to retreat in some areas and blocked their advance in others. Nevertheless, the SNM had achieved complete surprise in the opening phase of the battles and the army's casualties were high.

A possible reversal of the SNM's offensive would not necessarily mean the end of armed opposition to the Barre rule in northern Somalia. Summary execution of supposed rebel sympathizers merely added to the SNM hatred of the regime. Several of the 160 foreigners later evacuated from Hargeisa witnessed such executions. Earlier, the National Security Court had sentenced to death a former vice-president, Brigadier Ismail Ali Abokor, a former foreign minister, Omar Arteh, and six other officials accused of 'forming a sabotage unit, with the aim of causing chaos and undermining the unity of Somalia, in alliance with a foreign power'.

When the ageing President Barre dies or is overthrown civil war is likely in Somalia as the various factions struggle for power.

Analysis of the Invasion

Rebel forces of the SNM, having crossed from Ethiopia, occupied the south of Burao, which was then held by a garrison of only 100. It was quickly reinforced to 3,000, to face 1,000 well-trained rebels, supported by about 10,000 local sympathizers. The rest of the city's population of 400,000 fled. Colonel Abdi Aziz Ali, the army sector commander, said that he deliberately held back his assault for 46 days in the hope that he could induce the rebels to surrender rather than risk destruction of the city.

When Ali finally ordered a frontal assault, virtually every building in the southern half of Burao was destroyed during vicious hand-to-hand fighting. As the rebels fell back they destroyed key installations. By 19 July, the army controlled Burao but had suffered 1,000 men killed. Those rebels who survived fled to Hargeisa, to the west, where they joined a separate SNM force. This group, of perhaps 3,000 well-equipped troops backed by 15,000 militia, had attacked Hargeisa four days after the assault of Burao. They failed to capture military strongpoints but the north and east of the city were destroyed by gunfire and demolition. The entire population of 600,000 fled.

Before the army was ready to counter-attack in mid-August the rebels controlled most of Hargeisa. The army officer in command, Brigadier Ahmed Warsame, said that the rebels were determined to die rather than run. About 20,000 people in all died during the Hargeisa fighting. In all, 30,000 deaths occurred during the incursion and one million people were left homeless.

The rebels had gambled on their offensive bringing down the Barre government. The opposite seemed to occur. The nature of the SNM's campaign appeared to encourage Somalis from other regions to rally behind the regime. However, scattered rebel forces were still able to mount hit-and-run raids on roads and small towns. They had caused immense damage.

The government's military victory did nothing to enhance its reputation in the field of human rights. Amnesty International accused the government of systematic massacre of civilians, saying that the killings were deliberate executions of arrested people and 'part of a persistent pattern of gross human rights violations by the security forces'. It appealed to President Barre to stop the torture of prisoners. Most victims have been tortured to make them confess to involvement in political opposition or to provide information on other government opponents. A Canadian physician acting for the Canadian Centre for the Investigation and Prevention of Torture, who examined many Somalis, said that torture was 'a daily reality' in Somalia.[9]

References

1. Information on these battles is based on interviews with Eritrean officers and Ethiopian deserters. Diplomatic sources in Addis Ababa confirm the Ethiopian losses.
2 Oxfam assessment.
3. Statements from EPLF HQ.
4. Relief agency reports.
5. *Ibid.*
6. Ethiopian Army communiqué.
7. *The Guardian*, 6 April 1988.
8. *Adulis* Magazine, March 1988.
9. *Somalia: A Long-Term Human Rights Crisis*, Amnesty International British Section, London.

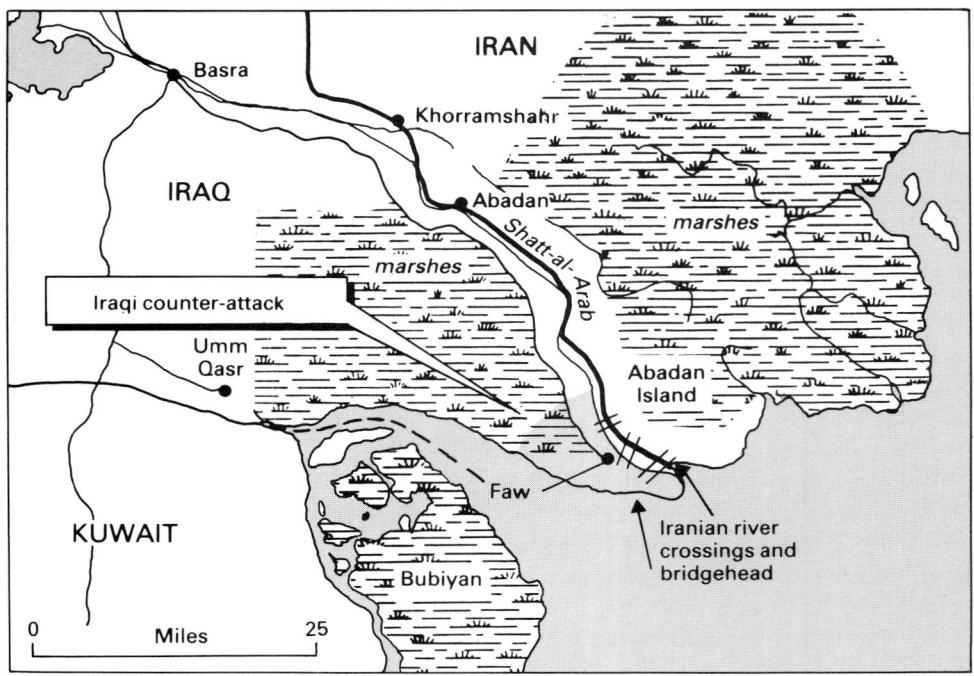

The Faw Battle

The Long Front

Iran–Iraq (Gulf) War

NO WIN, NO LOSE

Background Summary

The Gulf War began on 17 September 1980 when the Iraqi President, Saddam Hussein, attempted to capture Iranian territory which he claimed really belonged to Iraq. In dispute was the Shatt-al-Arab waterway, through which Iraq exported much of its oil. Iraq's powerful armed forces were expected to overwhelm the Iranians, whose best generals had been executed by religious zealots following the overthrow of the Shah in what was known as 'Khomeini's Revolution', in 1979.

The Iraqi infantry assault achieved tactical surprise but the Iranian lines did not break and the leaders in Tehran did not accept defeat. The first year was spent largely in artillery duels and patrol actions. In 1981 the Iranian army went on the offensive for the first time and drove out the Iraqis.

By now both sides had direct allies. Egypt, Saudi Arabia, and Jordan backed Iraq while Syria and Libya supported Iran. The Syrian-Libyan alliance with Iran caused friction in the Arab world, as Iran is not an Arab state. In July 1982 Iran launched *Operation Ramadan*, a massive infantry assault by waves of Pasdaran (Revolutionary Guards). They recovered some territory at immense cost in lives. In February 1983 they used 200,000 troops in an attack on twenty-five miles of front. Since Iraq had almost total air supremacy, the Iranian gain was small. This type of attack was repeated in April 1983, also without gain to the Iranians who by the end of the year had lost 120,000 men killed.

Great battles continued into 1984. More than 500,000 Iranians were engaged in *Operation Dawn 5* in February. By 1985 both sides, avoiding costly frontal attacks, spent much time and money in strengthening their defences. Iraq completed the construction of Fish Lake, a network of canals to protect Basra, the key southern city. The Iranians responded by digging long, deep tank traps.

During 1985 the Iraqi High Command attempted to cripple Iran's economy by bombing its oil installations and the foreign tankers using Iranian facilities. Saudi Arabia and Kuwait feared that the war would engulf them. Attempts by the great powers and by the UN to end the war were abortive. Iran presented the conflict as 'a war between Islam and heresy', while Iraq announced that it was fighting for the entire Arab race against 'vile Persian aggressors'. With forty nations selling arms and equipment to one side or the other—or to both—Iran and Iraq had the means and manpower to continue the war indefinitely.

In February 1986 Iran launched *Operation Dawn 8*. In early successes, troops crossed the Shatt-al-Arab and, at a cost of 25,000 men killed, captured the town of Faw on Faw peninsula. The next offensive was *Dawn 9*, 500 miles north of Faw. It was successful enough in terms of land captured to provoke Iraq into the use of mustard and nerve gas. The Iraqi High Command considered that chemical

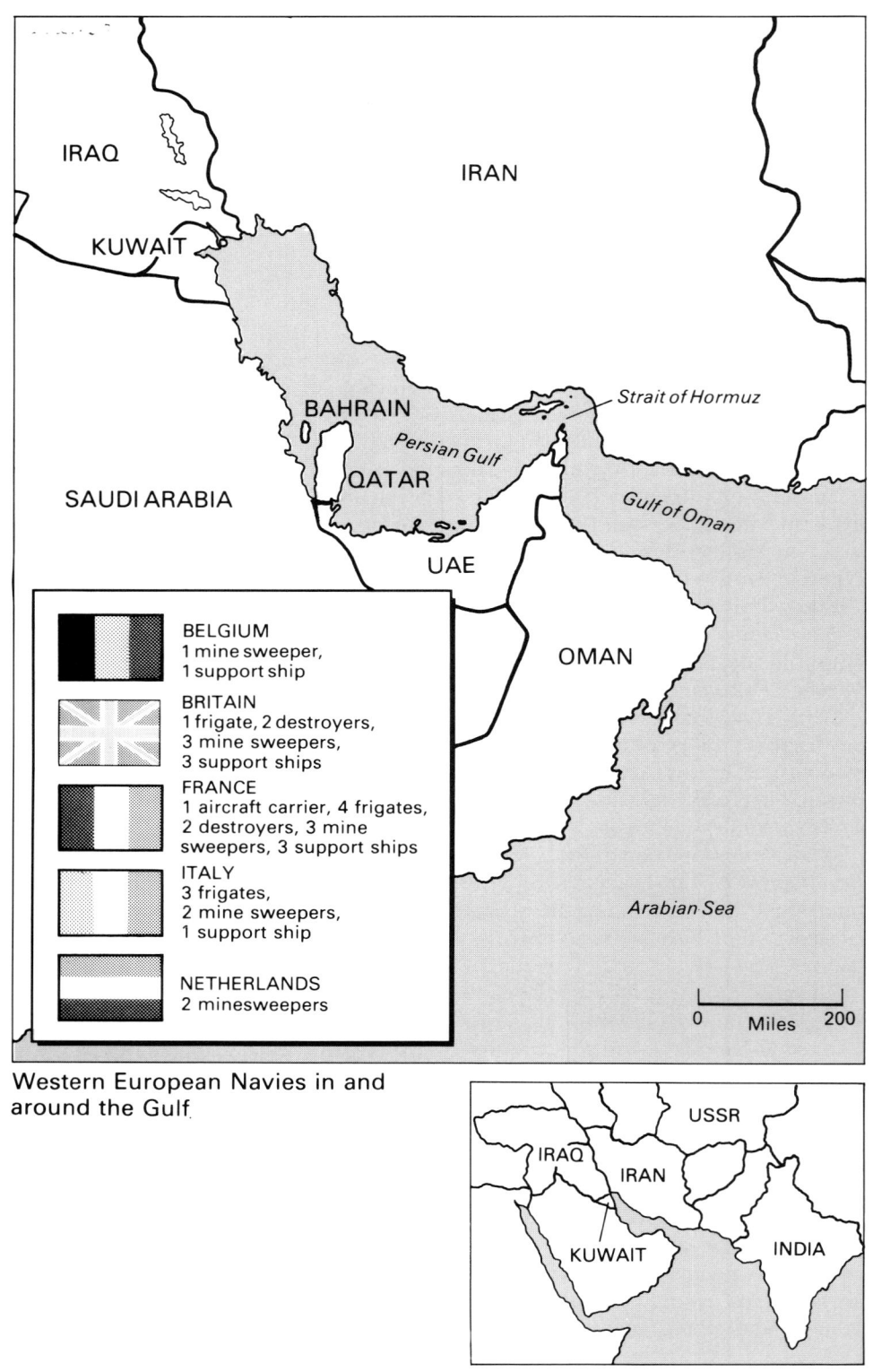

Western European Navies in and around the Gulf

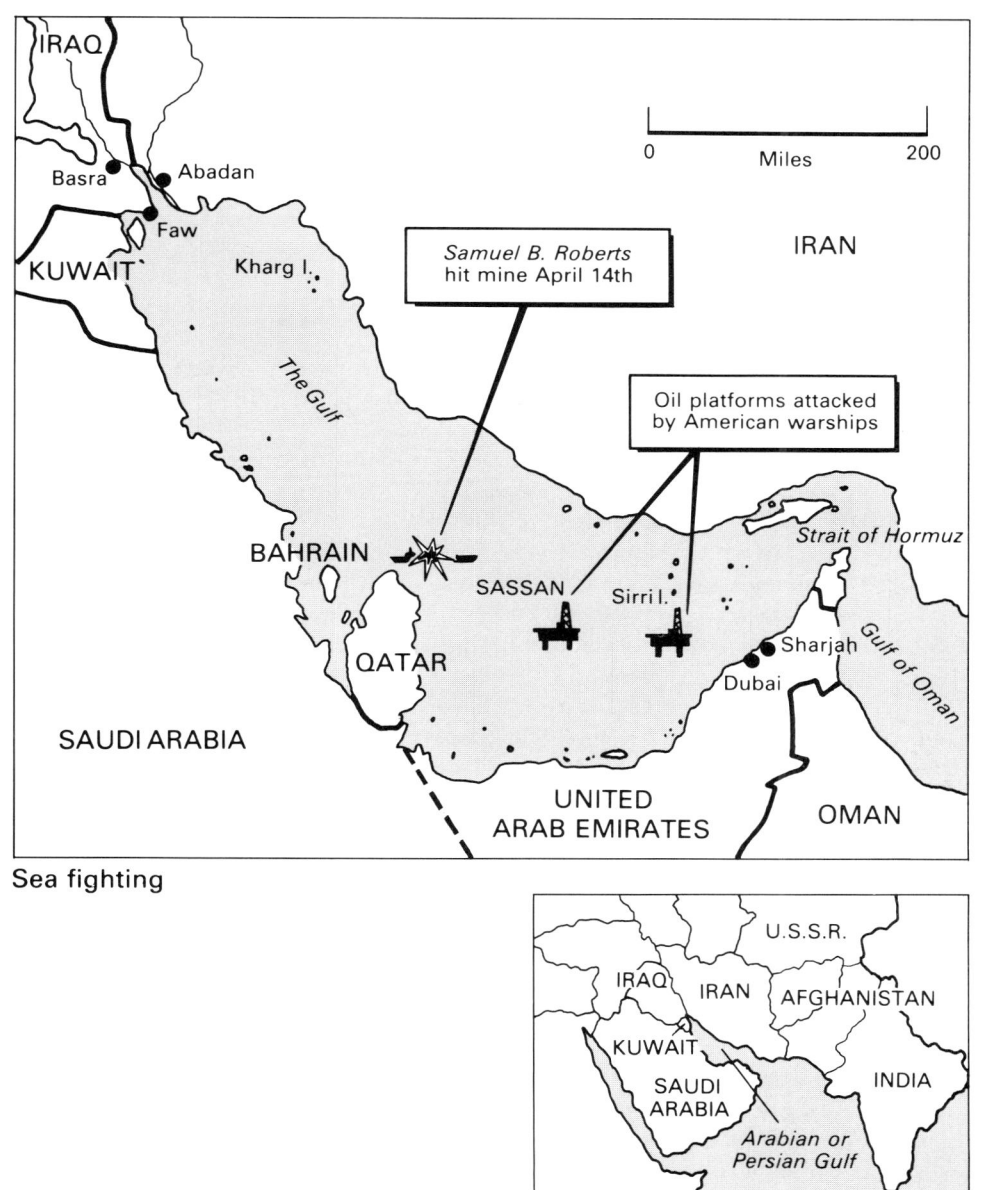

Sea fighting

weapons were necessary to counter Iran's advantage in manpower. Even so, Iraq itself had one million men under arms in March 1986, from a population of fifteen million.

In May 1986 the 2nd Iraqi Army Corps captured Mehran, just inside Iran and 160 km east of Baghdad. The Iranians counter-attacked, killing 500 Iraqis, wounding 2,500 and taking another 1,100 prisoner. Major General Abin Tawfiq, the Iraqi commander held responsible for the disaster, was executed in Baghdad.

The Iranians slowly became stronger, more professional and less inclined to rely on human-wave frontal assaults by 'martyrs'.

Summary of the War in 1987

On the night of 24 December 1986 Iran launched yet another offensive, *Kerbala 4*. About 60,000 infantry attacked on a 25-mile front and some crossed the Shatt-al-Arab. The Iraqis lost 10,000 men killed in stopping the enemy offensive. Having rapidly regrouped, the Iranians opened *Kerbala 5* on 8 January 1987, and established a bridgehead across the Jasim River. From their salient, they shelled Basra from a range of only six miles. In northern Iraq and in the Diana region the Iranians had other victories.

An Iraqi counter-attack—largely infantry—wiped out the Iranian salient but *Kerbala 5* left 20,000 Iraqi troops dead and the government alarmed. But the Iranians had 45,000 men killed and the Iraqis hoped that Iran would bleed itself to death. Saddam Hussein and his military leaders were confident that Iran could not possibly overwhelm the vast strength of Iraq in tanks, guns and airpower. Even so, Iran's air defences shot down about 100 Iraqi planes during *Kerbala 5*.

Iraq increased its attacks on Gulf shipping and on Iran's oil-loading terminals. Mirage warplanes hit Larak Island in Hormuz Strait, after a 600-mile flight.

The Iran capacity to attack increased sharply in 1987 because of weapons from China and others supplied by the US as part of the controversial and clandestine 'arms for Iran' operations. For instance, they acquired 2,000 TOW anti-tank missiles and spares kits for 235 Hawk surface-to-air missiles. The Iranians also received spares for the APQ-120 fire-control radars for their depleted force of F-4 Phantoms.

The Chinese delivered a version of the surface-to-surface Frog, which the Iranians fired at Basra with devastating effect. In October 1987 a missile similar to the Soviet Scud-B, with a reach of 180 miles, was in use. Most alarmingly, the HY-2 Silkworm, a Chinese mobile anti-ship missile, with a range of sixty miles, became operational. Radar-guided and carrying 1,000lb of explosives, a Silkworm can sink a supertanker. Iran had 240 of them in 1987.

In May 1987 the American destroyer *Stark*, on patrol in the Gulf, was hit by an Iraqi Exocet, supplied by France. This was the first attack on an American warship since the war began. The US government accepted that the attack, which killed several crew and caused great damage, was a 'mistake'. On the same day a Soviet tanker ran into an Iranian mine on the way to Kuwait. The Iranian government was preparing for an aggressive policy against all countries siding Iraq. The US government had agreed to permit Kuwaiti tankers to fly the American flag as a form of protection, a ploy which angered the Iranians.

The navies of the US, Britain, France, Belgium and the Netherlands had permanent patrols in the Gulf to protect the shipping of their respective nations. Both combatant nations had been seeking to 'internationalize' the war and they had at last succeeded.

The War in 1988

The year 1988 was the most eventful since the outbreak of the conflict, with the battle lines moving, each side trying to take the initiative and the increasing naval involvement of foreign powers. Strategies and tactics changed, the 'war of the cities' intensified and internal tensions were evident in Iran and Iraq.

During the winter of 1987-88 there was no major Iranian offensive, for the first time in the war, but early in April 1988 Iraq committed its Seventh Army Corps and Presidential Guard, both under General Maher Abdul Kashid, to an operation to retake the Faw Peninsula.

The Iraqis carefully lulled their enemies into a false sense of security. During the week before the offensive President Hussein and General Adnan Khairallah, the Defence Minister, conspicuously visited northern Iraq. Meanwhile, the Iraqi troops moved secretly to the Faw front. Finally, the attack went in on the eve of Islam's holy festival of Ramadan.

The Seventh Army battled down the river to Faw port while the Presidential Guard captured the central salt flats of Mamlaha and executed a pincer movement down the west coast. Naval units kept up a bombardment while the air force flew hundreds of bombing sorties to cut the Iranians' supply lines across the water. The government denied that it used the Kuwaiti island of Bubiyan to ferry troops and equipment across the Khawr channel, but reliable sources say that this is what happened.

The Iranians alleged that US helicopter gunships supported the Iraqi assault. This was an absurd claim, but US helicopter gunships and destroyers were active against the Iranian navy elsewhere—though never in collusion with Iraqi forces.

It was a well-planned and well-executed operation. Resistance was much less than the Iraqis had feared. Instead of the estimated 50,000–60,000 Iranian defenders only 10,000–15,000 were in position. This was because the Iran military leaders had decided that they could not hold Faw and the 15,000 soldiers were little more than a garrison.

The Iraqi offensive achieved surprise and marked a new policy—a change from static defence to hard-hitting offence. Until April 1988 the Iraqi High Command had been content with bombing and rocketing Iranian cities. It seems likely that the Iraqi action was a response to several Iranian attacks in the northern battlefront around Shalamche. The Iranians had overrun part of north-east Iraq in March 1988 though this offensive collapsed with no final advantage to Iran.

The loss of Faw was a blow to the Iranians, if only for its psychological value. It happened to be the only major territory they had captured since 1982. The Faw peninsula was not strategically important; the Iranians never once used it as a base from which to thrust north against Basra.

Following the loss of Faw, the Iranian government ordered full mobilization of all military-age males in the population of 45 million. In massive propaganda, Iran warned that it would 'crush the evil triangle'. In Iranian terms, this means the US,

Iraq and 'the Reactionaries'. This epithet is applied to Saudi Arabia, Kuwait and all Arab states which support Iraq.

On 14 May Iraqi warplanes flew 1,000 miles to the mouth of the Gulf to attack Iranian storage vessels off Larak Island. They hit five tankers, badly damaging four and killing more than twenty crew. Replacing the ships cost far less than the proceeds of the oil they carried.

Iran accused the US of helping the Iraqis by jamming the radar and radios of its aircraft. In blind revenge its gunboats attacked Japanese and Norwegian tankers.

The war settled down to two-way attrition. This was conventionally thought to favour the more numerous Iranians but Iran's freedom of manoeuvre was restricted by Iraq's new stock of Soviet ground-attack missiles.

By mid-1988 war weariness had spread in Iran. Two senior mullahs called publicly on Khomeini to accept an honourable peace. Their views may reflect those of a majority of the 140,000 mullahs but Iran seems incapable of change. In a parliamentary election its extremists emerged even stronger.

In May Brigadier General Ali Shahbazi was appointed Chief of Staff of Iran's armed forces in a shake-up of the military command following Iraq's victory in Faw and the American destruction of the Iranian navy. Shahbazi, who was appointed by Khomeini himself, replaced Brigadier General Esmael Sograbi, who became 'military consultant' to the Supreme War Council. Shahbazi is said to have an outstanding record in the guerrilla warfare headquarters in Ahwaz, south-west Iran. He has close links with the Revolutionary Guards Corps. When President Khamenei swore in Shahbazi, he said, 'The Pasdaran (Revolutionary Guards) and the army must work more closely together to co-ordinate their operations in every area. At present, more than any other time, the army is in need of sincere efforts.'

The army has always criticized the Revolutionary Guards for their human-wave tactics. Its generals have appealed for inter-service co-operation to work out better tactics. Shahbazi's appointment may produce them.

It seems likely that the Iranian leadership has faced the disagreeable fact that the war which Khomeini repeatedly says must be won is, after all, unwinnable. Still, Iran could not simply stop fighting with its main objective—the overthrow of Saddam Hussein—unachieved. Also in dire economic straits, it could not afford to welcome home a huge number of disillusioned troops when no alternative jobs are available.

The setbacks to Iran in 1988, particularly the loss of Faw and the destruction of its small navy, should not be taken as critical; they were psychological rather than military. The navy was never crucial to Iran and the loss of Faw was tactically inconsequential. Still a wealthy nation and led by strong-willed, ruthless Islamic extremists, in 1988 Iran was capable of years of warfare.

*   *   *

The Gulf Region will continue to be a region of east-west rivalry well into the 21st century, according to a study carried out by a team of senior Egyptian military strategists. The researchers said that with 60% of the world's known reserves of oil at stake, the industrialized Western world and the Soviet Union would inevitably vie for political and diplomatic influence indefinitely.[1]

The Sea War

December 1987 was the worst month in the Gulf for commercial shipping. At least twenty-nine ships were attacked either by Iran or Iraq. Iran was intent on waging a sea war in Gulf waters but did not put this fully into effect until 1988. Then, with the use of mines and raids by fast patrol boats, it tacitly declared war against all nations using the Gulf. The mines were laid by the *Iran Ajr*, which the Americans sank after catching it at work.

In April 1988 the US Navy had twenty-one warships in or close to the Gulf. They comprised six minesweepers, five guided missile boats, two frigates, two destroyers, two guided-missile destroyers, a guided-missile cruiser, a command ship, the *Coronado*, a combat store ship, an amphibious repair dock and a submarine.

At the same time thirty-two European warships were deployed in and around the Gulf. While the European navies lacked effective air cover and had less firepower than the US force, they had twice as many mine-sweepers as the Americans and their vessels were more modern and effective than their US counterparts. Britain's 'Armilla Patrol' has operated a protection service for British shipping in the Gulf since 1981.[2]

Iran's naval strength was three destroyers, eight frigates, two support ships and eight minesweepers, two corvettes, seven fast attack patrol boats and fifty Boghamma-type speedboats.

The critical period began on 14 April, when the frigate *Samuel B. Roberts*, escorting a US-flagged Kuwaiti tanker, hit a mine off Qatar. The explosion badly damaged the ship and ten seamen were injured. The following day a military meeting at the White House discussed the options. A major strike at the main Iranian naval base of Bandar Abbas was considered but rejected. By 16 April the Joint Chiefs of Staff had organized *Operation Praying Mantis* and sent orders to Rear Admiral Anthony Less, C-in-C Task Force. Three oil platforms, known to be command centres for Iranian attacks on shipping and the frigate *Sabalan*, a known raider of merchant shipping, would be attacked. The oil loss to Iran would be serious, since the rigs involved produced 15,000 barrels a day, or about 7% of Iran's daily production.

On 17 April Dutch and Belgian minesweepers found two more Iranian M-08 mines; there could be no doubt of their identity as they carried the same serial numbers as those previously discovered and identified. At 8.30pm President Reagan conferred with his senior advisers and at 9pm he briefed Congressional leaders. At 10pm he signed the Executive Order for fleet action. At 4am, British time, Downing Street was told of the impending attack—two hours before it took place. The Soviet and Chinese governments were informed as the attacks began.

The action began at 9.17am, on 18 April. Three US warships approached the Sassan oil platform and gave the Iranian crew five minutes to clear the rig. The first Iranian response was intense machine-gun fire but after the US ships fired a few warning rounds the Revolutionary Guards aboard abandoned the platforms. Helicopters lowered Marines to blow up the rig.

Three other US ships fired 1,000 rounds at an oil platform near Sirri Island. Across the Gulf for a distance of 400 miles events then moved rapidly in a way unplanned by the Americans.

10am An Iranian Boghamma speedboard fired at a helicopter from *Simpson* and the *Wainwright* launched missiles at two Iranian F-4 war planes, hitting one of them.

12.46pm Three Revolutionary Guards' speedboats attacked the *Willi Tide*, a US-registered supply ship off the United Arab Emirates (UAE) coast, causing some damage.

1.50pm US Intelligence intercepted orders from Tehran ordering Iranian frigates to attack 'all American ships'. The local US naval commander abandoned his attack on a third oil platform.

2.25pm Iranian speedboats attacked an American-operated rig in Mubarak field. They also rocketed and machine-gunned a British tanker.

3.15pm The Iranian patrol boat *Joshan* closed on the *Wainwright*, whose captain warned, 'It is my intention to sink you'. The *Joshan* fired a missile which the *Wainwright* deflected with chaff. The *Wainwright*'s missile hit the *Joshan*, as did three other missiles fired by the *Simpson*. The *Joshan* was sunk, with forty-four casualties.

4pm The Iranian frigate *Sahand* was warned away from American ships, but when its captain persisted Admiral Less radioed, 'The *Sahand* is in our vicinity. Take him.'

4.21pm The *Sahand* fired on US ships near Larak Island and Iranian shore bases fired five BM21 missiles.

4.34pm *Sahand* fired a missile at two American A6 warplanes, which retaliated with a surface-skimming Harpoon missile. It hit the *Sahand* almost simultaneously with a Harpoon from the destroyer *Strauss*. *Sahand* sank.

4.30pm Aircraft launched by the *Enterprise* fired on three Iranian speedboats, sinking one and damaging the others.

6.17pm An Iranian warship, the *Sabalan*, fired a missile at the *Jack Williams* and at an F-14 aircraft. They missed and two A6 warplanes dropped laser-guided bombs on the *Sabalan*, leaving it a wreck.

By now, Iran's navy had only two frigates left, both under refit, and a destroyer, the *Babr*. The US Defence Secretary, Frank Carlucci, ordered the American attacks to cease, 'unless fired upon'.

The immediacy and force of the American response showed that the US Command was happy enough to have an excuse to 'teach the Iranians a lesson', as it has wanted to do since 1979, following the humiliation of the embassy hostage crisis.

Chairman of the US Senate Armed Services Committee, Sam Nunn, stated that the Gulf conflict should not be allowed to develop into a US-Iranian war. The Iranian Prime Minister, Nir-Hussein Moussavi, responded by saying that it was only US intervention in the Gulf that prevented Iran from defeating Iraq. 'We will not forget the pure blood of Iranians shed by US mercenaries in the Persian Gulf', he threatened.

The National Liberation Army[3]

While Iraq had some reverses in the northern sector they were not serious and were more than compensated for by the success of the National Liberation Army (NLA) of the Iranian People's Mujahideen. This is an anti-Khomeini force made up entirely of Iranians and led by Massoud Rajavi, aged 43, and his equally political wife.

The Rajavis were expelled from France, where they had lived in exile following their escape from Iran in 1981. The French hoped that by throwing out the Rajavis they would mollify Iranian dislike of France and so secure the release of French hostages held by pro-Iranian terrorists in Lebanon.

The Rajavis, who had also opposed the Shah, found no difficulty in raising an army to fight Khomeini and his revolutionary regime. They claim that it now has a strength of 15,000. This is open to question but the NLA certainly has five bases in Iraq. The organization began its military operations in January 1987.

The NLA's relationship with Iraq is obscure. Spokesmen for the NLA repeatedly say that there is no formal military co-ordination with the Iraq armed forces. They claim to have 'complete freedom of movement'. However, this makes no military sense. The Iraqi High Command would certainly not allow any military command to do as it wanted. In any case, the anti-aircraft defences around the NLA bases are manned by Iraqi troops.

Well-armed, well-led and profoundly anti-Khomeini—though not traitors to their own country—the NLA is made up largely of young people from middle class and professional backgrounds. Many of them are university graduates or students whose education was disrupted by Khomeini's revolution. Nearly all the young leaders have a record of having fought against the Shah as well as Khomeini.

The NLA fighters are taking great political as well as military risks. They have staked everything on Saddam Hussein's ability to defeat Iran decisively and conclusively. They also have to trust Hussein not to abandon the NLA in some future deal with Tehran, yet Hussein is notoriously untrustworthy. The NLA received reinforcements during 1988 in the form of defectors from the Iranian armed forces, though each one is thoroughly vetted to ensure that he is not a Khomeini plant.

The Mujahideen see themselves, in effect, as an army ready to return to Iran and take over when the Khomeini theocracy collapses. Being intelligent, educated and well connected, some of the NLA men and women might well provide political leadership as well.

Finance for the NLA's bases in Iraq and their military activities is said, by the NLA itself, to come from donations by Iranians all over the world. However, the Gulf states make generous contributions.[4] Rajavi's staff claim great support for the NLA in Iran, though thousands of their activists were butchered in Iranian prisons and many more remain there.

One of the NLA's biggest operations was a brigade attack on the Iranian Army's 64th Division on 22-23 November 1987 in the Piranshahr region of north-west Iran. According to NLA communiqués, 3,030 Iranian soldiers were killed or wounded, 310 prisoners taken, 10 tanks and 100 vehicles destroyed. Among the equipment captured were 23 mm DHSK rocket launchers and 81 mm mortars. NLA losses were eighteen dead and fifty wounded. It is impossible to verify these figures. The NLA is said to have infiltrated several hundred fighters through the mountains to put them behind Iranian lines. When the fighting started the Iranians were attacked front and rear.

In another action, the NLA claims to have destroyed nine battalions and captured a large quantity of equipment, including four M-47 tanks. If this were true, the NLA claim to be transforming itself from a guerrilla force to a regular army would be justified.

The NLA claims to have killed or wounded 9,000 of their own countrymen, captured 900 and destroyed bases right along Iraq's western border. The claims are high but there is some evidence to back them. For instance, Iran's President, Ali Khamenei, disclosed in one broadcast that 1,200 Iranian soldiers had been killed by 'counter-revolutionary traitors'.

The Iranians take the NLA seriously as field opponents. On the front against the NLA they have wide and thickly-sown mine-fields. Significantly, the mines are anti-personnel type. The Iraqi army rarely makes an infantry attack, so the presence of the mines shows that the Iranians are afraid of the NLA.

The NLA uses mostly Soviet weapons and they have some European equipment. Officially, the organization has no rank but this really means no emblems of rank. In fact, there is a rank structure on the usual basis. An all-woman brigade was formed in 1988 under the leadership of Commander Makhabeh Hamshidi, aged 29, a former literature student in Tehran.

'War of the Cities'

The war of the cities was accompanied by much vituperative propaganda by both sides. When Iraq fired missiles, Baghdad Radio announced that they were 'to force Iran to understand that victory has become decisive for Iraq'. On another occasion Iranians were urged to kill Khomeini and then 'talk sense'. Avenging the war dead was a sacred responsibility, a spokesman announced. 'This is your night of vengeance, you who are in heaven', he said. 'On this blessed night the thirst of every Iraqi, Arab and every honest man will be quenched.' Fifteen missiles were fired at Tehran in twenty-four hours. The holy city of Qom was also attacked.

Tehran Radio directs most of its propaganda, when firing missiles, at 'the evil scum of Baghdad, Saddam Hussein'. It is frequently claimed that 'Iran is the only true inheritor of Islam' and as such will punish 'all the enemies of God'.

In a 40-day attack, 150 Iraqi missiles hit Tehran and Iran fired as many back. It is estimated that half of Tehran's population of six million moved into the mountains. Thousands of others lived in underground car parks.

The war of the cities can be seen as a type of violent propaganda since the attacks, no matter how frequent and destructive, could in no way affect the outcome of the conflict.

Iran's Chemical Weapons

During 1987 Iran began to develop chemical weapons but this fact did not become clear until 1988. In January the Prime Minister, Hussein Moussavi, revealed that his country had started to produce 'sophisticated offensive chemical weapons'.

The intention, apparently, was to use these weapons as warheads on missiles fired at Iraqi cities. The warheads are being manufactured at Damghan, a town near the Soviet border. The factory has a capacity of five tons a month. The first test-firing was made near Semnan, east of Tehran, when a nerve agent warhead was the subject of experiment.

The Iranians have no trouble delivering chemical weapons at long range. They have their own version of the Frog, with a range of forty miles and a version of the Scud-B which can travel 180 miles.

Iran's ambitions appear to be linked to the building of a large pesticides formulation plant near Tehran. The Frankfurt-based firm, Lurgi, a subsidiary of the Hoeschat Chemicals conglomerate, accepted a 44-month contract for the factory. The company was warned that there was clear evidence that agricultural chemical factories had been converted by the Iraqis to manufacture chemical weapons which they then used. The Iranians were certain to do the same. Nevertheless, Lurgi went ahead with the contract. A report from the Swedish International Peace Research Institute claims that commercial firms are unwittingly becoming highly involved in the rapid spread of chemical weapons to Third World countries.

The Nuclear Future

In November 1987 the Iraqi Air Force raided an Iranian nuclear plant at Bushehr in an attempt to block Iran's preparations for nuclear power and, later, nuclear weapons. The unfinished plant was damaged but the Iranians were soon rebuilding it. Their leaders have made it clear that they want nuclear weapon capability as soon as possible.

The Bushehr plant is a 1,200 MW facility and was started in the days of the Shah. The West Germans helped to begin two at Bushehr and the French two more at Darkhovin. Immediately after the Shah was deposed, Ayatollah Khomeini cancelled the programme, which was to cost $30bn. However, within weeks he reinstated the venture and a senior ayatollah was put in charge of it.

Iranian scientists who had fled abroad to escape Khomeini were lured back to work when told that it was their duty to save Iranian civilization. West German scientists also came back and one was killed in the Iraqi raid.

Iraq's own nuclear programme was set back years when Israeli warplanes wrecked their French-built Osiraq reactor in 1981. Neither Iraq nor Iran is close to achieving nuclear capability but their enmity is driving both of them towards its acquisition.

The US Error of Judgment

At 10.54 am on Sunday 3 July 1988 the US Navy in the Gulf made a catastrophic blunder. Captain Will Rogers of the USS *Vincennes*, the ship which had the most advanced air defence system afloat, mistook an Iran Air Airbus for an Iranian F-14 fighter and fired two Standard missiles at it. They destroyed the aircraft and killed all 290 people aboard.

Rogers had followed normal procedures. US captains were by now allowed to take any action they deemed appropriate against hostile force. 'Hostile intent' was defined as including any belligerent ship or aircraft approaching in a pattern that could lead to an attack. In fact, the Iranian Airbus was on a flight from Bandar Abbas to Dubai, 150 miles away. At the moment of take-off a battle was raging and the *Vincennes* was heavily engaged against two Iranian gunboats, but apparently the

Iranian aircraft captain was not informed about what was going on directly beneath him.

While the Iranians were partly themselves to blame for the tragedy, the central question for soldiers and politicians was why the world's most sophisticated radar system incorrectly identified an Airbus, which has so many differences from an F-14 fighter. Captain Roger's Aegis radar could have provided him with a picture of the Airbus' height, speed and direction of flight. The *Vincennes* and another US warship called the Iranian aircraft and warned it to stay way, but its transponder— the equipment which would normally have electronically notified possible attackers that the aircraft was a civilian one—may have been faulty. Wherever the fault lay, the incident was embarrassing for the US.

After the Cease-Fire

In August 1988 Iran accepted UN Security Council Resolution 598 calling for peace between Iran and Iraq. Immediately after the Iranian acceptance, Saddam Hussein sent his armies into Iran in an attempt to win more ground before the commencement of cease-fire talks. Hussein also demanded direct cease-fire talks before a cease-fire. A delegation of seven Arab foreign ministers hurried to Baghdad to urge Hussein to accept the cease-fire, which he reluctantly did. The war was far from over, since discussions over peace terms were expected to last for perhaps a year.

In prosecuting its war against Iran, Iraq has gone into debt to the extent of $110b. The Gulf states which have financed Iraq want to end their aid and call in their debts. Since Hussein is in no position even to pay interest on the money he owes, many observers expected him to keep the war simmering.

It was a simple fact that Iran had lost the war but Iraq had not won it; the end was neither decisive nor conclusive. Islamic radicals lost the war for Iran. Some Japanese experts called in to assess the destruction say that Iran will need 30 years to rebuild its economy. However, Iraq might well have lost the peace. Almost at once, Soviet, American, British and other diplomats sought to gain influence in Tehran. Iran offers strategic advantages that Iraq cannot match. It is nearly four times the size, with three times the population and has a long border with the Soviet Union. In the long term Iran, shorn of the power of the ayatollahs and mullahs, is likely to be more stable than Iraq.

Eliminating the Minorities

While Iraq took advantage of the end of fighting to attack its Kurdish population (see Kurdish War of Independence) Iran turned on the National Liberation Army. Abandoned by Iraq, the Mujahideen lost most of their commanders and troops in the plain just west of Kermanshah. Foreign reporters were kept out of the area, so that it has been difficult to build up a picture of what happened. This is the course of the NLA's disaster:

About 8,000 men and women soldiers of the NLA crossed the border in late July, following allied Iraqi troops who had captured Qasr-e-Sherin and Sar-e-Pol Zahab. Under heavy air cover, the Mujahideen advanced to Kerend and Islamabad, which Iraqi shelling and bombing reduced to rubble. The plan now called for the NLA to make a rapid drive on Kermanshah, where the population was expected to greet them in sympathy, and then move on to Hamadan and Tehran. But the Iraqi air force carried out only a few air strikes beyond Islamabad and the Mujahideen were left on their own. Iranian troops, with much more battle experience than the NLA, lured the Mujahideen towards Kermanshah and cut them off. Helicopter gunships and bombers then attacked the exposed columns of troops. They lost nearly all their armoured personnel carriers, light tanks and trucks. Iranian infantry swamped the Mujahideen as they tried to stand and fight.

The Iranian High Command said that 4,000 NLA troops were killed, a figure confirmed by unofficial sources. Survivors who took to the hills were hunted down and most were publicly executed in Kermanshah or other centres. Some were kept alive long enough to appear on television to condemn the Iraqis for betraying them and their own commanders for leading them into a trap.

Among the dead were Ali Zarkesh, NPA military commander within Iran and Abuzar Vardaspi, a prominent spokesman. Iraqi helicopters rescued a few other leaders in the last hours of the operation. Massoud Rajavi, the NPA leader, who did not take part in the cross-border offensive, is said to have ordered the execution of those of his commanders who opposed the operation and stayed behind. Had they been present during the crisis, Rajavi said, the plan need not have failed.

Many Mujahideen remained in Iraq and it was clear at the end of 1988 that they would resort to bomb attacks and assassinations within Iran. Their determination and dedication remained, despite the calamitous setback in Iran.

References

1. The research team was led by Major General Muhammad Tewfik Foda and the report was delivered in January to a seminar at the Nasser Military Academy, Cairo. The seminar was attended by officers from Sudan, Iraq, Kuwait, Somalia and the UAE.
2. Dominique Moisi of the French Institute of Foreign Relations, Paris, said: 'The Gulf experience was a big plus for Atlantic solidarity. The Europeans play a significant tactical and political role'.
3. Probably twenty Western journalists have visited some of the NLA camps in Iraq. The NLA is conscious of the need for publicity and produces its own communiqués. The claims made in them sometimes seem not only doubtful but incredible. They cannot be thoroughly checked but various indicators suggest a large degree of accuracy. A Western diplomat in Baghdad said: 'The NLA always look so neatly uniformed and they live in such comfort that it is difficult to take them seriously as fighting soldiers but they are quite ruthless. They are educated killers.'
4. Western diplomats in Baghdad and Cairo.

Holy War—Jihad

Background Summary

Jihad—the Arabic word for holy war—has several forms. It is fought openly and conventionally as in the Iran–Iraq war, covertly through assassination and in terrorist form through kidnappings and bombing, some of them suicide bombings. It is also fought through propaganda and economic warfare. *Jihad* is as old as Islam itself, that is, more than thirteen centuries. The present phase of holy war is largely being waged under the direction of the Shia Muslims of Iran and southern Lebanon, together with the more extremist of Sunni Muslims, such as Colonel Gaddafi, President of Libya.

Jihad is not merely a war waged by fundamentalist Islam against the Christian West and against the Jews. It is also aimed at all Muslim monarchs, as monarchies are anathema to strict Shia Muslims. Other enemies are regimes declared to be 'reactionary', such as that of Egypt, and those which Muslims accuse of having betrayed Islam, of which Morocco is an example. Gaddafi, who has long seen himself as the *Mahdi* or 'expected one' of Islam, regards his opponents as enemies to be destroyed in Holy War.

Various wars have an element of *jihad*. Apart from the Iran–Iraq War, they include: the Bangladesh—Shanti Bahini war; the Afghanistan war; the war being waged by Indonesia against the guerrillas of East Timor; the inter-related wars in Lebanon; and the Philippines' war against Muslim insurgents. (For a full description of the phenomenon of Holy War and activities since 1979 see **WAR ANNUAL 1**).

Summary of Holy War in 1987

Holy war operations and attacks were planned and co-ordinated within the Iranian embassies in London, Rome, Vienna and Paris. A party of eight Iranian terrorists was arrested in Paris on 22 March 1987 and identified as being under the direct control of the Speaker of the Iranian parliament, Hojatolislam Rafsanjani. It was reported that the Iranian ambassador to the Vatican, Ayatollah Khosrow-Shahi, was believed to control a network of operations in Spain, Italy, West Germany, Britain and France.[1] Khosrow-Shahi discredited himself by an absurd claim to have converted the Pope to the Shia Islam faith and he was replaced. For several months the Iranian embassy in West Germany was the major operations centre, running twenty-two terrorist networks.

To satisfy Tehran, the French expelled activists hostile to Khomeini in France and paid back US\$300 million of a billion-dollar loan lent by the Shah of Iran's government in the 1970s.

Throughout 1987 Libyan missions in several countries recruited mercenaries for Gaddafi's Islamic Legion and its branch, the Pan-American Islamic Legion. Maltese newspapers, among others, carried full-page advertisements seeking recruits. Gaddafi induced Mauretanians, Rwandans, Nigerians, Sudanese and others to rally to his banner as 'warriors for *jihad* . . . soldiers for Allah'. These men fought in the Libyan war against Chad.

Holy War in 1988

Despite a supposed reconciliation between Libya and Iraq, the co-operation between Tripoli and Tehran continued. Libya sent 120 artillery officers to Iran at the end of 1987. They were to be deployed at the front with Iraq and would control Iranian artillery and missile units.[2]

Co-operation between Libya and Iran extended to Western Europe, where their intelligence teams worked closely together. French investigators examined the Iranian connection with the *Eksund 11* affair, named after the ship seized off the French coast on 7 November 1987. Loaded in Tripoli with enough weapons to equip 6,000 men, the ship was heading for Ireland. (See NORTHERN IRELAND TERRORIST WAR). However, French and British investigators concurred that the shipment was too large for the IRA alone. Spanish terrorists as well as Middle Eastern holy war teams in Europe were to share it.

Another combined operation came to light following an explosion on the small Italian island of Tremiti, on 9 November 1987. A Swiss, Jean Louis Nater, blew himself up. His associate also Swiss, was arrested shortly afterwards. Italian security forces suspected Libya of having sponsored the two Swiss after a series of Libyan threats against Italy.

Saudi Arabia—A Major Enemy

Serious difficulties arose between Saudi Arabia and Iran after the 1979 Iranian revolution. The Saudis supported Iran's imperial regime until the last moments of the Shah's reign. After his downfall Tehran Radio began fierce attacks against the Saudi regime, which it accused of being corrupt and pro-American. 'Appropriate action' against the Saudis was threatened.

During the 1986 pilgrimage to Mecca—the *Hadj*—the Saudis arrested 100 Iranians trying to smuggle in explosives. These would-be terrorists were returned to Iran.

During the *Hadj* ceremonies in Mecca in July 1987 Iranian fanatics hostile to Saudi Arabia organized a riot in which 402 people were killed before the security forces regained control.

Some observers suggested that the riot could have been provoked by ultra-radical Iranian fundamentalists opposed to any rapprochement between Iran and Saudi Arabia. More likely it was a deliberate act by the Iranian government as part of its known policy of undermining the royal house of Saud. Beyond this, diplomats in Riyadh suggest, there were those within the ruling family who were eager to break with Iran and so decided to respond brutally to the Iranian pilgrims' demonstration.

A source close to Iranian Prime Minister Hussein Mussavi claimed that the demonstration was organized in co-operation with Saudi authorities in charge of the pilgrimage. He contended that an order for the police to fire on demonstrators came from the Saudi Ministry of the Interior. Iran, this source said, was warned weeks in advance by Turkish intelligence sources that 'part of the Saudi ruling family was looking for an incident that would finally destroy relations between Iran and Saudi Arabia'. Government officials in Riyadh denied that the police fired but this denial is hardly credible. Khomeini pledged to 'root out' the Saudi dynasty and put the holy cities of Mecca and Medina under international control.

Iran's pre-eminence in *jihad* was made clear by Khomeini on 7 January 1988 when he claimed that his government's will could even override the precepts of the Islamic holy book, the *Koran*. The Ayatollah, in effect, compared his government to that of the Prophet Muhammad in Medina, in the years before his death in 632. Muhammad ruled with prophetic authority, through the consensus of the community. To represent the Prophet as an inspired dictator would seem to refashion Muhammad in Khomeini's image, rather than the other way round.

The key part of Khomeini's claim was this: 'Our government is a branch of Muhammad's absolute vice-regency. It takes precedence over all religious practices such as prayer, fasting, or the *Hadj* pilgrimage. I openly say that the government can stop any religious law when it feels it is correct to do so. The ruler can close or destroy the mosques wherever he sees fit. The government can unilaterally abrogate its contracts with and obligations towards the public whenever such contracts are against the interests of the country and Islam. The government can prevent its citizens from performing the *Hadj* pilgrimate, which is one of the divine duties.'[3]

Apologists for Khomeini's extraordinary action in presuming to 'take precedence over all religious practices' said that he merely wanted to control Iranian pilgrims and prevent a repetition of the 1987 riot.

However, eighty-five per cent of Muslims follow the Sunni path, in which clerics have no special authority. They were offended that a clergyman of the Islamic faith's minority fifteen per cent claimed authority over the *Koran*'s injunctions to daily prayers, the month of fasting and the *Hadj* pilgrimage. These three, together with the declaration of faith and the charitable tax, form the sacrosanct five pillars of Islam.

Khomeini's declarations were distinct moves in *jihad* and were intended to further strengthen the Shia supremacy in holy war.

Early in 1988 President Hojatolislam Sayed Ali Khamenei introduced a holy war scheme under which Iranian citizens would financially sponsor a soldier for three months. The sum needed was 200,000 *rials*, about $200 at black market rates. The 'fiscal *jihad*', as a journalist called it, reflected the government's attempt not only to raise more money but to involve more of its older citizens in holy war. In fact, Khamenei's 'invitation' was really an instruction to contribute to war funds.

The Haramine Conference

Leaders of extreme Islamic groups held a conference in London in January 1988 to plan further moves in holy war. That the meeting took place in London, under the eyes of Western and Arab intelligence agencies, showed the confidence of the *jihad* planners. More than 400 delegates from forty Islamic countries gathered at the Royal National Hotel in Bloomsbury for the three-day meeting which was named the Haramine Conference, a reference to the two holiest shrines of Mecca and Medina. Many of the delegates were high on the suspect lists of intelligence agencies.

Dr. Climent Sidiqi, chairman of the Muslim Institute of Britain, which organized the conference, returned from a visit to Iran shortly before it opened. While in Tehran he had attended a meeting of 'Islamic Revolutionary Forces' which allocated $68 million in 1988 to export *jihad* and to foment trouble in Saudi Arabia.

During the working sessions of the London meeting, delegates discussed plans for 'liberating the Islamic *umma*'—that is, Muslims throughout the world. Saudi Arabia was called 'the arm of US imperialism extending into the heart of the Islamic world'. A Nigerian delegate described in detail what he called 'the Saudi conspiracy against West Africa'.

To the surprise of Western intelligence agencies, the majority of the men attending the conference were Sunni Muslims, yet they voted to accept Khomeini as the true spiritual leader who represents the authentic voice of Islam for both Sunni and Shia Muslims. Analysts regard this as an alarming development. While Sunni Islam has many millions of fundamentalists, it had been assumed that they were without the leadership necessary to make them into dangerous *jihad* fighters. The Haramine Conference showed that leadership exists at high level.[4]

Challenge to President Mubarak

Jihad is the most serious challenge to President Husni Mubarak of Egypt. It was responsible for the assassination of President Sadat in 1981 and uprisings in Egypt. Suppressed by the police, the *jihad* fighters have split into small cells. One was behind the unsuccessful attempts on the lives of two former Ministers of the Interior, Hassan Abu Basha and Nahawi Ismail, in 1988.

The most violent *jihad* men in Egypt are supported by Iran but number no more than 5,000. Much more numerous is the clandestine movement of *Gamaat al Islamiya*, which is particularly strong in the universities. Despite suppression by the police, it is active and increasingly violent.

Khaled Nasser, son of the former Egyptian President, emerged as one of *jihad's* most dangerous leaders. Accused in Cairo of complicity in the murders of Americans and Israelis, he fled the country and went to Yugoslavia, before making his base in Algeria. Nasser is a member of 'Egypt's Revolution', a fundamentalist group with Iranian and Libyan links.

More seriously, Nasser is the leader of a holy war organization known only as 'The Arab Army'. This group was created by Nasserite networks and included some members of the Egyptian intelligence services. The organization was said to have been dismantled in August 1987 by the Egyptian police acting on inside information.

A Libyan, Ahmad Qaddafadam, betrayed the organization, apparently acting on instructions from Tripoli. Egyptian police were closing in on 'The Arab Army' and Libyan leaders decided that, as they were eager to revive an old friendship with Egypt's leaders, they would give them 'The Arab Army' as a goodwill gesture. The Libyans also considered that any publicity on the true nature of the organization would create major political problems for the Mubarak regime. They were correct. The Egyptian government suppressed news of the case and Nasser's name had to appear abroad before it was acknowledged by the Egyptian Press.

The police did not succeed in fully dismantling 'The Arab Army'. The explosion in April 1988 of a bomb in Alexandria, which damaged both the US consulate and an office of Egypt's state intelligence, proved this.

Nasser, who believes that the Middle East is ripe for fundamental political changes, sees 'The Arab Army' as a 'liberation army'. It is being organized in Europe, and by early February 1988 Nasser had initiated consultations on how it should be structured. One of his colleagues was the Algerian fundamentalist, Ahmad Ben Bella.

Increased drug trafficking between Egypt and Rumania, involving cocaine and heroin, is being used to finance Nasser's activities.[5]

Jihad in Afghanistan

The war in Afghanistan brought into being a Muslim international brigade of volunteers to fight alongside the Mujahideen guerrillas and embrace the *jihad* against the Russians, both as a religious duty and as a training ground for future revolution in their own countries.

In an attack in February 1988, thirty young Saudis, Egyptians and Pakistanis were among the force which overran the outpost of Sumungkay, near Khost. The Egyptians in the group were sympathizers of the Muslim Brotherhood holy war movement.

The significance of the international brigade is that it shows the readiness of Muslims to take part in a fighting *jihad*. It is known that *jihad* leaders throughout the world are encouraged by the ease with which an international brigade was raised. A speaker at the Haramine Conference said that training of volunteers anywhere in the world was not a problem. They could be trained in Libya, Iran, Lebanon, Pakistan, South Yemen or Syria. (*See Afghanistan Resistance War*).

Holy War Hijack

The hijacking of Kuwait Airways Flight 422 in March 1988 was an act of holy war and the Arab gunmen were acting with the support of Iranian factions. The hijackers were Shia and they forced the plane to make its first landing at Mashdad, Iran, one of Shia Islam's holiest centres. There was evidence that while the aircraft was at Mashdad other terrorists, as well as arms and explosives, were taken on board.

References

1. Jack Anderson, *Washington Post*, 20 January 1966.
2. *Middle East Insider* (weekly confidential newsletter) 23 November 1987.
3. Statement issued by Iranian missions in Europe.
4. Information from certain delegates to the conference.
5. Diplomatic sources in Cairo and Tripoli, also *Middle East Insider*, 29 February 1988.

India–Pakistan War

DESERT AND MOUNTAIN TENSION

Background Summary

India and Pakistan share a 2,000-mile border that stretches from the Arabian Sea north-east to the great mountains of the Karakoram Range. In mountainous Kashmir the Indian and Pakistan armies have been in a state of war—though not continual fighting—since 1947. India holds two-thirds of Kashmir and Pakistan the other third; but Pakistan claims the entire region on the ground that the population is two-thirds Muslim. Another argument is over water, since the rivers that flow through Pakistani Kashmir have their source in India. Pakistan is even more worried that India could isolate it from its ally, China. India holds the Siachen Glacier, which overlooks the strategic 800-mile Kakakorah highway from Peking. UN observers are permanently stationed in Kashmir but they cannot prevent fighting between Pakistan and India. In 1985 infantry fighting took place near Siachen Glacier and Pakistani and Indian aircraft fought above the glacier.

Summary of the war in 1987

During 1986 the Jammu sector was the scene of great military activity and tension. The Pakistani Army dug a 30-foot-deep, anti-tank canal along the border and guarded it with its own tanks. With tension mounting, India and Pakistan came to an agreement. Pakistan withdrew an infantry division and an armoured division from the area of Khemkaran, which links Kashmir and Jammu with the rest of India. India pulled back a division. This reduced the likelihood of hostilities in the north but it did nothing to calm the Pakistanis in the south. Here, in the Rajasthan desert, India carried out *Operation Brass Tacks* with 150,000 troops. Pakistan regarded this as threatening.

The War in 1988

In September 1987 Indian forces attacked and captured the Quaid Observation Post on the Siachen Glacier. Pakistan later responded with a battalion attack on Indian positions in an indirect attempt to recapture the strategic Post.

This fighting quickly led to a large-scale build-up of forces in the area. Both sides built forts and gun positions on mountain slopes. Early in 1988 fierce fighting broke out around the Bilafond-La Pass, one of five Passes in the Siachen sector. None of this made much news except in the major newspapers of the belligerent countries but any clash between India and Pakistan must be taken seriously since an all-out war could lead to turmoil throughout southern Asia. Indian Prime Minister, Rajiv Gandhi, repeated that India was determined not to surrender any ground in

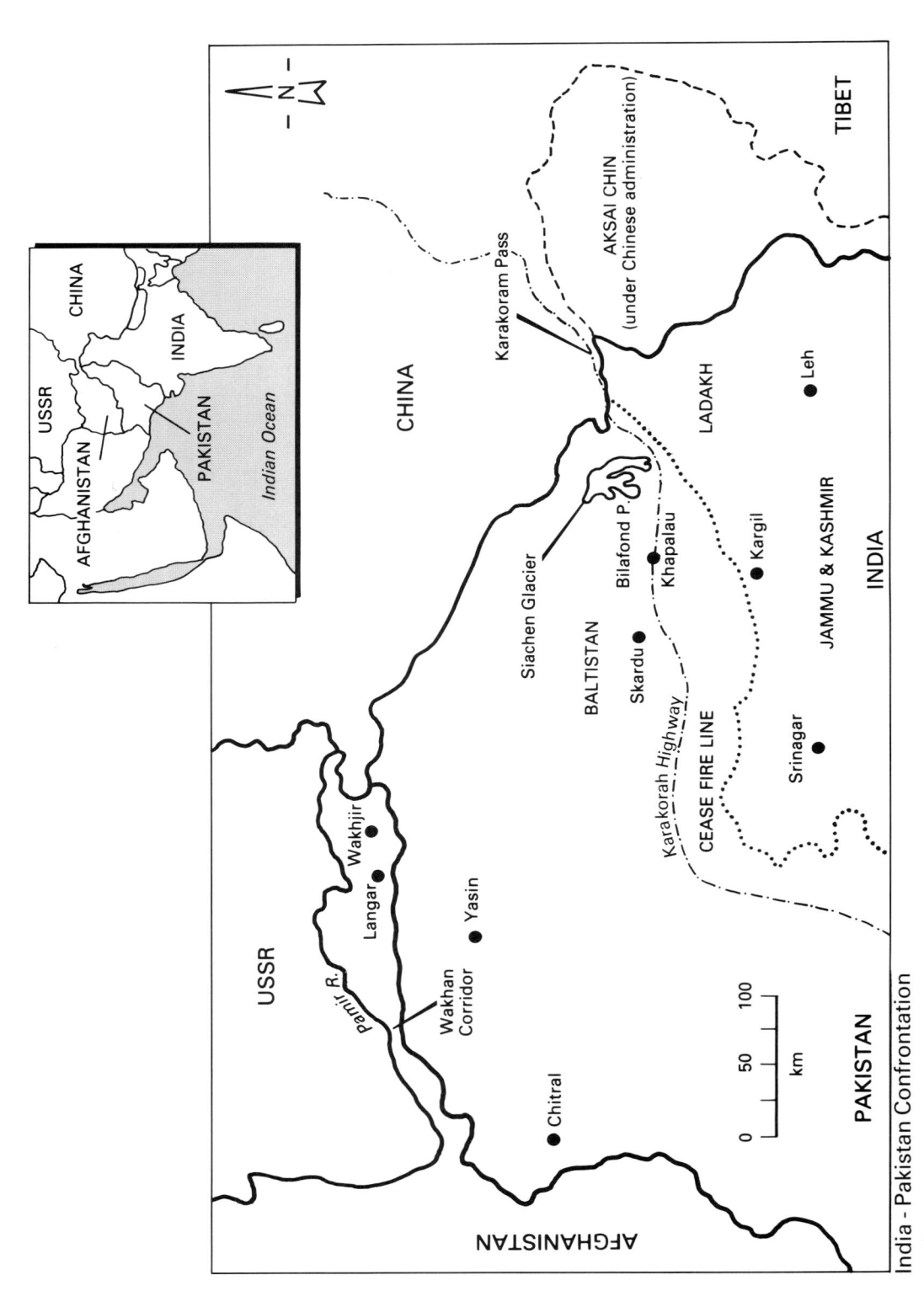

India - Pakistan Confrontation

the Siachen area. 'Pakistan will get a befitting reply if it attacks', he said. The Soviet news agency TASS accused Pakistan of 'a new armed provocation on the border with India'.

In the glacier area Pakistan held a thin line of forward positions along a fifty mile line at heights ranging from 17,000 feet to 24,000 feet. In continuously harsh weather, the Pakistani troops suffered severely. Supply was dependent on local porters who operate from Khapalau, forty-two miles from the Pakistani line.

It has long been thought that Pakistan has benefited most from the Afghan war, since great quantities of US weapons and equipment destined for the Afghan Mujahideen guerrillas have been stolen for Pakistan's army stores. However, India has benefited far more by being a passive Soviet ally in Afghanistan. Many Indian officers served as advisers to the Afghan army and air force. They had valuable experience in high, rugged terrain and on their advice India increased its helicopter and heliborne capability.

The Pakistanis note the qualitative difference in Indian equipment in Siachen and northern Ladakh. Here the Indians are using Cheetah helicopters specially modified by France's *Aerospatiale* to Indian specifications. The Cheetahs are used for supply work, evacuation and special forces insertion.

India is developing air assault forces modelled on those of the Soviet Union and Afghanistan. According to Pakistan intelligence reports, the Indian air force has several Hind and Hip helicopter squadrons, whose crews are officers with experience of combat missions in Afghanistan. The Pakistani Army is acutely aware that in any future confrontation India's air power would probably be decisive.

In a war game in 1987, the Indian High Command simulated a war against China along the Tibetan border. On Day 1 the Indian Air Force flew 500 sorties and achieved air supremacy in seventy-two hours. In all they flew 1,000 deep strike sorties and 500 close air support and 500 interception sorties. At the end, the Indian government was sure that it could prevent Chinese forces from supporting Pakistan.

Pakistan is supplying arms to the extremist Sikh separatists of Punjab and has organized logistical help for them by arranging safe houses and travel to the arms bazaars of the North-West Frontier. According to the Governor of the state of Punjab, Sidhartha Ray, Pakistan wants to bring about the 'disintegration of India'.

Pakistan sees a strategic threat from India and its defence plans are for a short war. The assumption is that Pakistan could hold on for two weeks while international pressure compelled India to negotiate a ceasefire. Pakistan's defence strategy is being assessed on three general assumptions. First, India has ambitions to play a greater regional role and sees Pakistan as the principal block. Second, the willingness of India to pay a high price in any war is questioned by the Pakistanis. Third, Pakistan would not be able to concentrate on an Indian armoured thrust in the north but must take into account its own soft underbelly in Sind, in the south. Pakistan's 'worse-case scenario' is that of being squeezed by an Indian-Soviet military and diplomatic axis.

Since the Afghanistan government gave the Soviet Union full control over the Wakhan Corridor, Pakistan has felt even more exposed. The Corridor gives the Russians a long front against Pakistan and makes it even easier for them to cut Pakistan's links with China.

The Pakistan–India war remains low-key. However, while Pakistan and Indian officials refer to it as a border dispute in international forums, in their own countries they call it 'the war'.

Jammu-Kashmir is India's only Muslim state and the Muslims, all pro-Pakistan, are becoming more rebellious and organized.

India's Sikh–Hindu and Gurkha–Hindu Wars

Background Summary

The Sikhs of the Punjab embarked on a civil war against the central Indian government in 1980. This was the result of a dispute which began in 1947, at the time of independence and when India and Pakistan were partitioned. The Sikhs gained the impression that they would be given a Punjabi-speaking state which they would call Khalistan. Chandigarh would be the capital and the new state would get its share of water and electric power. India could not meet the Sikhs' forty-five demands and Jarnail Singh Bhindrinwale, leader of the nationalist *Akaki Dal* party, turned the Golden Temple in Amritsar into a great fortress. He preached implacable religious fundamentalism against the Hindus. Mrs. Gandhi, the Prime Minister, ordered Indian commandos to capture the Golden Temple in June 1984. In this battle, code-named *Blue Star,* sixty Indian soldiers died and 600 Sikhs, including Bhindrinwale, who was aged only thirty-six. Sikh members of Mrs. Gandhi's bodyguard assassinated her in October 1984.

A Sikh terrorist campaign against Hindus began and Hindus slaughtered 2,000 Sikhs. Joginder Singh, Bhindrinwale's aged father and the new leader, began a holy war—unbridled terrorism—against Hindus. Sikh moderates were murdered when they tried to reach a settlement with the new Prime Minister, Rajiv Gandhi. The Sikhs established an operational headquarters in Britain and sent instructions to Sikhs in India. Other underground groups were set up in Canada and the US.

Sikhs make up less than two per cent of India's 800 million population but they constitute a fifty-two per cent majority in Punjab. Also, they have a great influence over India's economy, politics and army. Sikh participation in the army of one million has stayed at around twelve per cent for a decade, but the bright image of the Sikh soldiers was tarnished as a result of the Gandhi assassination.

Summary of the War in 1987

The Indian government insists that India will not again be divided. To surrender to Sikh demands would encourage the 1.4 million Gurkhas in West Bengal who demand a state of their own. Also, various Muslim groups among the 100 million Muslims in India seek independent homelands. Throughout 1987 the Sikhs were equally insistent on their 'rights' and terrorism was frequent enough to justify the labelling of this conflict as a terrorist war.

There were four known attempts on Rajiv Gandhi's life in 1987. Senior army officers, judges and Bengali politicians were murdered. The authorities, in 1986,

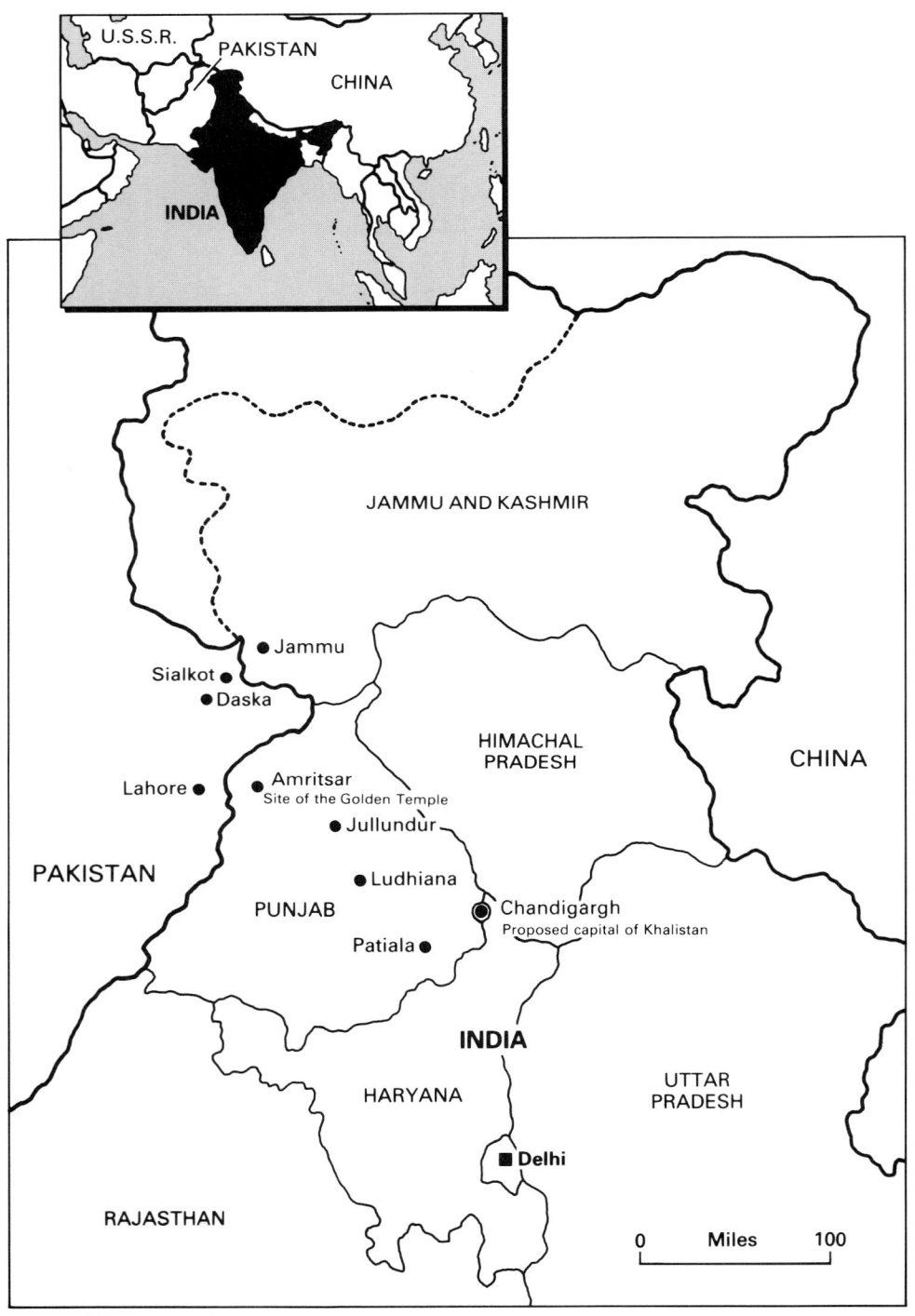

India's Sikh-Hindu War

had created a special national security formation of police commandos modelled on the British SAS, who quickly acquired the name of the Black Cats, from their black uniform. Tough and fast-moving, they were expected to reduce the incidence of terrorist attacks, though even the Black Cats could do nothing to stop indiscriminate terrorism. Sikh gunmen killed many Hindus by throwing bombs into wedding parties and public transport. Even more named groups became prominent, notably the Khalistan Liberation Army and Khalistan Commandos. Sikhs killed more than 1,000 people in 1987; it was the worst year of violence.

The War in 1988

On 21 March Sikh terrorists fired rockets for the first time in Punjab. The target was the Central Reserve Police Force in a temple on the outskirts of Phagwara. Ballistic experts confirmed that the rockets were of Soviet manufacture. The Sikhs use Chinese AK47 rifles, smuggled in from Pakistan. The security forces, most of whose men have only the outdated British SMLE .303 rifles, cannot hope to match the AK47.

The Golden Temple again became the scene of a pitched battle in May. Sikh gunmen were known to be in hiding in the massive complex of buildings and passages and 3,000 police of the National Protection Group, including 200 Black Cats, were sent to Amritsar. Black Cat marksmen set up sandbagged positions on a hotel facing the temple's main entrance. Other Black Cats, wearing bullet-proof vests and armed with Israeli Uzi submachine-guns, were deployed outside the western wall.

In the four-acre complex, the fighters set up fortifications in a water tank and two minarets. The authorities resisted the temptation to besiege the temple and in fact, did so only after a Sikh sniper shot a senior officer of the security forces in the face.

After three days of fighting the government tried to negotiate peace through the head priest of the Golden Temple, Jasbir Singh Rode, Jarnail Bhindrinwale's nephew, but this was abortive. Before being taken to prison Rode said: 'I appeal to all Sikhs to come forward and fight for the Golden Temple. Let them come in groups to Amritsar and let them face bullets if they have to.'

On 14 May a commando squad captured a communal kitchen and several buildings. With water supplies running low inside the barricaded buildings, the police hoped that they could starve out the gunmen, estimated to number 100. When the defenders sent messages that they preferred death to surrender, a loud-speaker broadcast appealed to the gunmen to allow their women and children to leave. It was characteristic of the Sikhs to meet this appeal with a burst of gunfire, although they had earlier allowed 800 non-combatants to leave.

The officers in charge of the siege tried to limit the Sikhs' movements. They wanted to avoid storming the temple since this would be seen by the Sikh community as further desecration. The Sikh terrorists holed up in small rooms around the marble walkway that surrounds a holy lake in the middle of the complex, and knocked holes through walls so that they could move around.

The Black Cats' strategy was to alternate heavy machine-gun and rocket fire with offers to accept the Sikhs' surrender. These tactics worked. Two of the most notorious terrorists, wanted for several horrific massacres, killed themselves by swallowing cyanide.

After ten days, the Black Cats flushed out the terrorists, thirty of whom were killed. The security forces suffered no casualties. The victory was a much-needed boost for Rajiv Gandhi. His élite troops managed to regain control without entering the sacred precincts and Gandhi thus avoided further alienating the Sikh population.

However, the most powerful terrorist groups remained intact and Sikh terrorism was to continue in Punjab. The secessionist Sikhs came together under the leadership of 'chief general' Labb Singh, head of the Khalistan Liberation Force, the Bhindrinwale Tigers and the *Babbar Khalsa.*

By May 1988 Hindu migrant labourers were in full flight from Punjab for fear of being attacked. Sikh terrorists began to explode bombs at railway stations in the expectation of increasing both the Hindus' panic and their urge to leave the state. Each year about 800,000 migrant workers go to the Punjab looking for work in the prosperous agricultural state. Nearly 4,000 left for their homes after thirty workers at a canal project were shot dead. Sikhs burst into a farmhouse near Amritsar and shot dead another nine labourers from Uttar Pradesh state.

The Gurkha–Hindu War

Many Gurkhas from Nepal have over the years crossed into India looking for better economic prospects and then stayed on in Darjeeling, where they now constitute more than sixty per cent of the population. But they have complained they get the worst jobs, no matter how well educated they are, while the good jobs go to Bengalis.

Separatist agitation became serious in 1986 when the government of the state of Meghalaya expelled hundreds of Nepalese. The six million living in West Bengal and elsewhere in India feared the same fate and increasingly pressed for their own state. The separatists' movement and the Gurkha National Liberation Front has evoked little sympathy because of its violence. In attacks in 1987 and 1988 Gurkha extremists burned down 100 buildings, including Darjeeling's Tiger Hill tourist lodge. At least ten people lost their lives, raising the death toll in 1987-88 to 150.

In 1988 the West Bengal government reacted strongly. It brought in large numbers of paramilitary police, who burned down entire villages, such as those of Chimni and Maneybangyan. The main victims were innocent civilians.

Under pressure, the armed Gurkhas flee across the border into Nepal, which they use as a base for their attacks on the security forces and government property. Senior police officers believed that the Gurkha activities in early 1988 were the start of a full-scale insurgency, which they claimed was supported by Nepal.

Israel and the Palestinians

THE INTIFADA

Background Summary

When Israel's boundaries were established by the armistice agreements of the Arab states' 1948-49 war against Israel, it emerged holding three-quarters of the territory of western Palestine. Jordan already took up the area of eastern Palestine. Of the rest of western Palestine, the West Bank was annexed by Jordan in 1950 and the Gaza Strip passed to Egypt. During the 1967 war, Israel captured and occupied the West Bank, including East Jerusalem, as well as Gaza, Sinai and the Golan Heights. Israel extended its civil law to East Jerusalem at the end of June 1967 and claimed full sovereignty in 1980, reuniting the city as its state capital. On 25 April 1982 Sinai was restored to Egypt under the terms of the Egypt–Israel Peace Treaty of March 1979.

The future of the West Bank—or Judea–Samaria—and of Gaza could not be easily determined since both had become bases for Palestine Liberation Organization (PLO) terrorist activity against Israel. A territory of 2,200 square miles, the West Bank comprises the highlands of Judea–Samaria and the hot, arid rift valley of the River Jordan. Of its population of 850,000 Palestinian Arabs about twenty-five per cent live in towns, mainly Nablus, Bethlehem, Ramallah, Bireh and Jericho, sixty-three per cent in villages and the rest in refugee camps. Another 130,000 Arabs live in East Jerusalem. Gaza, a strip of land of about twenty-nine miles by five, has a population of 550,000 Gazans and Palestinians, of whom about 60,000 are refugees.

After Israel had assumed control over the areas in June 1967, their government was the responsibility of the military authorities and, therefore, of the Ministry of Defence. From 1970 Israel was the only country working to rehabilitate the refugees and improve their living conditions. It contributed regularly to the funds of the United Nations Relief and Works Agency (UNRWA)—$29 m. in 1987. It funded and implemented its own rehabilitation programmes, sometimes despite UNRWA opposition. Before December 1987 nine programmes had resettled 10,000 families who had agreed to leave the refugee camps. Each family was given a plot of land, on which seventy per cent built their own homes according to their needs and preferences. Refugees acquired ownership of their houses as soon as they finished building them. However, with its limited resources, Israel could not solve the problems of the refugee camps.

The Camp David Accords of 1978 stipulated that the inhabitants of the administered territories were to have autonomy and self-government during a five-year transitional period, after which their ultimate status would be decided. It became clear during negotiations between Israel and Egypt that Egypt and the Palestinians considered autonomy to mean an independent Palestinian state; Israel, however, had in mind a form of administrative self-government. This and the increase in the number of Jewish settlements on the West Bank became a source of friction.

In August 1985 the Israeli authorities implemented stronger controls to contain demonstrations. Schools and universities were sometimes closed in reprisal for participation by students in riots. The PLO consistently tried to re-establish cells in the West Bank and Gaza with the intention of fomenting unrest in the territories and causing trouble in Israel itself.

Intifada—Why and How

On 18 December 1987 four Arab residents of the Gaza Strip were killed in a road accident. False rumours were soon circulating that their deaths were caused deliberately in revenge for the murder earlier in the month of an Israeli salesman, Shlomo Sakal, by Yasser Arafat's terrorist squad 'Force 17'. Within two days unrest was rife on the Gaza Strip and West Bank. The uprising or *intifada* had begun.

Another immediate cause may have been the Israeli decision to deport from Gaza one of the leaders of the extremist *Islamic Jihad* movement. The volatile youth of the territories may have been inspired by the exploit of a glider pilot sent against the Israeli Army in the north of the country by the Popular Front for the Liberation of Palestine—General Command (PFLP-GC). (*See Conflict in Lebanon*) Historic dates occurring just before the uprising such as the 70th anniversary of the Balfour Declaration on 2 November and the UN Partition Resolution on 29 November, may also have had some effect.

Within days of the spontaneous outbreak of unrest, the PLO's activists and front organizations on the West Bank and Gaza were actively exploiting it. They included the Shabiba youth organization. Extremist religious organizations also became involved in inciting further unrest.

Confrontations took place between Arab demonstrators and Israeli troops. These soldiers were trained to fight invaders from beyond the state's borders and they were ill-equipped and ill-prepared to deal with thousands of youths throwing stones and petrol bombs and firing steel balls from catapults. They were forced to resort to live ammunition and clubs, while the government deported known agitators.

Violent protests in the Arab sector of Jerusalem involved hundreds of youths and tied up Jerusalem's entire 600-man police force. The Israeli political leaders and the public were taken by surprise by the daring and defiance of the protestors. Israeli soldiers, unfamiliar with the territories, were shocked by the hatred they encountered. The demonstrators set up barricades of burning tyres and wooden crates and chanted Palestinian and Islamic fundamentalist slogans as they taunted the soldiers. The rioters held their ground until the troops fired tear gas or charged into the crowds brandishing truncheons and carrying M-16, Galil and Uzi rifles and submachine-guns. Palestinians attacked Israeli soldiers and civilians with knives and axes.

Khalid al-Harran, a PLO leader, said in an interview with the Lebanese newspaper, *Al-Sayyad*, that the riots could not attain the dimensions of a civil revolt because of the economic difficulties which would ensue but promised that the PLO would raise funds for a protracted civil revolt. In the meantime, the PLO, its leaders and institutions began a propaganda war. As early as 10 December 1987, Chairman Yasser Arafat called on the inhabitants of the West Bank and Gaza to step up the *intifada*.[1] In an interview with the Saudi paper *Al-Medina*[2] he exhorted the Palestinian people to 'wage a *jihad* until our land is liberated'. The PLO called on the residents of the territories to 'organize people's committees, to strike and to punish anyone stepping out of the national ranks or breaking the strike'.[3]

False reports were disseminated, accusing the Israelis of using poison gas or cutting off water supplies to refugee camps.[4] Arafat urged violence and sacrifices: 'Advance and kill. Move from street to street, from house to house, from corpse to corpse.'[5]

The deputy director of Nasser Hospital in Khan Yunis, Gaza, Ahmed Marzouk A-Shaab, was beaten and seriously injured by Palestinians for having helped people wounded in the rioting to reach Israeli hospitals.[6] The *Washington Post* correspondent, Glen Frankel, described how rioters dealt with merchants and workers. 'Some were compelled to stay away from work by youths with stones and threats.'[7]

Islamic Jihad, the most violent and dangerous of all the Muslim groups operating in Gaza and the West Bank, was particularly active. It called for immediate *jihad* against Israel. A leader of this group told an Israeli journalist, 'We want to liberate our land only by force, to kill all heretics, the Jews and Zionists among them. We have groups. They meet in a house and decide to kill a Jew.'[8] *Islamic Jihad* was led by Skeikh Abd Al-Aziz Odeh and Dr. Fathi Shaqaqi, graduates of Zaqiziq University, a radical Islamic centre in Egypt.

On 22 December 1987 the Security Council adopted Resolution 605 'deploring' Israeli policies and practices, especially the use of live ammunition, which had resulted in the death or wounding of Palestinians. Interviewed on television in 7 January 1988, the Prime Minister, Yitzhak Shamir, said the disturbances were 'a new phase of the Arab war against the state of Israel'. The security forces were trying to restore calm and order while exercising maximum restraint. He hoped that the deportations would have a calming effect.

After a visit to the administered territories by the UN Assistant Secretary-General, Marrack Goulding, a UN report was issued stating that the only way to ensure the protection of the people of both the territories and Israel would be a comprehensive, just and lasting settlement of the Arab-Israel conflict.

The Israeli Defence Forces Chief of Staff, Lieutenant General Dan Shomron, reassured an increasingly alarmed Israeli public that the army was in control of the situation. At the same time he rushed in reinforcements to triple the military deployment in the West Bank and Gaza. As the violence continued, Israel came under mounting international pressure to stop using live ammunition against the protestors. The Defence Minister, Yitzak Rabin, rejected the demands and said that he would do everything to protect the lives of the soldiers and restore order in the administered territories.

The brutal activities of some soldiers, in beating Palestinian youths and otherwise maltreating them, was condemned in many parts of the world and in Israel itself. Israeli courts sentenced some soldiers to periods in prison.

The 'military' tactics of *intifada* were interesting. Groups of youths and sometimes young boys were incited by a few older men to throw stones and fire catapult missiles at soldiers. When the goaded soldiers' patience snapped and they charged, the Palestinians ran and hid in the warren of alleyways. Sometimes they ambushed the pursuing soldiers, occasionally with petrol bombs. The troops invariably responded with pursuit, but later they used tear gas, rubber bullets and live ammunition. Apparently it did not occur to the Israeli commanders that a better tactic was to pull the troops out of range of the stones and catapaults. As the attackers would never move far from the safety of their narrow streets there would then have been no danger of the soldiers being hit; and consequently no point in throwing stones. The principle of cordon-and-control was almost totally ignored for that of rush-and-arrest.

Ominously, from Israel's point of view, the reaction of the Israeli-Arabs—Arabs with Israeli citizenship—was hostile. In a unique display of solidarity with the Palestinians, the 700,000-strong Arab community held a general strike to show solidarity with the West Bank and Gaza Arabs. Violent protests took place in Nazareth, Umm El Fahm, Lod and Jaffa, an Arab neighbourhood of Tel Aviv.

The disturbances added a new sense of urgency to the long-standing debate between Israel's Right-wing Likud bloc and the Left-leaning Labour Party over how to bring peace. Labour Leader and Foreign Minister, Shimon Peres, advocated handing over the West Bank and Gaza Strip to Jordan, except for East Jerusalem and some areas of the West Bank considered vital for Israel's security. The Likud, headed by Yitzhak Shamir, opposed giving back any territories captured in the 1967 war.

After twenty years of what has been called *Pax Hebraica*, when only small forces were needed in the territories, it seemed that Israel could be facing a desperate yet increasingly confident people who felt that they had nothing to lose.

The Israeli Defence Forces did not issue any emergency mobilization orders or reduce its manning levels on the borders, but Chief of Staff Shomron said he was concerned at having to curtail some training programmes in order to draft soldiers into the territories. Some soldiers were given riot-control training.

On 12 March 1988 three terrorists took over a bus in the Negev desert near Beersheba and held the passengers hostage. They murdered one of them before a Border Police unit stormed the bus. Two passengers died and eight were wounded. The terrorists were killed. A report of this incident in the *Jerusalem Post*[9] carried the headline 'The Day that the Daydream Ended'. This was a reference to the Israelis' confidence that following the Egypt–Israel peace treaty, terrorism in the southern part of Israel had gone for ever. The attack, though part of the *intifada*, worried the PLO leadership because, being aimed at Israeli civilians, it 'spoiled the purity of the uprising'.

On 16 April an Israeli raiding party killed Khalil El-Wazir (Abu Jihad), the PLO's military commander, and a founder member of Fatah, Arafat's own group within the PLO. To carry out this coup the raiders travelled to Tunisia by sea and shot Abu Jihad in his villa. It was Abu Jihad who had transformed the spontaneous revolt of the territories into something like continuous guerrilla warfare. Israel had long held Abu Jihad responsible for the 1978 coastal road massacre in Israel when more than thirty civilians were killed. In the administered territories, Abu Jihad's killing caused the worst violence of the *intifada*.

It was clear by mid-1988 that the Palestinians, having suffered more than 200 deaths from Israeli bullets, no longer thought of their activities as 'demonstrations' but as war. Certainly *intifada* was war to the Arab leaders who met at a summit meeting in Algiers in June. They promised to help the Palestinians and the PLO by 'all means in our power'. They recognized the PLO as the sole representative of the Palestinian people and offered Arafat £148m for a 'fighting fund', with much more to come.

Pragmatic Palestinians

Not all Palestinians on the West Bank oppose Israeli administration. Many well-educated young Palestinians, disenchanted with the PLO's activities and with the fruitlessness of Arab politics in general, have publicly demanded Israeli citizenship. Without denying the principles claimed by the PLO, these younger people claim that by exploiting Israel's commitment to democratic rights they could circumvent the constraints of Israeli occupation.

Many individuals have openly sought to co-operate with Israel, often at great personal risk. Many have been murdered by PLO supporters. Others joined the Village Leagues operation, a form of co-existence and even of economic co-operation in rural areas. The Leagues vanished under threats from PLO groups. Some important West Bank people, such as Elias Freij, the mayor of Bethlehem, tried to separate Palestinian from Arab politics. Yet others present the 'acceptable face' of the PLO in the territories. These are personalities who repeatedly stress their loyalty to the PLO and receive much financial assistance from some PLO leaders to keep open channels to certain Israelis and to Western diplomatic diplomats in Israel.

Intifada Organization

No mass movement on the scale of the Palestinian *intifada* could be sustained without some form of organization, co-ordination and direction. These were provided at various levels. At local levels clandestine committees ran the uprising by distributing leaflets and by working to ensure that the rebellion did not simply die down. The membership of these committees was secret but most Palestinians with any political or social awareness knew who the members were.

The radio station *Voice of Jersualem*, broadcasting from Syria, issued many instructions about confronting the Israeli security forces. The station is run by the Popular Front for the Liberation of Palestine General Command (PFLP-GC) led by Ahmed Jibril. It is one of the most militantly rejectionist and anti-Arafat terrorist groups.

However, Arafat and the PLO continued to be the rallying call for the demonstrators, if only because Arafat remained the only well-known name. Such invocation of Arafat's name did not mean that the demonstrators would necessarily be willing to follow his diplomatic line.

By March, many instructions were reaching the organizers within the West Bank and Gaza by coded messages broadcast over the several radio channels available in Israel, including PLO radio in Baghdad, Syrian radio, *Voice of Jerusalem* and probably Jordanian radio. Messengers carried verbal messages—Arabs have a remarkable ability to memorize long passages. During the periods of strikes, when many Arabs from the West Bank and Gaza did not report to their places of work in Israel, money was also secretly brought in from outside.

Islamic Movement Opposes PLO

By September the *intifada* had brought into being the Islamic Resistance Movement, the most extreme of the underground Palestinian groups. It is generally known as Hamas, which means 'zeal', and is the Arabic acronym for 'Islamic Resistance Movement'. Hamas is a result of the increasing frustration with PLO leader Yasser Arafat's failure to turn the uprising's perceived achievements into concrete political and diplomatic gains. Hamas began to feed on a growing fear on the West Bank that the uprising was going nowhere.

Hamas wants an Islamic state in all of Palestine, including Israel. It opposes an international peace conference because it believes that such a conference would bring about a territorial compromise. Hamas posters proclaim, 'The end of Israel is a Koranic inevitability.' A leaflet distributed throughout the West Bank in September 1988 carried the statement, 'Yes to the revolution of the mosques. Let those calling for peace be silent. We will tell the sons of Zion that we will not forget Haifa and Jaffa. We are coming.'

In the same month the Hamas organizers challenged the Unified Command for the Uprising, the underground steering committee dominated by the PLO, by calling for and enforcing general strikes other than the ones designated by the command. This resulted in inter-Arab street brawls. It emerged that the unofficial spiritual leader of Hamas is the Gaza sheikh, Ahmed Yassin. Another prominent spiritual leader is Sheikh Bassam Jarrar, a young mullah on the West Bank.

Hamas is actually an offshoot of the Muslim Brotherhood, the fanatically fundamentalist movement which is deeply involved in Jihad (q.v.). Its popularity in the refugee camps of Gaza was clear from the moment it began to operate there but its appeal in the West Bank caught PLO activists by surprise. Its support base is in more remote and conservative rural areas where sixty per cent of West Bank people live. It has a communications network in the mosques that cover both Gaza and the West Bank.

In its covenant, Hamas rejects compromise with Israel because it claims all of Palestine as an Islamic trust that cannot be surrendered. Many Israeli leaders, including senior Foreign Office officials, have long wanted to believe that their difficulties with the Arabs, including the Palestinians, were fundamentally political. This was never the case, despite the importance of political differences. The Muslim Arabs hate the Israelis primarily because they are Jews and Hamas made this clear as the *intifada* continued.

As the violence intensified, the Israeli army introduced a new rifle firing smaller plastic bullets which, unlike the older and larger ones, can penetrate into the body. They are capable of causing death or serious wounds, though soldiers were under orders, according to the Defence Ministry, to fire only at the legs of rioters throwing stones and petrol bombs.

References

1. PLO Radio, Baghdad.
2. 25 December 1987.
3. Spokesman, PLO Radio, Baghdad, 24 January 1988.
4. Arafat to a news conference; reported by Gulf News, Agency, 12 January 1988.
5. PLO Radio, Baghdad, 30 December 1987.
6. Israeli Press, 15 December 1987.

7. *International Herald Tribune*, 8 January 1988.
8. *Ha'aretz*, 20 January 1988.
9. 19 March 1988.

Kurdish War of Independence

Kurdish War of Independence

Background Summary

The Kurds are the world's largest ethnic minority with no homeland and little hope of achieving one. With no desire for unity in the 3,000 years of their known history, the 16-22 million people of Kurdish origin began their own split with the break-up of the Ottoman Empire.

They occupy an area which straddles the borders of five countries—Iraq, Iran, Turkey, Syria and the Soviet Union. None has any sympathy for their nationalist aspirations and the Kurds have been bloodily repressed, most recently by the Iranians and Iraqis. Unfortunate alliances have also plagued the Kurds. For instance, Mustafa Barzani, leader of the Iraqi Kurdistan Democratic Party (KDP) allied himself to the Shah of Iran in the early 1970s and fought against the Iranian Kurds. In 1975 the Iraqi government offered the Shah territorial concessions if he would abandon the Kurds, which he did. The KDP was caught between the Iranian and Iraqi armies and suffered badly. In 1983, with the Gulf War in progress, the KDP helped Iranian troops to cross into Iraq. The rival Patriotic Union of Kurdistan (PUK), led by Jalal Talabani, trained Iranian Kurds to fight Khomeini's troops.

In Turkey, the Kurdish Workers' Party (PKK), a nationalist and Marxist-Leninist organization, has had great influence. 'Apo' Abdullah Ocalan formed the PKK in 1978 and its militants became known as Apoists. They were outlawed after the Turkish army coup of 1980 and Ocalan took refuge in Syria, where he still has his headquarters. Trained in Syria, the exiled militants have crossed into Iran and Iraq and from there have waged guerrilla-terrorist warfare against Turkey.

Since 1985 the KDP, 15,000-strong and led by Idris Barzani, son of the famed Mustafa Barzani, have also fought as guerrillas against the Iraqis. They tied down many Iraqi troops in Kurdistan at a time when the Iraqi President, Saddam Hussein, needed all available troops to face the Iranians. The much-divided Kurds had other groupings, including the Socialist Party of Kurdistan (Pasok), the Iraqi Dawe Party, a Shia Muslim group, and the Turkish Workers Party of Kurdistan.

Since 1975 much of the Kurdish countryside has been destroyed in one way or another by one enemy or another. For instance, whole villages have been razed and their farmland despoiled and made barren.

Summary of the War in 1987

The Kurds were fighting on four fronts. Well supplied with Kalashnikovs, rocket-propelled grenades, mines and explosives, they were militarily significant in Turkey, Syria, Iran and Iraq.

Iranian-backed Kurds fighting against Iraq received large supplies of modern weapons and equipment and went on the offensive, besieging garrisons and even towns. They badly damaged major power stations and cut the strategic road from Kirkuk to Turkey. In effect, the Kurds created a second front against the Iraqis along a 650-mile border.

When Idris Barzani died during an Iraqi air raid on 31 January 1987 his brother Massoud became leader of the KDP and began the tortuous process of trying to unify the Kurdish factions.

In Turkey the ruthlessly oppressed Kurds became more militant and violent. Their language had been banned for years and thousands of mililtants were held in prisons. Operating mostly from within Iraq but sometimes also Syria, the Kurds, members of Ocalan's PKK, attacked both civilian and military targets. After they attacked the village of Tasleden and massacred women and children, the Turkish air force bombed their mountain camps and killed several hundred Kurds. The Iraqi government permitted the Turkish Army to mount hot pursuit operations inside Iraqi territory. The air raids greatly angered the Iranians, who believe that Turkey's secret and ultimate objective is to regain some ground lost to Iraq after World War I—the oil-rich Kirkuk and Mosul regions.

During 1987 the conflict between the Turkish Army and the Kurdish insurgents in the remote eastern Turkish provinces turned into a full-scale war. The Turkish generals and government claimed to be cracking down not merely on a troublesome terrorist minority but on Communist terrorists. Influential Turks were advocating a large-scale military operation, including a 'pre-emptive takeover' of northern Iraq.

The Syrian government was unable to control its ethnic Kurds, who also raided into Turkey. The Turkish government pressed the Syrian President, Hafez Al Assad, to stop these cross-border attacks. The ultimate Turkish weapon against Syria would be to deny them water from the great Euphrates River, which rises in Anatolia.

While many Kurds were fighting with Iran against Iraq, about 11,000 were fighting against Iran in Iranian Kurdistan. These guerrillas were members of a breakaway group of the Kurdistan Democratic Party led by Abdorrahmen Qassemlou. He was not dependent on Baghdad but did receive some aid from the Iraqis. Whenever Iranian troops were sent into Kurdistan they invariably managed to push the Kurds out of the main towns but the outnumbered Kurds, as always, managed to hold the rugged, mountainous ground.

The *pesh mergas*, the Kurdish name for the resistance fighters, had a formidable and frightening reputation among their enemies.

The War in 1988

Iraq

In January 1988, at Deeralok, near Amadya, in northern Iraq, the KDP's army decisively defeated an Iraqi force, killing or wounding 600 men and taking a similar number of prisoners. The battle lasted six days, long enough for the Iraqi command to have massively reinforced its troops and to have attacked the Kurds from the air; the Kurds have no aircraft. However, the opposing forces, fighting in rugged country, were too closely engaged for the Iraqi pilots to distinguish friend from foe. Also, while two entire Iraqi armies, 150,000 men in all, were in

Kurdistan, they were so overstretched that they could not help the regiment being mauled by the Kurds. The KDP captured 1,000 weapons.[1]

Undeniably, the Kurds are a serious and continuing threat to the oil-producing areas around Kirkuk and the twin pipelines that carry most of Iraq's oil exports to the Mediterranean coast through Turkey. Harassment operations occur almost daily, often in conjunction with Iranian fighters from the Islamic Revolution's Guards Corps (IRGC). The successes of their attacks are always exaggerated in accounts published by Ramadan HQ in Tehran, but they are useful to Iran in trying to defeat Iraqi troops.[2]

The Iraqi government acted brutally and ruthlessly against its own Kurds throughout 1988, with many terrorist atrocities, including poison gas attacks, against civilians. At least 500,000 families were forcibly resettled many hundreds of miles away in the regions close to the borders with Kuwait and Jordan.[3] The Kurds' alliance with the Khomeini regime is wholly tactical and they strongly oppose the Iranians' intention to turn Iraq, should they capture it, into an Islamic republic. However, they feel that they could be no worse off under the Iranians than under the Iraqis.

Amnesty International claimed in 1988 that the Iraqi government was using rat poison to eliminate Kurdish dissidents opposed to the Saddam Hussein regime. A PUK leader in the northern town of Marga gave a dinner for leaders of the Kurdish Socialist Party and other anti-Iraqi groups where they discussed their plans of campaign. A women agent of the Iraqi *Jiraz al Rasd*, the most secret branch of Iraqi Intelligence, was present under cover. She served *irun*, the salted mixture of yoghurt and water which the Kurds drink. Thalium poison, which she had put in the drink, killed three of the Kurds and made the others seriously ill. The survivors were taken across the border to hospitals in Tehran but as the antidote for thalium poisoning was not available some of the afflicted men were flown to London. Here a consultant confirmed that they were suffering from thalium poisoning.

Amnesty said that killing of suspected government opponents had been a continuing human rights concern in Iraq. In the past three years it had called for investigations into reports that the Iraqi security forces had hanged, shot, beheaded, poisoned and bled to death its political opponents.

The Kurds know that they cannot trust Saddam Hussein. When he needed help from the Kurds he amicably received Jalal Talabani of the PUK in Baghdad. In an interview with Hazhir Temourian, a Kurdish journalist from Britain, Talabani said:

> Hussein promised to put a stop to the Arabisation of Kirkuk and join me on television to declare a new charter for Kurdish autonomy. Then it became clear that the Iraqi army could successfully defend Basra against Iran and Saddam Hussein went back on his word. He has resumed his policy of destroying Kurdish villages and deporting the population for resettlement, never to be seen again. He uses chemical weapons against our civilians every day. So now it's either him or us.[4]

The PUK and KDP are enemies but for tactical purposes they formed, in 1987, a National Front of Kurdistan (NDF). One of the greatest benefits was to be the increased manoeuvrability of the fighting forces. In practice, this took some time to become effective because of jealously guarded areas.

The joint strength of the KDP and PUK in 1988 was formidable. The KDP had

15,000 fighters and could call on a militia of 30,000; it controlled 6,000 square miles of northern Iraq. The PUK also had 15,000 trained and experienced fighters and controlled 24,000 square miles.

Chief spokesman for the PUK, Newsherwan Mustafa, while on a visit to Europe, said 'From Khanaqin to Zhako all areas are now open for the *pesh mergas* to operate in freely'.[5] In October 1987 KDP 1,000 guerrillas had overrun an Iraqi army base at Kani Masi in Dahok province. Soon afterwards guerrillas shelled the Iraqi-Turkish highway. Before the groups came together in coalition only tactical operations such as these were possible. With the NDF functioning efficiently, in 1988 attacks were being mounted on strategic and economic targets, such as airfields, bridges and oil installations.

Hazhir Teimourian brought back valuable information from his trip into Kurdistan. Leaders of both the PUK and KDP told him that they were prepared to operate a more ambitious military strategy. Hoshyar Zebari of the KDP reported that his forces were moving away from their guerrilla tactics to the assault of larger military targets and capture of small towns. Talabani claimed that the PUK could capture the cities of Kurdistan, but its fighters would be vulnerable to Iraqi air attack unless their Iranian allies embarked on a major offensive to keep the Iraqi warplanes occupied. In addition, the PUK did not have the logistical apparatus to feed the people of the cities.

The Iranians have certainly courted the Iraqi Kurds by giving them plentiful supplies of weapons and material, including—for the first time in 1988—medium calibre artillery, anti-tank and anti-aircraft missiles.

Kurdish resistance against Iraq, however courageous, may not be rewarded. The worst-case scenario for them would be peace between Iraq and Iran. Many experienced Iraqi divisions would then become available for an overwhelming offensive against the Kurdish regions. If the PUK and KDP were to co-operate at political level without the usual mistrust and reservations they might establish a Kurdish republic while Iran and Iraq are otherwise engaged.

Turkey

Beginning in 1987 and continuing throughout 1988, the Turkish government expanded and intensified its programme to provide 'village guards'. Sometimes voluntarily, but more frequently under pressure from the security forces, men were armed and paid to protect their own village against PKK marauders. The village guards were in an unenviable position because the PKK treats everyone who obeys the soldiers as though they too are 'members of the oppressive regime', and punishes them accordingly. Many village guards have been butchered by the PKK.

The organization sometimes showed its contempt for authority by staging a coup at times when security had been heightened. While Prime Minister Ozal was in the PKK area, with a massive security presence, the PKK raided a village, shot dead twenty-five people in broad daylight and escaped without difficulty. They made a similar murderous raid during a visit by President Kenan Evren.

Atrocities were so frequent in the PKK's domains that the KDP had no association with the PKK, while the PUK, which was once very close to it, told the PKK that it would sever all connections unless its attacks were limited to military targets.

The biggest reported encounter of Turkey's four-year Kurdish insurgency took place on 1 April 1988 in the mountains north-east of Nusaybin. Turkish troops, mostly commandos, surrounded a PKK group in their cave hide-outs. In a seven-hour small-arms fight, a Turkish helicopter pilot and two soldiers were killed and twelve were wounded. Twenty guerrillas were killed.

The Turkish operation followed PKK attacks on three villages in which they killed ten civilians. The helicopter pilot was the key figure in the affair. At very low level he had trailed the guerrillas into the mountains and then directed the commandos to the spot. He was shot down while giving instructions for the final assault on the PKK men. Western military attachés in Ankara say that the Turkish command has not learnt to use scout helicopters efficiently and has no armoured helicopters in its fleet of 482 combat aircraft.

The Kurdish regions of Turkey are abysmally under-developed. The main city of Diyarbakir, with a population of nearly half a million, has only two factories. Only eighteen miles from the main highway and in some cases only yards from a NATO base there are villages with neither electricity nor running water and peasants have no furniture. The Turkish Prime Minister, Turgut Ozal, has been responsible for better conditions for Kurdish militants kept in Diyarbakir military prison. Ozal seemed to be trying to incorporate Turkish Kurdistan into the Turkish community, partly because he was under pressure from the European Community, which Turkey wants to join. Kurdish resentment of the Turks may be too deep for Ozal to overcome.

The Iraqi Onslaught

Following ceasefire agreements between the Iranians and Iraqis, the Iraqis abandoned their Iranian Mujahideen allies (see *Iran–Iraq War*) and the Iranians similarly abandoned the Iraqi-Kurds who had supported them in their war against Iraq. At the same time, the Iraqi regime of President Saddam Hussein was able to give more attention to his aim of crushing Kurdish resistance for good.

The first sign that Tehran was reducing its support for Iraqi Kurds came six days before Iran accepted UN Security Council Resolution 598. On 12 July, Iranian forces announced their withdrawal from positions in Kurdish areas of Iraq. Thousands of rebels were trapped inside Iraq and became short of supplies as the Iranians stopped weapons and ammunition deliveries.

This was the moment for which Saddam Hussein and his army staff had been waiting. Kurdish military positions and civilian settlements were attacked by infantry, tanks and aircraft. Chemical weapons were widely used (see *Trends: Chemical Warfare*) and Kurds fled in their tens of thousands, mostly into Turkey, home to the majority of ethnic Kurds. The situation was ironic. In September–October 1988, while some Turkish soldiers were guarding the disarmed KDP fighters against Iraqi attack, others were chasing KDP assassination squads. While Iraq was trying to govern its Kurds with brutality and terror, Turkey was trying to live up to its rhetoric on Kurdish equality.

Turkey did not want to call for aid from foreign countries because this would imply that it could not cope with the refugee problem but diplomats said that sooner or later the government would be forced to seek aid from the UN and other relief agencies. The Turks were concerned over the publicity given by the US,

Britain, France and other countries to the 'Kurdish problem'. Editorials in some leading Western newspapers talked about a revision of the 1922 Treaty of Savres which recognized the Kurds' right to a state of their own after the collapse of the Ottoman Empire. This suggestion angered the Turks.

For their part, Iraqi Kurds were particularly bitter about world governments and organizations which, they said, were content to mouth vague and futile condemnations of chemical weapons without ever actually naming the Baghdad government. Iraqi Kurds were also sickened by the silence of Iranian Kurdish leaders who never once condemned the scorched-earth policy Baghdad had been pursuing since May 1987 against their fellow Kurds in Iraq.

Sooner or later, the Iranian Kurds will have to pay the price of the Iran–Iraq peace. Once peace is restored the Iranian *peshmergas* will lose many of the advantages they had been enjoying from their 'tactical alliance' with Iraq. They will also encounter increasing problems in their struggle which, by the end of 1988, had not reached the proportions of a real conventional war as in Iraqi Kurdistan.

References

1. Diplomatic sources in Baghdad.
2. Diplomatic sources in Tehran.
3. Kurdish sources, verified by UN Secretariat and by sources in Baghdad.
4. Published in *The Middle East*, April 1988.
5. Interview.

South-East Asia Wars

VIETNAM IN KAMPUCHEA: VIETNAM–CHINA:
THAILAND–LAOS: ACTION IN SOUTH CHINA SEA

Vietnam's War Against Kampuchean Guerrillas

Background Summary

Kampuchea was formerly Cambodia. Vietnam invaded the country in December 1978 to 'protect the south-western flank from hostile influence', namely China. China and Vietnam are inveterate enemies and from the beginning of this war China supported the Kampuchean Resistance groups, particularly the Khmer Rouge party led by the infamous Pol Pot, whose men killed probably two million Kampucheans, out of a total population of seven million. They died because they opposed Pol Pot—or were suspected of doing so. The Soviet Union supported Vietnam. The other groups were Son Sann's Khmer People's National Liberation Front (KPLNF) and Prince Sihanouk's *Armée Nationale Sihanoukienne* (ANS). These three parties formed an unstable alliance.

Heng Samrin became Prime Minister and collaborated with the Vietnamese army, which had invaded Kampuchea to 'liberate the nation from Pol Pot'. It was a laudable ambition, but the Vietnamese had no intention of leaving once they had restored order. Heng Samrin put Kampuchea's army under Vietnamese command.

The opposition groups took to the jungle. In 1979 the Chinese mismanaged an invasion of Vietnam in support of the Kampuchean insurgents. The conflict became a war of resistance against foreign occupation but not a genuine guerrilla war as the Kampuchean fighters did not live off the land. They established bases and fixed lines of defence.

By 1985 Vietnam had 160,000 troops in Kampuchea and the army's assaults, using an artillery barrage followed by an infantry assault, were devastating. The KPNLF and ANS lost all their bases and the Khmer Rouge lost its mountain stronghold, Phnom Malai.

The Resistance fighters retreated to Thailand where they established bases as well as camps for their 250,000 civilian refugees. Despite intense Vietnamese pressure, by the end of 1985 the KPLNF was able to mount attacks against Vietnam posts. The Vietnamese laid more than one million mines along the 450-mile Kampuchea–Thailand border in an attempt to seal it against Resistance incursion. In the period January–May 1986 the Vietnamese Army, now 180,000 strong, moved into eastern Thailand in further attempts to prevent the guerrillas from entering or leaving Kampuchea. Many civilians and some guerrillas were wounded by cluster bombs and fire from Soviet-supplied helicopter gunships. In that year the combined Vietnamese army of occupation and their Kampuchean army allies suffered 7,000 casualties compared with the guerrillas' 5,000.

Kampuchea: Guerrilla Routes

Some KPLNF exploits were spectacular. For instance, in September 1986 about 200 guerrillas ambushed a convoy of thirteen river boats carrying 572 Vietnamese troops. They sank all the boats and killed many Vietnamese. In a second similar river ambush in October the Vietnamese lost 300 men.

Summary of the War in 1987

The guerrillas numbered 66,000 men in three main groups. The Khmer Rouge consisted of 35,000 men, KPLNF 16,000 and ANS 10,000. The KPLNF had another 4,000 poorly-armed reservists.

In numerous raids, the guerrillas entered Kampuchea along four main trails and sometimes carried out attacks behind the Vietnamese lines. Well-led sabotage teams hit targets as far into the country as the capital, Phnom Penh. The morale of the Kampuchean army deteriorated in the face of the guerrillas' success and several hundred soldiers deserted to them. Some units mutinied rather than attack their fellow countrymen.

In an alliance known as the Coalition Government of Democratic Kampuchea, the guerrillas produced an eight-point peace plan. In essence they wanted the Vietnamese out of the country, after which Prince Sihanouk would become President and Son Sann the Prime Minister. The UN would supervise free elections. However, the Vietnamese wanted their puppet Heng Samrin as Prime Minister and would not accept any Khmer Rouge member in the government. The Vietnamese feared that the Khmer Rouge would take over Kampuchea as the last Vietnamese army unit withdrew. Many people in South-east Asia and beyond shared the view that Pol Pot's atrocities would be repeated.

The War in 1988

Reports circulated in South-east Asia during 1988 that China was no longer wholly behind Pol Pot and would drop him and his colleagues if this would lead to a settlement in Kampuchea[1] that was widely accceptable. The Chinese government openly and surprisingly stated that the Khmer Rouge could not be the dominant power in any future government, which must be headed by Prince Sihanouk. Chinese and US officials believed that, in a crisis, China could force Pol Pot into exile but diplomats in South-east Asia said that Chinese control over Pol Pot was much less than generally believed.

In anticipation of a Vietnamese withdrawal, which the Khmer Rouge believed would come in 1988, Pol Pot's staff built up war supplies and carefully husbanded them. Pol Pot's obvious strategy for the Khmer Rouge was to be the strongest group in the event of the Vietnamese leaving. Because of Khmer Rouge secrecy it was difficult for UN relief officials to enter the group's refugee camps, which contained 72,000 people, to deliver food. The UN has a strict embargo on relief food reaching the Khmer Rouge fighters.

In May 1988 a document which reached the Thai government caused great misgivings. It was a Khmer Rouge plan for seizing power, together with details about wiping out all opposition once again. The document could not be authenticated and could have been a forgery by enemies of the Khmer Rouge. However, diplomats in Bangkok said that even if it were a forgery, it accurately

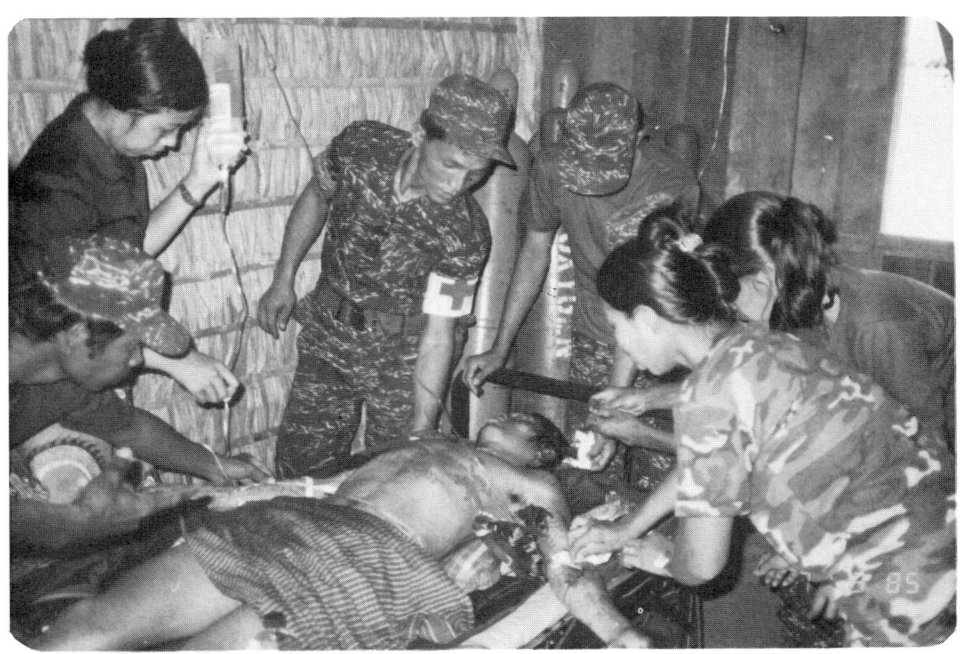
A wounded KPNLF guerrilla evacuated to the field hospital. (Bun Ny Chea.)

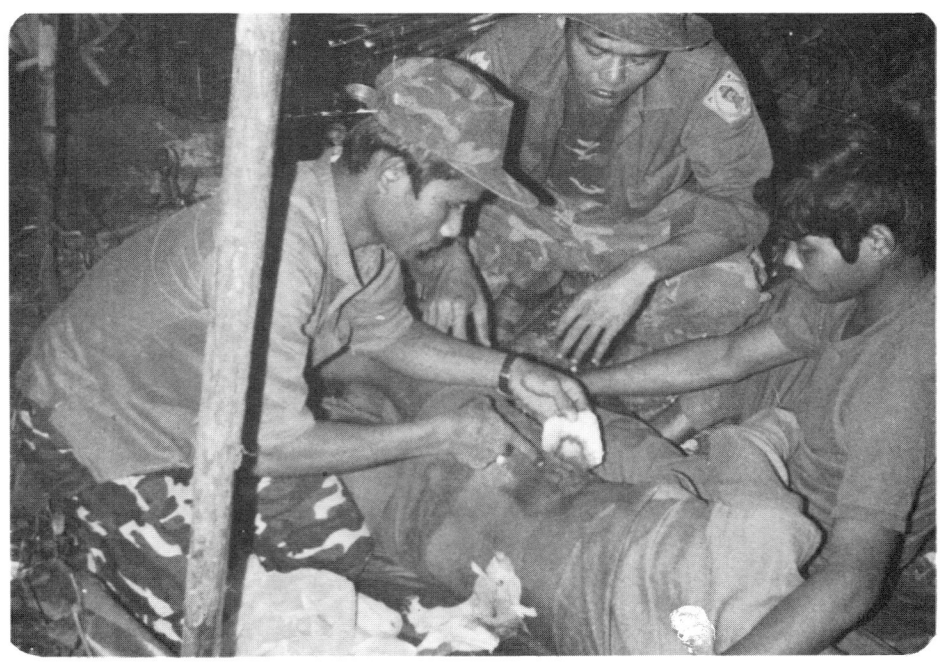
Treatment is adequate at field level but the KPNLF lacks qualified doctors. (Bun Ny Chea.)

Vietnamese mines have been dismantled by KPNLF guerrillas at the camp of Baksei. Prince Sihanouk, leader of the movement, examines the mines. (Bun Ny Chea.)

The KPNLF fighting men on parade. (Bun Ny Chea.)

As KPNLF fighters evacuate a position under attack from Vietnamese troops, a lone rearguard covers their retreat. (Bun Ny Chea.)

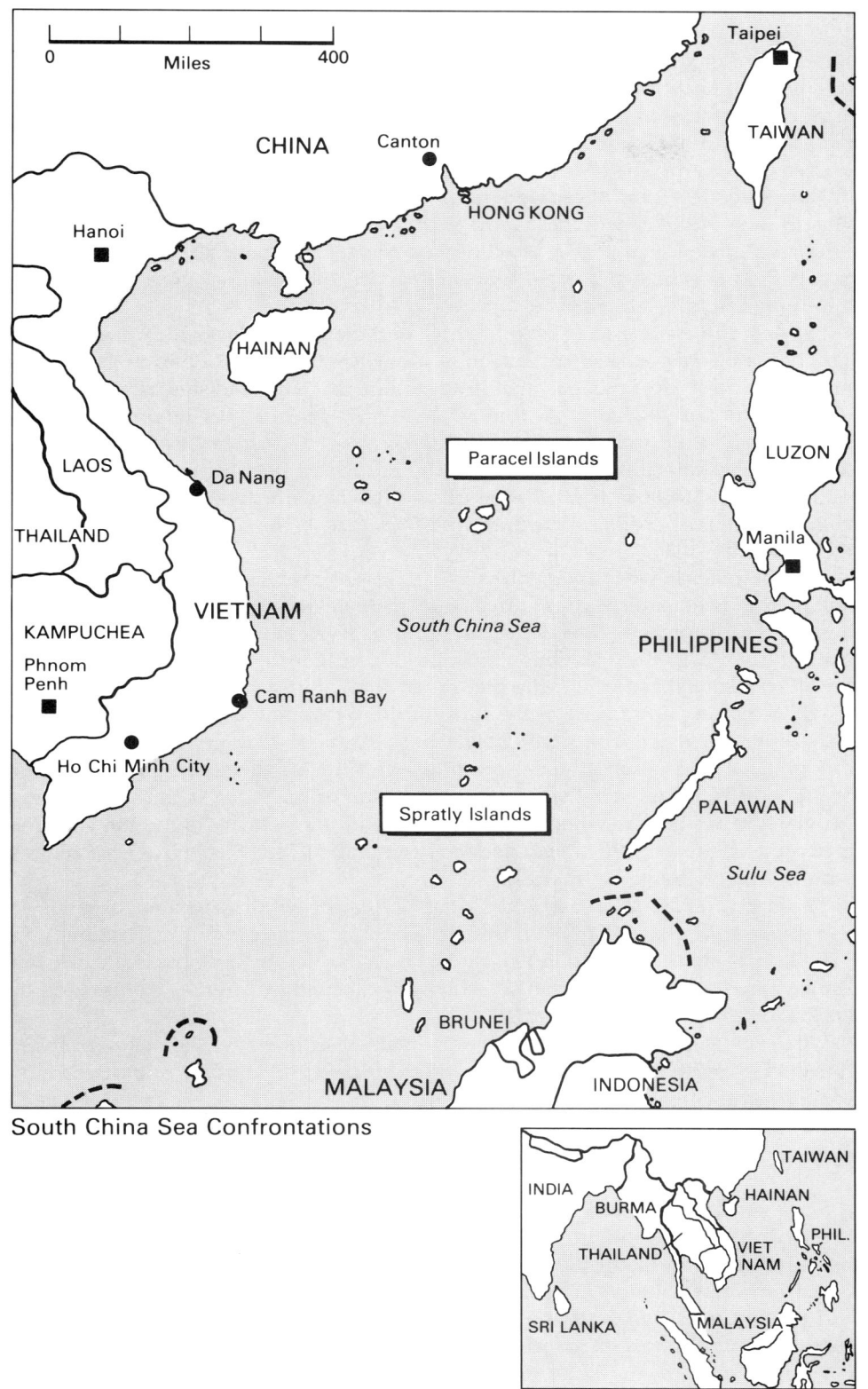

South China Sea Confrontations

stated Pol Pot's intentions.[2] The Khmer Rouge embarked on a public relations campaign to show that it was now respectable. This did not deceive visitors to its army camps; almost without exception they reported that the organization was still committed to total control of Kampuchea.

Every year since 1982 Vietnam had pulled out some men, most recently 20,000 in November 1987, but these were simply troop rotations disguised as withdrawals. On 25 May 1988 when the Vietnamese government announced, through the Foreign Minister, Nguyen Co Thach, that it was to withdreaw 50,000 troops by the end of the year, the decision surprised all parties to the conflict. Nguyen Co Thach indicated that all Vietnamese troops would leave by 1990.

Unknown to the world's public, the Prime Minister of Thailand, General Prem Tinsulanonda, had earlier visited Moscow and spent forty-five minutes talking to Mr. Gorbachev. He explained that it was unfair that Thailand should have to bear the tremendous burden of Kampuchean refugees in its territory and be endangered by the spillover of the Vietnamese war. Gorbachev told Prem that he would discuss withdrawal with the Vietnamese. Within days Nguyen Co Thach was summoned to Moscow. It is believed that Gorbachev informed him that the Soviet Union could not continue payments of $3m. a day for Vietnam's campaign in Kampuchea.

The Vietnamese government already had serious problems, without running the risk of the Soviet's displeasure. In 1988, three million of Vietnam's 63.5 million people were reported to be on the verge of starvation. The nation was virtually bankrupt. In May the Vietnamese ambassador in Bangkok was visiting embassies, even Western embassies, seeking pledges of food aid for his country.[3]

While fighting continued in desultory fashion throughout 1988, peace conferences were convened in various cities. Prince Sihanouk emerged as the key figure, though he was not always the most popular one. He said that he might be prepared to join Hun Sen, who had become Prime Minister of Kampuchea, in forming a new two-party government in Kampuchea. This would mean abandoning the coalition government-in-exile, which included the democratic KPLNF as well as the Chinese-backed Khmer Rouge communists.

The angry Son Sann accused the Prince of 'playing Vietnam's game' by risking a Resistance split. The KPLNF controlled Site 2, a refugee camp in Thailand with 170,000 people. After Phnom Penh it is the second biggest Kampuchean city. But Prince Sihanouk knew that the KPLNF was weakened by internal feuding and he hoped to talk Son Sann around.

Whatever might happen at however many conferences, the main problem remained Pol Pot and the Khmers Rouges, who still had a lust to rule the country whatever the cost in human lives.

Thailand–Laos Conflict

Since 1975 Thailand and Laos have been in dispute over a thirty-square mile strip of hilly land along their common border. Actual fighting has been intermittent but in February 1988 the Thai Army advanced into the area. The rough terrain was a big problem for the Thai Troops. Once the Laotian Command had pushed men into a few commanding hills—which it did quickly—the Thais knew they could retake them only with heavy loss. Foreign diplomats estimated that about 300 Thais were killed and 500 wounded, some in a mined forest. Sheer incompetence was a major factor in the Thais' poor showing; seventy Thais were killed by their own side's fire.

When the Thai Air Force sent in bombers to support the ground troops, several were shot down by enemy SA-7 and SA-9 missiles. A Thai F-5E fighter bomber was brought down by a missile during the fighting and a Thai spokesman said that Vietnam was involved. Vietnam still has 25,000 troops in Laos, after withdrawing another 25,000 in 1987.

The official Laos news agency reported that the Thai troops had been unable to advance. 'All the claims of recapturing certain positions were false and aimed only at encouraging demoralized Thai troops', it said.[4]

The following day, Thai warplanes made further bombing attacks but it is unlikely that they caused any great damage in the thickly-forested terrain. No independent observers were able to visit the area but diplomatic sources in Bangkok said that the fighting would continue at a 'low level'.

Both Thailand and Laos have said that they want talks to end the fighting but Bangkok demands the complete withdrawal of Laotian troops before negotiations start.

Following the battle *débacle*, a new coalition of opposition parties moved a vote of no confidence in the government. The government of Prem Tinsulanonda, once army commander-in-chief, was in no danger of falling. However, the political hopes of the present commander-in-chief, General Chavalit Yongchaiyudh, were ruined.

Thailand's army had a similar experience in 1987 when Vietnamese troops occupied positions on Thai hills near the Chong Bok Pass, where the frontiers of Thailand, Kampuchea and Laos converge. A Thai brigade tried to drive them out and lost 200 men before it withdrew. From this piece of stolen ground Vietnamese guns have frequently shelled the border areas in Thailand where they suspect that Kampuchean guerrillas have found refuge.

Action in South China Sea

On 8 February 1987 Chinese and Vietnamese frigates opened fire on each other in the Spratly Islands of the South China Sea and on 14 March a more serious engagement took place. Each navy had one ship sunk and others damaged, and 120 Vietnamese sailors were drowned. The fighting underlines the tension over the Spratly Islands and Paracel Islands. China regards the Nansha (Spratlys) and Xisha (Paracels) as sovereign territory and has made them administrative districts of Hainan Province.

When Chinese forces protected scientific exploration ships in the area in 1987, Hanoi Radio broadcast a stern warning. 'Faced with foreign military manoeuvres, including warships and submarines, our people and our armed forces will protect our sovereignty over the archipelago.' Vietnamese troops were already on some of the 200 islands.

In June 1988 China had twenty-two warships in the Spratlys region while Vietnam had about thirty, but China had greater and stronger naval reserves. Vietnam has forty-five fast attack boats but only seven old frigates and no submarines. China could quickly send double this force to the Spratlys. Chinese

Vice Foreign Minister, Qian Qichen, told a press conference, 'We do not wish to see an all-out war. There will be no war if Vietnam refrains from provocations against China and withdraws all its troops from the islands and reefs.'[5]

While Hainan is nearly 1,000 miles north of the extreme south of the Spratlys, its Hong-6 bombers have a range of 4,000 miles. China has 800 land-based aircraft, including the Jian-7 fighters, and fifty seaborne Hong-6s. China is capable of in-flight refuelling, supply of ships at sea by helicopter and has new warships and supply vessels capable of longer-range patrols. Vietnam's advantage is that it has forty-eight MiG-23s which could cover the Spratlys and the Paracels from south Vietnam.

Other countries have interests in the islands. Malaysia claims sovereignty over the southern Spratlys, some of which lie only twenty miles from east Malaysia, and has been conducting naval operations in the islands for at least nine years. Joint Malaysian-Indonesian fleets patrol the region and Canada conducted naval exercises with ships from the nations of the Five-Power Defence Agreement (FPDA). These are Australia, Britain, New Zealand and Singapore, with Brunei's membership pending.

The Philippines also claims the Spratlys, which it calls the Kalayaan Islands. International negotiations were pending in 1988 and China seemed ready to accept some claims by Malaysia and the Philippines but neither these countries, nor Vietnam, seemed likely to be so accommodating. Further armed clashes seemed imminent, especially if Taiwan, yet another claimant to the islands, were to challenge China. The Philippines occupies nine of the islands, Malaysia three and Taiwan the largest of them.

In 1974 China pushed the Vietnamese out of the Paracel Islands. At the time they were occupied by South Vietnam. The Communist government of North Vietnam backed the Chinese action. But when the North took over South Vietnam in 1975, all pretensions about Communist brotherhood vanished. Now Vietnam loudly claims the Paracels but is unlikely to regain them.[6]

The Chinese, new to gunboat diplomacy, have shown that they know how to use it. In 1974 South Vietnam's superpower backer, the US, had already pulled its troops out of Vietnam; thus Vietnam was virtually powerless when the Chinese moved into the Paracels. Now, with the Soviet Union withdrawing from Afghanistan and in the grip of *glasnost*, Vietnam will get no help from the Russians over the Spratlys.

The islands are significant in two ways. They lie astride the important sea lanes of the South China Sea and they are believed to be perched on valuable oil and gas reserves.

Vietnam–China Border Tension

Military actions by both sides occur much more frequently than either Hanoi or Beijing likes to admit. At least 300,000 of Vietnam's 1,250,000 armed forces are stationed along or close to the rear of the 400-mile frontier, while China has as many men facing south.

The Chinese Army appears to have higher morale and is better clad than the Vietnamese soldiers, who are grossly underpaid. Even a Lieutenant Colonel is paid only the equivalent of $15 a month. Many officers also have civilian jobs in order to support their families. The rank-and-file are unable to do this and their families have to fend for themselves.

However, the Vietnamese are strong in matériel. The army has 2,200 tanks, mostly T-34/-54/-55/-62, and 1,600 armoured personnel carriers of modern manufacture. Surface-to-air missiles appear to be restricted to SA-7 but there are plenty of them.

Vietnam's logistical strength is misleading because the Soviet Union keeps it short of spare parts. The country's real strength is in its manpower. Apart from its huge army, it has the People's Regional Force of 500,000, the People's Self-Defence Force of one million, the Armed Public Security Force of 60,000 and Border Defence Forces of 60,000.

Hostilities with China are mostly in the form of cross-border artillery duels, especially in the region of Dong Dang. In March 1988, following a minor border incident in the west, a battalion of Vietnam infantry crossed the border and a small-arms fight ensued. In April Chinese tanks made an incursion simultaneously with troops landing in the Spratly Islands. This was a warning to Vietnam that open hostilities could ensue if China's possession of the islands was disputed.

Psychologically, Vietnam holds the ascendancy despite low morale in the army. The Chinese were promptly and bloodily repulsed when they invaded in 1979 and neither side has forgotten it.

References

1. The KPLNF supports the use of the name Cambodia in English, Cambodge in French and Kampuchea in Khmer. This was announced in a Press release from the Office of the President of the KPLNF, December 1987. The ANS has the same policy. The term Kampuchea is now so entrenched in the West that the organizations will have difficulty in reverting to Cambodia.
2. Thai Foreign Office.
3. Diplomatic sources in Bangkok.
4. 16 February 1988.
5. Report from a correspondent who was present.
6. *Jane's Defence Weekly* reported on the China Sea confrontation on 28 May 1988.

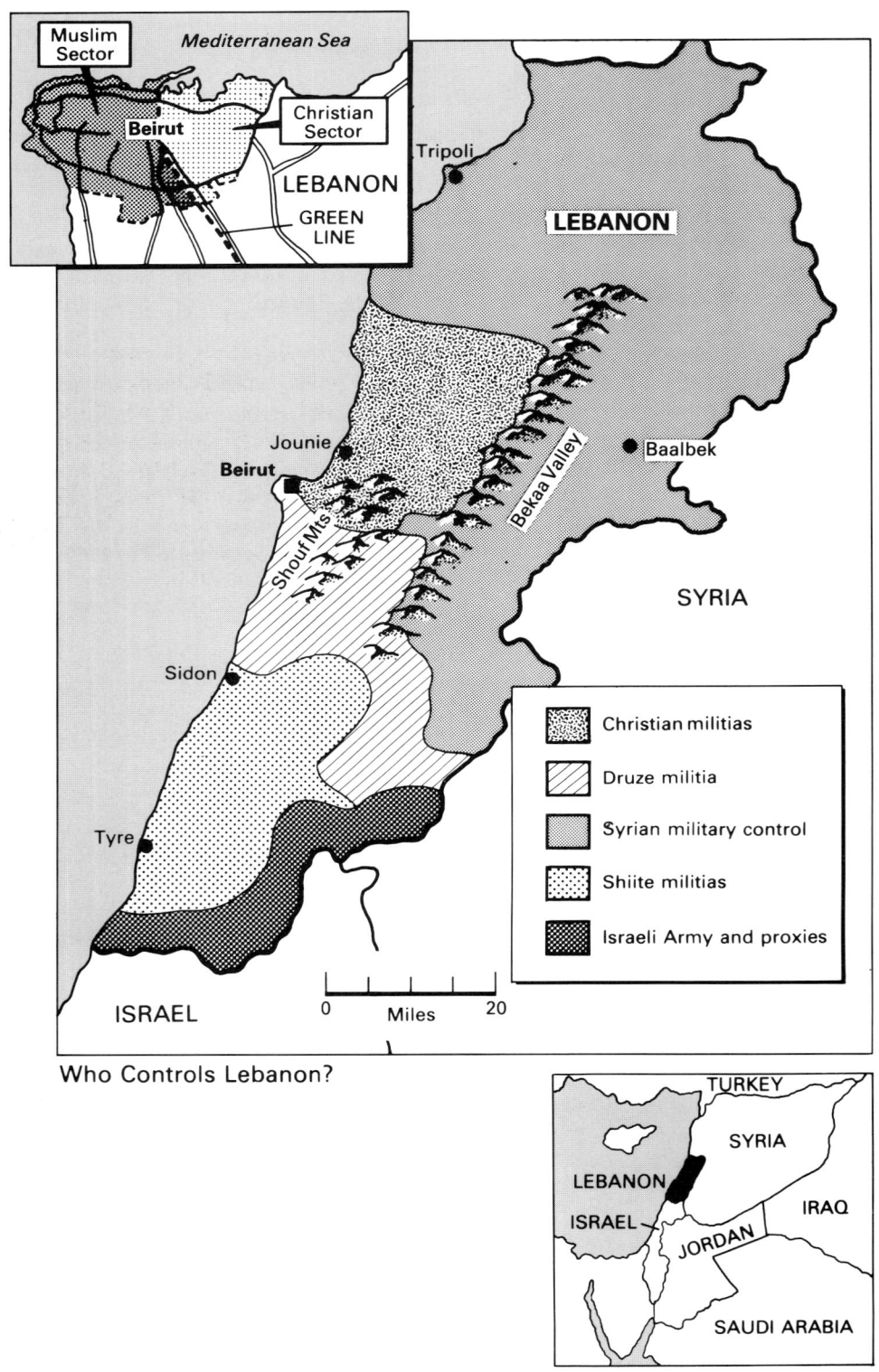

Who Controls Lebanon?

Conflict in Lebanon

Background Summary

This conflict began in 1975 as a form of civil war, mainly between the 'Lebanese Forces'—the name of the Maronite Christian militia—and terrorists of the Palestine Liberation Organization (PLO). After bloody expulsion from Jordan in 1970, the PLO settled in Lebanon where it became a state within a state. The PLO region was known as Fatahland, after Yasser Arafat's PLO faction. When the Christians appeared to be losing to the PLO, the Syrian Army went to their aid, but later the Syrians changed sides and backed the PLO.

As other groups were drawn into the conflict it became complex. Involved were: Shia Muslims of the south, Sunni Muslims of central-west Lebanon, and the Druse of the hills, notably from the Shouf Mountains. More than 100,000 people were killed in the next eight years, mostly in massacres.

In 1978 the Israelis mounted *Operation Litani* into southern Lebanon, in retaliation for Palestinian raids against Israel. The UN sent in a multinational force, the United Nations Interim Force in Lebanon (UNIFIL). On 6 June 1982 Israel launched *Operation Peace* for Galilee and defeated both the PLO and Syrian forces.

The PLO split into two, with the Arafat faction evacuating Beirut in October 1982. Christian militiamen massacred at least 800 Palestinians in two refugee camps.

Meanwhile Iranian Shia Muslim agitators reached the Bekaa Valley in large numbers, and became the extremist *Hezbollah* (Party of God) movement. US Marines, French paratroopers and Italian and British soldiers were sent as peackeepers to Beirut where they were out of their depth in what had become a holy war. American and French casualties were heavy as a result of Shia suicide attacks. All four nations withdrew. Israel also made a phased withdrawal but suffered casualties in attacks made by suicide 'martyrs' driving car-bombs. With the help of the South Lebanese Army (SLA), the Israelis set up a security zone along the Israel–Lebanon border.

In Beirut during 1985, Maronites, Druse, Shia Muslims, Sunni Muslims and Syrians, in shifting alliances, fought savagely. The Sunni militia was practically wiped out by allied Syrians, Druse and the Shia militia, *Amal*. In Tripoli, northern Lebanon, 500 Sunnis were killed while fighting the combined Syrian Army and various militias.

In a siege operation which became known as the Camps War, *Amal*, backed by Syria, tried to destroy the camps in which 50,000 Palestinian refugees lived.

Hezbollah was strong in Beirut by 1986 and was often in armed conflict with *Amal*. Meanwhile gunmen from Arafat's PLO faction filtered back to Lebanon and took control of territory from Sidon to the Maghdousheh Heights. UNIFIL

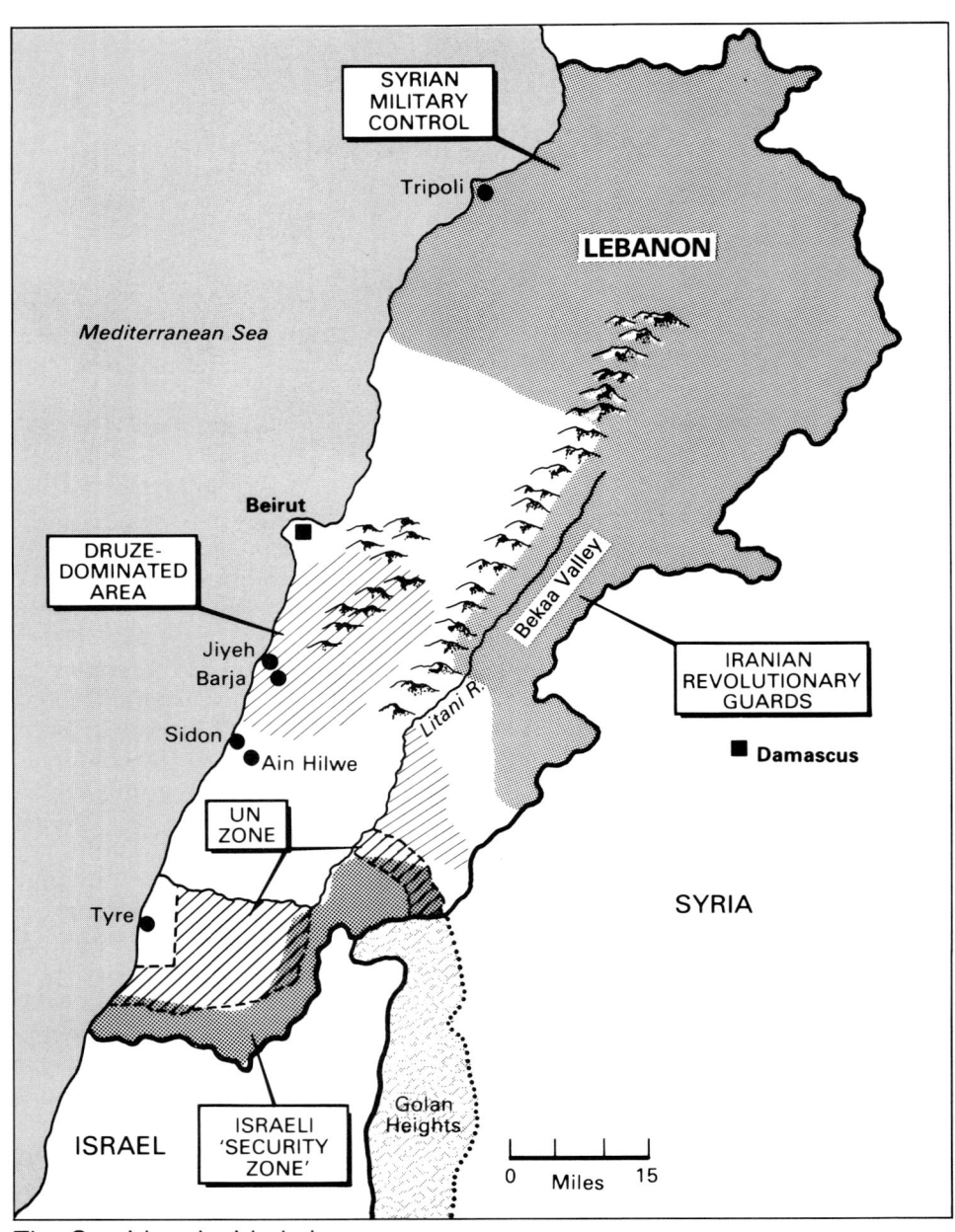

The Outsiders Inside Lebanon

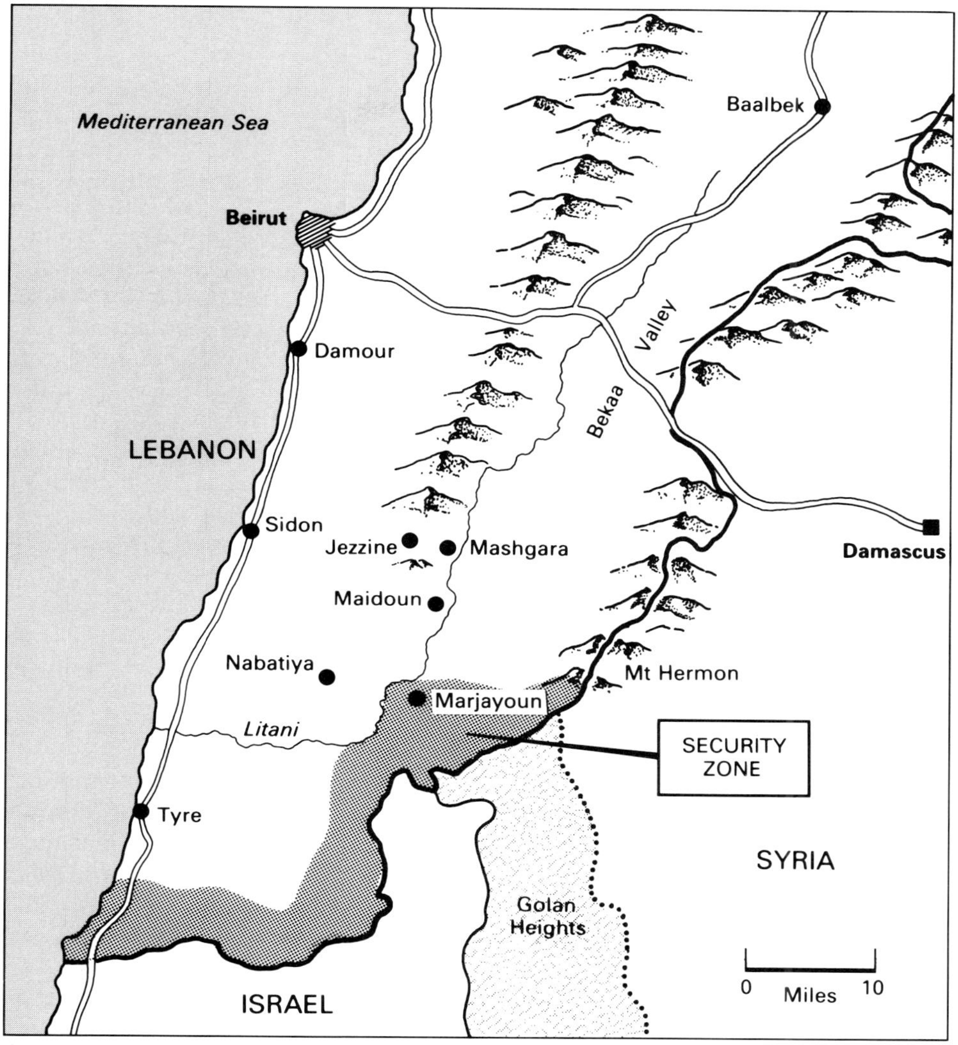

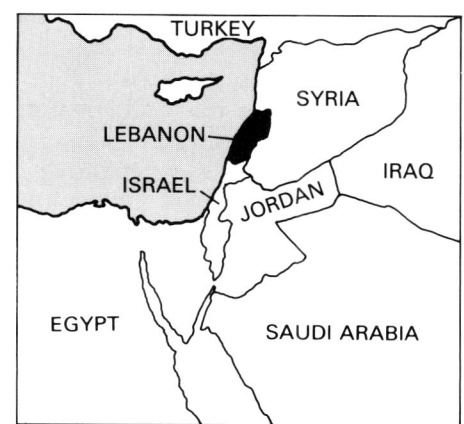

Mediterranean Sea

Beirut

Damour

LEBANON

Sidon

Jezzine ● ● Mashgara

Maidoun ●

Nabatiya ●

Litani

Marjayoun

Mt Hermon

Tyre

Baalbek

Bekaa Valley

Damascus

SECURITY ZONE

SYRIA

Golan Heights

0 Miles 10

ISRAEL

Area of Israeli Operation: May 1988

TURKEY

SYRIA

LEBANON

ISRAEL

IRAQ

JORDAN

EGYPT

SAUDI ARABIA

peacekeepers, under attack from Shia fighters, turned its checkpoints into small fortresses.

Summary of the War in 1987

Two wars took place simultaneously during much of 1987—*Hezbollah* against *Amal* in south Beirut and both against the South Lebanon Army and Israeli forces in southern Lebanon. Despite its working alliance with *Amal*, *Hezbollah* steadily encroached on *Amal* territory and took over one village after another in the south. While here a degree of tense co-existence existed between *Amal* and *Hezbollah*, in Beirut fighting was so savage that the Syrian Army moved into certain areas to impose a ceasefire and curfew. The Syrians 'executed' scores of *Hezbollah* fighters in an attempt to protect their *Amal* protegées but Syrian troops did not attempt to enter *Hezbollah*-held suburbs.

The Syrian Army remained active in northern Lebanon against the Islamic Unification Movement, known as *Taweed*. Following a *Taweed* street ambush of Syrian troops, the Syrians rounded up 200 hostages and massacred them.

Several enormous car bombs were detonated in crowded streets in Beirut and Tripoli and about 500 people were killed. Throughout the year *Hezbollah* maintained its campaign of capturing British, French and German hostages.

The War in 1988

Syrian Army's Intervention

With *Amal* and *Hezbollah* competing for control of Lebanon's 1,500,000 Shia Muslims, *Amal* was doing so badly—having lost nine of the ten Beirut localities it had formerly controlled—that Syria intervened. The local Syrian commander, Brigadier Ghazi Kenaan, surrounded the area with 7,000 troops and on 27 May then sent in 1,500 of them. The *Amal* fighters were immensely relieved. The *Hezbollah* fanatics, acting on orders from Iran, put their weapons aside but did not surrender them.

The operation, ordered by President Assad, was presented as an example of Syrian armed strength. However, it was not a victory over *Hezbollah*. *Hezbollah* did not fear a confrontation with the Syrian Army, gave up no territory, surrendered none of its 'rights' and produced none of its hostages. The Syrian soldiers did nothing but 'take up positions'.

Brigadier Kenaan told foreign reporters brought in specially to witness the Syrian operation: 'You can rest assured and reassure people that the war for the southern suburbs is over.' But foreign diplomats were in no doubt that *Hezbollah* rather than Syria had won the test of wills. Assad's unusual military softness was connected with his four-strand foreign policy. He is hostile to Iraq; he values his alliance with Iran because it, too, is hostile to Iraq; he maintains hostility towards Israel; he demonstrates Syrian power in Lebanon. What mattered most in Beirut in the summer of 1988 was the alliance with Iran, which 'owns' *Hezbollah* and its 7,000 members. *Hezbollah*'s prime concern throughout 1988 was, as its leaders frequently announced, 'to resist Israel'.

Members of the Supreme Shia Islamic Council of Lebanon bitterly attacked the role of Iran in Lebanon. Two Shia clerics in particular, Sheikh Shamsheddin and Sheikh Qabalan, said repeatedly in 1988 that Iran had no right to demand unquestioning loyalty from the Shias of Lebanon. Addressing the Iranians, Qabalan said:

> I reject you. I have experienced you well, leave us alone before it is too late. Our bones are blue with hatred. Many may be angered by these words, but the Iranians have made us shed tears of blood. Let them cry with us for the blood that has been spilled in the southern suburbs. It is precious and will cost dearly. If we are unable to punish them, Allah will.[1]

More than 800,000 Shia Muslims live in southern Beirut. According to *Amal* sources, *Hezbollah*, in alliance with the 2,000 Iranian Revolutionary Guards, killed 11,000 civilians and wounded many thousands more between January 1987 and June 1988.

Northern Border Raids Against Israel

During 1987-88 PLO raiders made hundreds of attempts, by land, sea and air, to infiltrate into Israel, primarily from the north. Some of the squads were sent on terrorist operations from organizations that are affiliated with Syria and based in Syrian-controlled territory. The growing rapprochement—sponsored by Colonel Gaddafi—between the PLO's Yasser Arafat and the Syrian President Assad, was an indication that extremists were intent on maintaining the strategy of violence in order to continue the conflict with Israel.

Between 13 September 1987 and 26 April 1988 these were the most serious incidents from the Israel point of view:[2]

13 September 1987: A raiding squad was intercepted in the Golan Heights south of Kuneitra. Three terrorists were killed in the clash.

16 September 1987: Using a hang-glider, a terrorist from the group Popular Front for the Liberation of Palestine—General Command (PFLP-GC) crossed Israel's northern border and entered an army camp near Kiryat Shemona. Here he killed six Israeli soldiers and wounded seven. Another hang-glider terrorist was intercepted in the air while still within the security zone of southern Lebanon. Both raiders were killed.

22 December 1987: Two terrorists broke through the security fence and were spotted near a military camp. They escaped back into southern Lebanon.

20 January 1988: A terrorist squad from Arafat's *Fatah* was intercepted near Kibbutz Menara and three were killed. One Israeli soldier was killed.

4 February 1988: A *Fatah* squad was intercepted near Kubbutz Yiftah. In a shoot-out, two Israeli soldiers were killed and one wounded. A terrorist was killed and another wounded.

28 February 1988: A dinghy carrying terrorists belonging to Ahmed Jibril's PFLP-GC faction was intercepted by a naval patrol and sunk.

5 April 1988: A party was intercepted as it was trying to break through the northern security fence near Kfar Yuval. All seven men were either killed or captured.

15 April 1988: A naval patrol intercepted terrorists in a dinghy near Sidon and killed them.

26 April 1988: Two terrorists penetrated the security fence near Har Dov, where they attacked an Israeli truck, wounding its driver. An Israeli unit killed the raiders during a shoot-out.

Operation in the Bekaa Valley[3]

Following the long series of attacks against Israeli targets either within Israel or in the security zone, the Israeli High Command launched an operation on 2 May 1988 to drive *Hezbollah* raiders from the village of Maidoun, which they had fortified.

Artillery fired 1,200 rounds from ten 175 mm and eight smaller guns to provide cover for about 2,000 paratroops. Helicopter gunships also backed the soldiers as they fought their way to Maidoun, which is well north of Israel's security zone and within three miles of positions held by the Syrian Army in the southern Bekaa Valley. The Syrian-held village of Meshgara came under Israeli shellfire, but the Syrians, assured through diplomatic channels that the Israeli operation was not aimed at them, did not respond.

In Maidoun, about forty *Hezbollah* gunmen were killed in a day of fighting, as were three Iraelis. By evening the Israelis had dynamited much of Maidoun and withdrew, though they stayed north of the security zone for a few days to demonstrate to everybody in the region that cross-border raids would draw retaliatory attacks of great force.

Lebanese Army versus Lebanese Forces

The Christian militia of East Beirut, always known as the Lebanese Forces, has no connexion with the Lebanese Army. The Army commander is General Michel Aoun and commander of the Forces is Sami Geagea. In May 1988 the two organizations skirmished in Beirut and many observers feared that a war could erupt at any time.

Tension began when the Lebanese Army, in April, began to deploy in East Beirut as part of a plan to bring the two sectors of the capital under government control in advance of a presidential election. The Army hoped that the move would allow parliamentarians to elect a new head of state in relative calm. The parliament building is located on the Green Line that divides Christian and Muslim areas in Beirut.

The Lebanese Forces reacted by placing 1,800 militiamen, armed with rocket-propelled grenades and medium machine-guns at eighteen roadblocks close to similar roadblocks manned by army troops. The Lebanese Forces increased the tension by bringing reinforcements from Kesrouan and Byblos.

General Aoun was trying to show that he was in charge of Christian areas because he apparently hoped to be elected president of Lebanon. Aoun is hostile to the Lebanese Forces. The price of defusing the tension in East Beirut was a heavy one for the army. Following meetings chaired by President Gemayel and attended by army commanders, an agreement was reached under which most checkpoints were dismantled. The Internal Security Forces, yet another organization, was ordered to set up new checkpoints, mount patrols and arrest armed men in Christian areas. This was a blow to the prestige and authority of the army.

UNIFIL's Essential Role

To a degree that is not widely appreciated, unarmed UN observers and peacekeeping forces play an important role in preventing yet another major eruption of violence. For more than three years the UN forces have faced a steady and dangerous level of violence, much of it committed by Iranian-supported extremists who want to end UNIFIL's presence in Lebanon.

UNIFIL's 6,000 personnel succeeded throughout 1988 in stemming the level of violence. Even many of its Israeli critics have come to admit that its role is crucial.[4] For residents of southern Lebanon it is obvious that UNIFIL's presence is a key to preventing chaos. The force has created a zone of relative security and impressive economic vitality. Most important, UNIFIL acts as a buffer that reduces the intensity and frequency of violence.

The Shia *Amal* movement strongly supports UNIFIL. The Shia leaders see UNIFIL as a surrogate for a legitimate, effective and functioning government which exists nowhere else in Lebanon. While *Amal* has played a major role in resisting the Israeli presence in Lebanon, it always carefully limits the level of 'permissible resistance' to the Israeli security zone itself. In this way it hopes to preclude Israeli military response.

Hezbollah is viciously critical of UNIFIL for 'serving Israel's interests'. UNIFIL gives Israel no aid whatever but, as the *Hezbollah* leaders see the situation, if UNIFIL could be removed, the Israeli security zone would be even more exposed to attack by the Islamic Resistance Front. Extremists who accept this argument took up arms against UNIFIL in 1988 and the level of anti-UNIFIL violence reached troubling heights.

Should UNIFIL withdraw, the immediate loser would be *Amal*, which is committed to preventing a reinstallation of the armed PLO presence that previously undermined peace in the south. *Amal*'s siege of the Palestinian refugee camps in the Beirut area (see **WAR ANNUAL 2**) had as much to do with thwarting PLO aims in the south as in the environs of Beirut. It is obvious therefore that Palestinian fighters and *Hezbollah* gunmen have become allies against Israel.

References

1. Interview quoted, in Arabic, in *Ash Shiraa*, 18 May 1988.
2. Israeli Defence Forces' spokeman. All the incidents mentioned were confirmed by various international journalists.
3. Journalists accompanied the IDF force. A Syrian source told me that the army commander in the southern Bekaa Valley had six hours' notice of the Israeli operation.
4. Interview with an IDF officer.

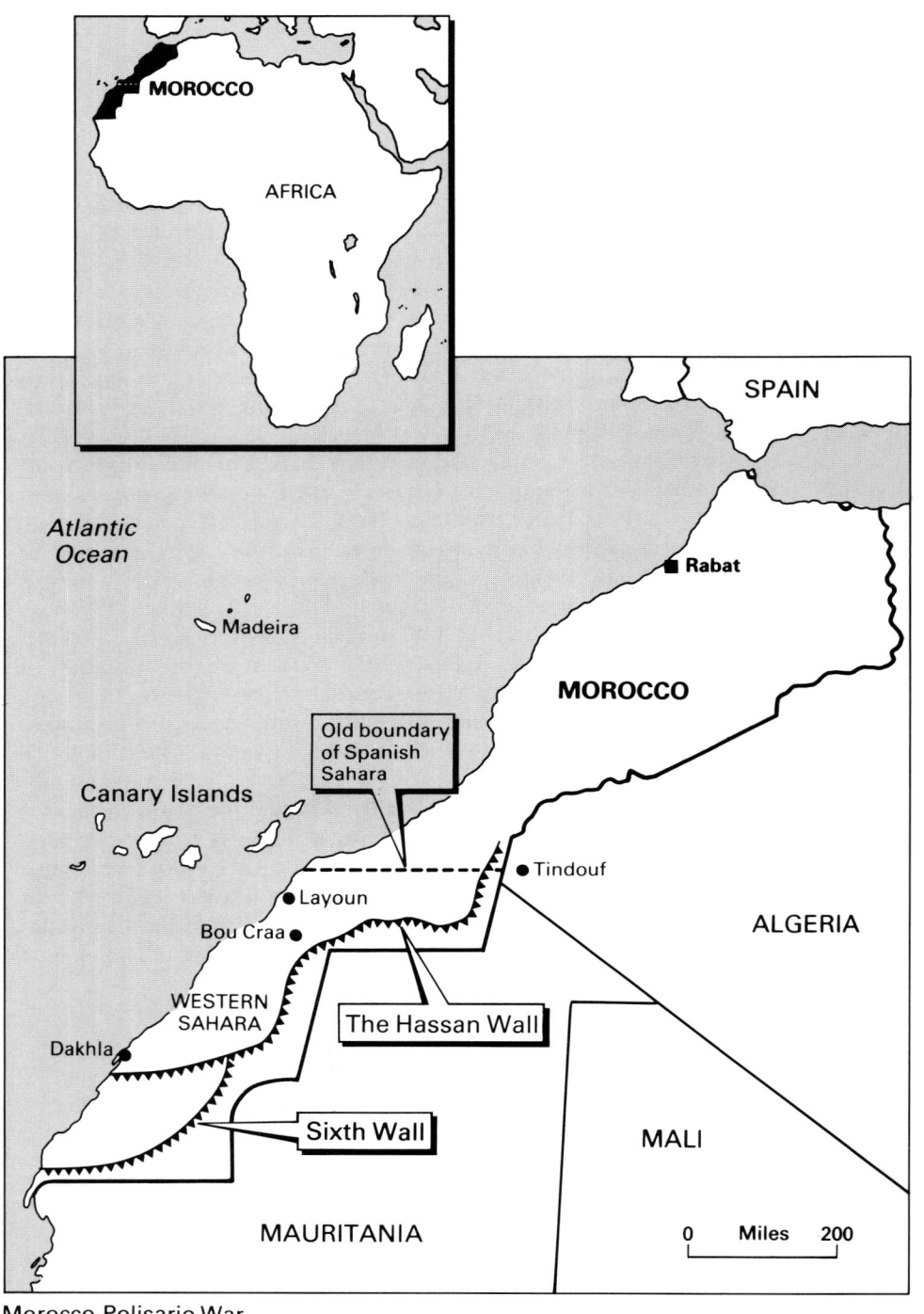

Morocco-Polisario War

Morocco—Polisario War

HIT, CAPTURE AND RUN

Background Summary

The war is over the ownership of Western Sahara, a former Spanish colony. Morocco and Mauritania claimed the territory but in 1975 an international court found that neither country had a legitimate claim and that the overriding principle was self-determination by the estimated 300,000 inhabitants, the West Saharans or Sahrawis.

When Spain withdrew in 1976, Morocco and Mauritania partitioned the country. The Popular Front for the Liberation of Saguia el-Hamra and Rio de Oro (Polisario) declared the whole area to be the Sahrawi Arab Democratic Republic (SADR). After military reverses, Mauritania agreed to a ceasefire and Morocco claimed the entire area.

The highly mobile Polisario guerrilla army made it impossible for Morocco to occupy the region. The Moroccans then based their strategy on the Hassan Wall, a system of defences begun in 1980. The Sahrawis were squeezed into the north-east or into refugee camps in neighbouring Algeria, which supports Polisario. The Organization of African Unity (OAU) recognized SADR, as did other countries, but Morocco would not negotiate with Polisario.

SADR leaders believed that in time Islamic fundamentalism, already rife in Morocco, would bring down the monarchy of King Hassan and the Moroccan people would then reject the enormous cost of the war. Polisario had only one powerful friend, the Soviet Union. Morocco could count on help from the United States and France.

By 1985 the Moroccan Army had taken over nearly all the northern part of the disputed territory, leaving only the stony plains of Rio de Oro for the guerrillas. The ever-lengthening Hassan Wall dominated the territory and in 1985 it stretched for 1,000 miles. About twelve feet high, it was protected by barbed wire, radar and ground sensors.

Summary of the War in 1987

The Hassan Wall restricted Polisario's military operations but no amount of Moroccan pressure could limit its social growth and the growing foreign recognition for SADR—sixty-five countries. In 1987, as in previous years, Polisario showed off its array of captured Moroccan equipment, including British Cascavels, Austrian-French SK-105 tank destroyers, South African AML/E1 and ninety armoured cars and French mobile administration systems.

On 26 February 1987, the 11th anniversary of the founding of SADR, 110 Polisario armoured Land Rovers, in a well-planned raid, broke through the Hassan

Wall, demoralized the Moroccan soldiers in that sector and returned with Spanish Santana troop-carriers, a French AMX tank, dozens of mortars and bazookas and thousands of small arms.

The Hassan Wall had grown still longer—to 1,500 miles—and actually comprised five or six separate walls. It was a remarkable feat of military engineering but it was not impregnable. Polisario radiers could cross it almost at will by night but it was impossible for them to survive for long, especially during daylight hours.

The War in 1988

The Moroccan Army announced that Polisario had 'fallen away' to 10,000 members, while the organization's friends said that it had 50,000 fighting men. In fact, it had no more than 3,000.[1] It had not 'fallen away' to this number; 3,000 had been its strength since 1986. For the type of hit, capture and run war which Polisario fights it needs no greater number.

Politically, SADR grew even stronger, as the number of nations recognizing it increased to seventy-one. The OAU's president, Kenneth Kaunda of Zambia, visited the unofficial capital, Tindouf in Algeria, and the refugee camps to show the OAU's solidarity with SADR.

SADR General Secretary, Muhammad Abdel-Aziz, announced on the occasion of the Kaunda visit that his people wanted 'the whole land of Western Sahara or martyrdom'. The Moroccan government ridiculed SADR by claiming that it was purely an Algerian creation and that if Algeria withdrew its support Polisario would collapse within weeks.

The supposition is academic since it became ever clearer that the conflict was a proxy war, a dispute over pre-eminence in the region. For the Algerian government of President Chadli Benjedid, the war keeps an antagonistic Morocco occupied without bringing the countries into direct conflict.

The war cost Morocco $1m. a day in 1988,[2] thus it was not willing to relinquish any of its claims. The Hassan Wall garrison grew from 110,000 in 1987 to 150,000 in 1988. The Moroccan use of cluster bombs and napalm against Polisario indicated a level of desperation which contrasted sharply with the government's assertion that Morocco had really won the war and was merely waiting for Polisario to realize this.

The Moroccans could certainly not lose the war. The US, France and Saudi Arabia were replacing every bullet and bomb used by the Moroccan forces. In any case, Polisario's 3,000 fighters could not capture Moroccan towns or destroy army bases.

Equally, Morocco could not win the war since there was no way in which the Polisario guerrillas could be wiped out. The cluster bombs and naplam caused few casualties and appeared to have no effect on morale. Early in 1988 the Polisario leaders intensified attacks on garrisons along the wall. They were able to do this only because their intelligence was excellent. They knew exactly where they would find a Moroccan unit new to duty on the wall and even where a particular commander was not considered efficient. Some of this information came from scouts, some from Moroccan prisoners.

According to information from a reliable source,[3] Polisario—with Algerian army help—has had the use of pilot-less reconnaissance drones fitted with television cameras which spy on Moroccan positions behind the wall. This could explain the astonishing success of some Polisario raids. The number of Moroccan prisoners in Polisario hands grew from 2,000 to 2,500 in 1988.

The Hassan Wall undoubtedly keeps the greater part of Western Sahara free of Polisario activity and by mid-1988 about 100,000 Moroccans had been settled in Moroccan-held territory. However, SADR was effectively a state in being, with good administration, according to Kenneth Kaunda and the many other politicians and statesmen who visited it. Based on a communalist society and greatly different from the old traditionalist society of north-west Africa, SADR runs its refugee camps efficiently and keeps its people in good health. The tent-capital, Tindouf, has a population of 160,000.

Morocco, with armed forces totalling 215,000, as well as an equal number of paramilitary forces, could pass large units through the Hassan Wall and make a sweep through the country bounded by the Wall on the west and the frontiers of Mauritania and Algeria on the east.[4] But the Polisario guerrillas would merely disappear across the borders into the trackless wastes and return to fight another day.

On the basis of steady success against great odds and with few casualties in its own ranks, Polisario could well be the world's most efficient guerrilla 'army'.

UN Peace Initiative: Polisario Offensive

On 11 August 1988 the UN Secretary-General Perez de Cuellar announced that he had proposed a 'compromise that covers all aspects' to bring about peace between Morocco and Polisario. After a ceasefire, he suggested peace negotiations under the auspices of the UN and the OAU, with Algeria and Mauritania as observers. A referendum on self-determination would be held under UN and OAU supervision.

Creating conditions for such a referendum would be difficult. Polisario insisted that Moroccan troops and administrators be withdrawn from the territory during the referendum; the demand was rejected by Morocco. However, the peace plan was conditionally approved by both sides.

Less than three weeks later, on September 23, one of the largest battles of the war took place around the Oum Dreiga section of the Hassan Wall. Polisario took the initiative by sending into battle about 1,000 men in two light infantry battalions and one mechanized infantry battalion; a Polisario battalion numbers 350 men. They moved in thirty armoured personnel carriers backed by field artillery.

The Moroccan army command, which rarely comments on operations, admitted that 51 of its soldiers were killed and 95 wounded but diplomatic sources put the overall figure at 270, including 25 Moroccans taken prisoner. Colonel Abdelsalam Al-Abidi, CO of the 3rd Regiment Motorized Infantry, was among the captured and he later died of his wounds.

Polisario suffered 124 casualties, according to Moroccan sources, but Polisario itself made no statement about losses. Its communique noted that the operation was 'outstandingly successful'. The purpose was to show Morocco that Polisario was entering peace talks strong and determined, not as a weakening loser. The fact that Polisario's claims were carried by the Algerian newsagency APS indicated to diplomats that the Algerian government endorsed the Polisario attack, despite its having re-established links with Morocco.

SADR leaders said that provided the referendum was fairly conducted it would abide by the result. King Hassan produced a new idea—turning the kingdom into a federation of self-governing provinces. This would give him titular sovereignty over the disputed territory and deprive the Sahrawis of foreign representation. On such terms a lasting peace seemed unlikely.

References

1. There may be many more trained men than this but 3,000 is the operational number. The figure comes from a Western European intelligence source and is confirmed by two African statesmen who have visited Tindouf.
2. This amount is a UN estimate, corroborated by a US State Department source.
3. Diplomatic sources in Algiers.
4. I am told that in January 1988 the Army General Staff planned such a dragnet sweep and that it reached an advanced stage of preparation before King Hassan heard of it and ordered it to be cancelled. He realized that should the sweep fail, as it almost certainly would, Morocco would look militarily inept and be politically embarrassed. I cannot confirm that the operation was planned.

Mozambique Guerrilla War

'BRUTAL HOLOCAUST'

Background Summary

Mozambique has been a battlefield since it became independent from Portugal in 1975. The Mozambique Liberation Front (Frelimo), the Marxist faction which won control of the new nation, embarked on an economic programme that favoured big state farms and industralization schemes at the expense of peasant families. Villagers were forced into communes, often where the Portuguese colonial administration had herded people into strategic hamlets. In addition, the Frelimo leaders opposed strong religious beliefs and sometimes repressed them. By these measures and by mismanaging the economy they brought the country close to ruin.

In 1977 Ken Flower, chief of the Rhodesian Central Intelligence Organization, created the Mozambique National Resistance (MNR), which is better known as Renamo. White-ruled Rhodesia planned to sabotage the assistance which black regimes, such as Frelimo, might give to the Zimbabwean Resistance.

Fighting between Frelimo and Renamo gradually destroyed Mozambique. In 1982 South Africa, which has a long border with Mozambique, embarked on a campaign to ensure that it would never become a threat to South African security. Units of the South African Defence Force (SADF) engaged in destructive guerrilla-type warfare of their own, while the South African government financed, trained and armed Renamo guerrillas.

The Nkomati Accord, of 1984, signed between South Africa and Mozambique, was intended to stop aid to Renamo. In return, Mozambique's President Samora Machel prevented terrorists of the African National Congress (ANC) from using his territory as a base for operations against South Africa. The US became involved because the Reagan administration feared that Mozambique was following Angola into the Soviet-Cuban camp.

Frelimo had reversed many of its socially destructive policies by the early 1980s. The policy of state farms was abandoned, the private sector was encouraged and new, strong links with the church were sought. However, much irreversible damage had been done by then.

In Mozambique's 303,769 square miles of difficult terrain, half of Renamo's 9,000 fighters were beyond proper command and control; yet all benefited from supplies sent by Portugal, Morocco, Saudi Arabia and Zaire.

Frelimo had 15,000 soldiers supported by 3,500 Zimbabwean troops. President Machel relied on Russian and Chinese aid.

For much of 1986 the Renamo guerrillas controlled two-thirds of the country and terrorized some urban areas, even in the capital, Maputo. Because of

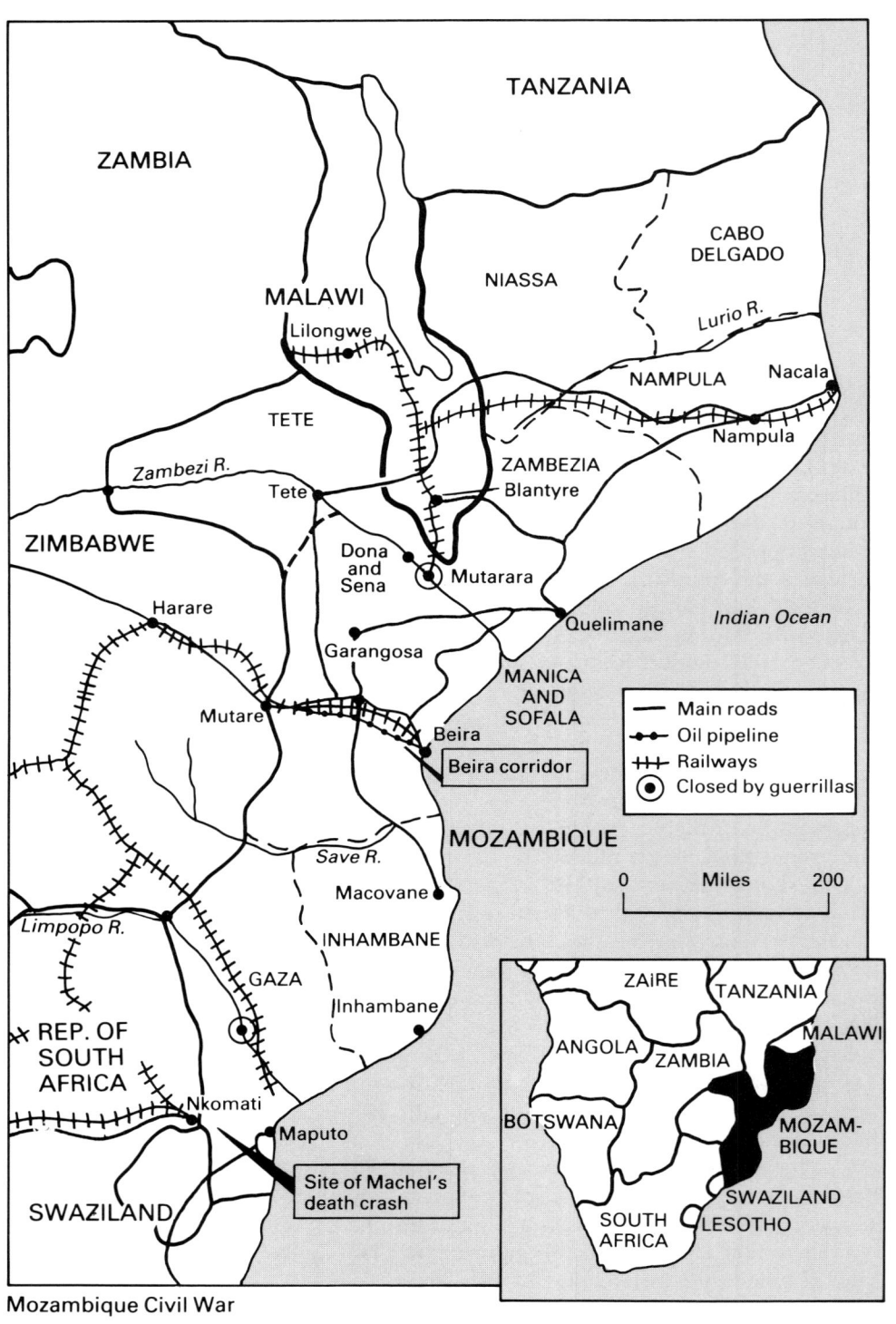

Mozambique Civil War

terrorism—by both sides—250,000 people had become internal refugees. In June 1986 the Renamo leader, Alfonso Dhlakama, claimed to have 18,000 men under arms, 2,000 of them in 'conventional battalions'. In fact, they were no more than large gangs. They fought in a semi-conventional fashion, as at Inhaminga in June 1986 during an inconclusive pitched battle against government troops.

Renamo operated from Malawi for much of 1986 until its President, Hastings Banda, came under so much pressure from Zimbabwe and Tanzania that he drove out the guerrillas.

Summary of the War, October 1986-December 1987

On 19 October 1986 President Machel was killed in a plane crash while en route from Zambia to Maputo. He was succeeded by Joaquim Chissano, a moderate politician who was formerly Foreign Minister. In March 1987 Chissano reached a mutual defence agreement with Malawi. In the meantime, Zimbabwean operations in Mozambique in support of the government increased. With Zimbabwe's help, Frelimo reversed Renamo's 1986 gains. Zimbabwe had 10,000 servicemen in Mozambique in 1987. In addition, there were 1,500 Cuban, 200 East German, 350 Soviet and eighty North Korean military 'advisers'. Despite the government's apparent strength, Renamo was active in thirteen of the fourteen provinces during 1987.

The War in 1988

In April 1988 the US Deputy Assistant Secretary of State for Africa, Roy Stacey, said: 'What has emerged in Mozambique is one of the most brutal holocausts against ordinary human beings since World War II.' His blunt assessment sums up much of the military activity in the country throughout the year.

Stacey accused Renamo of 'waging a systematic and brutal war of terror against Mozambican civilians through forced labour, physical abuse and wanton killing'. He was speaking at a UN-sponsored conference in Maputo which raised $143m. emergency aid for Mozambique.

For the US to turn so decidedly against Renamo, which it had long supported against the Marxist regime, was remarkable. The change occurred following a report by Robert Gersony, consultant to the US State Department's Bureau for Refugee Programmes.[1] Gersony spent three months in Mozambique and neighbouring states gathering information and interviewing witnesses. His report made shocking reading. Renamo, he said, used 'systematic and co-ordinated' violence against civilians. They were shot, executed with knives, axes and bayonets, burnt alive, beaten to death, asphyxiated and drowned.

Thousands had been trapped in 'unspeakable conditions'. Older children were forced to act as porters for Renamo troops on the march and, though they walked from 6am to 8pm, they were not permitted food on the way. Any child who could not keep up or dropped a load was beaten, sometimes to death. Girls and women were forced to 'provide sex'. Those who resisted were beaten as, if they objected, were their husbands or fathers.

Renamo fighters repeatedly attacked villages in areas controlled by the government and razed them. According to Gersony, Renamo raiders often murdered village officials. A group of officials with their wives and children were burnt alive in their homes and the villagers were forced to witness the 'execution'. In a particularly vicious attack on the town of Homoine the rebels massacred 400 civilians.

Gersony's document recorded cases of 'target retribution' against small children whose parents had fled. Some were murdered, others had ears, lips, nose or limbs cut off.

Social workers in Maputo are trying to relieve the nightmares of abducted youths who do finally reach safety. Fernando Maposse, aged 14, was captured and forced to join the rebels, but escaped after accidentally killing two members of his own band in a skirmish against government troops. Maposse said that the rebels crept like animals through the bush and consulted a witch doctor before deciding when to attack. Another youth was tortured and abandoned when he refused to kill members of his own family. The rebels chopped off an ear and the fingers of the boy's right hand.

Mozambican soldiers were also guilty of atrocities, the Gersony report stated, but they were responsible for three per cent of murders of civilians compared with ninety-four per cent attributed to Renamo. After the Gersony report, the US administration announced that Mozambique, despite being a Marxist state, was moving in the right direction through developing its ties with the West.

Food Convoys Without Escort

Renamo, whose followers had increased to probably 24,000, is not the only group that Mozambicans fear. Local warlords and bandits armed with AK-47 rifles murder and plunder at will. About eighty per cent of the nation of 13.5 million people was being torn apart by mindless violence in 1988. Together with the outlaws, the rebels had driven more than one million people from their homes and put an end to food production by an estimated two million farmers.

The guerrillas hindered relief efforts by looting emergency provisions and destroying what they could not carry away. At Christmas 1987 the International Red Cross halted airlifts from Maputo to rural villages after Renamo threatened to shoot down the planes. Land routes were no safer. More than 400 people were killed in ambushes on the main road from Maputo north in one three-month period. Travelling in convoys guarded by incompetent Frelimo troops, relief vehicles were easy prey.

Aid agencies argue that helicopter gunships, armoured cars and modern communications equipment are needed to run supplies through Renamo blockades. Until mid-1988 no Western nation had agreed to provide weapons or equipment. Even without gunships, some aid continued to get through. Western donors supplied $22.5m. in trucks and tractors between 1984 and 1988. The international relief agency CARE managed to move 11,000 tons of food and other supplies each month, mainly by rail and road. However, the routes are tortuously long. The trip from the distribution centre of Tete to the Zumbo area on the western border is 200 miles but the journey needed a ten-day 500-mile detour through Zimbabwe and Zambia to avoid Renamo rebels.

In January, President Chissano removed General Sebastiao Mabote as army chief-of-staff and replaced him with General Antonio Hama Thai, who had planned a successful offensive against Renamo in the central province of Zambesia. However, by early 1988 the government army, which had a nominal strength of about 30,000 in ten provincial commands, had disintegrated except for a few units which remained disciplined. The Railway Security Battalion was one of them. The Cubans, Russians, North Koreans and East Germans could not restore any real cohesion or command.

Contrary to Press reports, the army's equipment was good and generally well serviced; the foreign advisers could at least see to this.[2] The army had fifty armoured reconnaissance vehicles, thirty of them BRDM-1/-2, 100 armoured personnel carriers and sixteen mechanized infantry combat vehicles.

Renamo claimed, during 1988, that all its weapons and supplies were captured from Mozambican regular forces and occasionally from Zimbabwean troops supporting the Mozambique government. Mozambican and American officials disputed this and said that South African intelligence services supplied the rebels. Such assistance was supposed to have ended after the signing of the 1984 Nkomati agreement.

The South African interest in backing rebels in Mozambique is to disrupt communications. If the roads and railways are destroyed, Zimbabwe, Botswana, Malawi and Zambia are forced to send their goods through South Africa. In this way Pretoria keeps southern Africa in a stranglehold.

'Betrayal' of Renamo

Despite Renamo's well-documented atrocities, throughout 1987-88 a small, dedicated group of wealthy US businessmen and evangelical Christians lobbied to persuade the Reagan administration to aid the rebels. The Renamo supporters, who have a Capitol Hill office called the Mozambican Research Centre, claimed that the Gersony report was 'politically motivated and inaccurate'. The State Department was 'betraying' the Reagan doctrine of helping anti-Communist insurgents.[3]

In Mozambique, in March 1988, an Australian missionary, Ian Grey, was sentenced to ten years in prison for security offences that involved carrying messages from the American group to Renamo. The Renamo supporters tried to engage Colonel Oliver North, the former White House National Security aide at the centre of the Iran-Contra scandal, but he said he was too busy.

Renamo's View of Strategy

Until 1988 it had been virtually impossible for foreigners to comprehend the ferocity of Renamo guerrillas. They could understand how Right-wing groups would want to oppose a Marxist regime, but slaughter of peasants who wanted only to continue their farming life was not only cruel but irrational.

Then, in a rare and brief interview, the elusive Alfonso Dhlakama explained something of his policy.[4] He said that military strategy was 'merely to make problems for the enemy'. In line with this thinking, the Renamo command made no attempt to control or restrict the activities of the army.

In fact, Renamo has no unified command and the movement is riven with enmities and feuds. After thirteen years of operations, it was still not an army, merely a collection of gangs with a distant allegiance to Dhlakama, since it is through him that arms supplies are sometimes organized.

Also in 1988, Evo Fernandes, Renamo's former secretary-general, explained Renamo's objective: 'In the villages we must destroy the presence of Frelimo and the authority of the state. When that is done we take the people away to our schools.' He was referring to Renamo's brutal indoctrination centres.

In January 1988 two Renamo leaders, Mateus Lopes and Joao de Silva Ataide, were killed while returning from a meeting with Dhlakama inside Mozambique. The official explanation was that they died in a car accident. Other Renamo officials alleged murder; they said that the culprits were members of a group of senior officials who opposed efforts to negotiate an end to the war.

A Mozambican official told a British reporter: 'This is a war from the Middle Ages. In some areas the government is seen as an intruder into a world of age-old traditions. It breeds a very vicious reaction, a desire to destroy any vestige of central or modern authority.'[5]

British-Trained Troops Take the Field

The first troops to be trained by British military advisers in neighbouring Zimbabwe finished their twelve-week course in December 1987. They amounted to only a company in strength and the British programme, at a cost of £3.5m, trains only 350 troops a year, far too few to have any rapid impact on the war. While the troops are rated the best in the army they are largely ineffective because of the failure to supply them in the field. For instance, when word of a massacre of villagers at Homoine reached the army base at Maxice, on the coast, the soldiers had to walk the twelve miles to Homoine because there was no transport.

Instruction in tactical warfare, river crossing and use of weapons has greatly helped the Western-trained units but their morale is constantly sapped by shortages of food. Some soldiers get only one real meal each week and they often drink contaminated water.

Most of the Frelimo soldiers guard projects connected with particular foreign sponsors. Troops at Ungubana defend a British-funded operation to rebuild the 355-mile Mozambique railroad that follows the Limpopo River from Zimbabwe to Maputo. The elite 'Tigers Battalion' guards the European Community's great agricultural project near Maputo. Italy feeds troops stationed near Italian dam and irrigation works.

A private British firm, Defence Systems Ltd., trains government troops to counter Renamo strikes on rehabilitation work on the Nacala railroad in the north. Late in 1988, Defence Systems, whose instructors are mostly ex-members of Britain's SAS, won a contract to help set up a force to protect the power lines of the giant Cahora Bassa hydro-electric plant in Tete Province.

Of all the special forces trained by Mozambique's allies the Soviet-trained 'red beret' commandos have probably made the biggest difference to the war. The 'red berets' are spearheading the new offensive in the northern province of Zambezia. The overall problem is that with so many separate special forces protecting the foreign-financed development projects the logistics problem becomes ever more difficult in a country whose transport and communications are so poor.

References

1. The Gersony Report was published in March 1988. The British Foreign and Commonwealth Office stated that it had known for a long time that Renamo was 'responsible for premeditated atrocities' and that the 'very disturbing' Gersony paper was substantiation of the British view.
2. A diplomat with military experience, based in Maputo, said that Frelimo had 'little concept of tactics for convoy protection'. Another said that the army was reluctant to track down rebels after an attack.
3. Dan Burton, a Republican Congressman from Indiana is one of Renamo's main American supporters. James Blanchard, a Louisana businessman, told the *New York Times* that he had given Renamo $75,000 in two years.
4. Quoted in a report by Richard Dowden in *The Independent*, London, 24 February 1988.
5. *Ibid.*

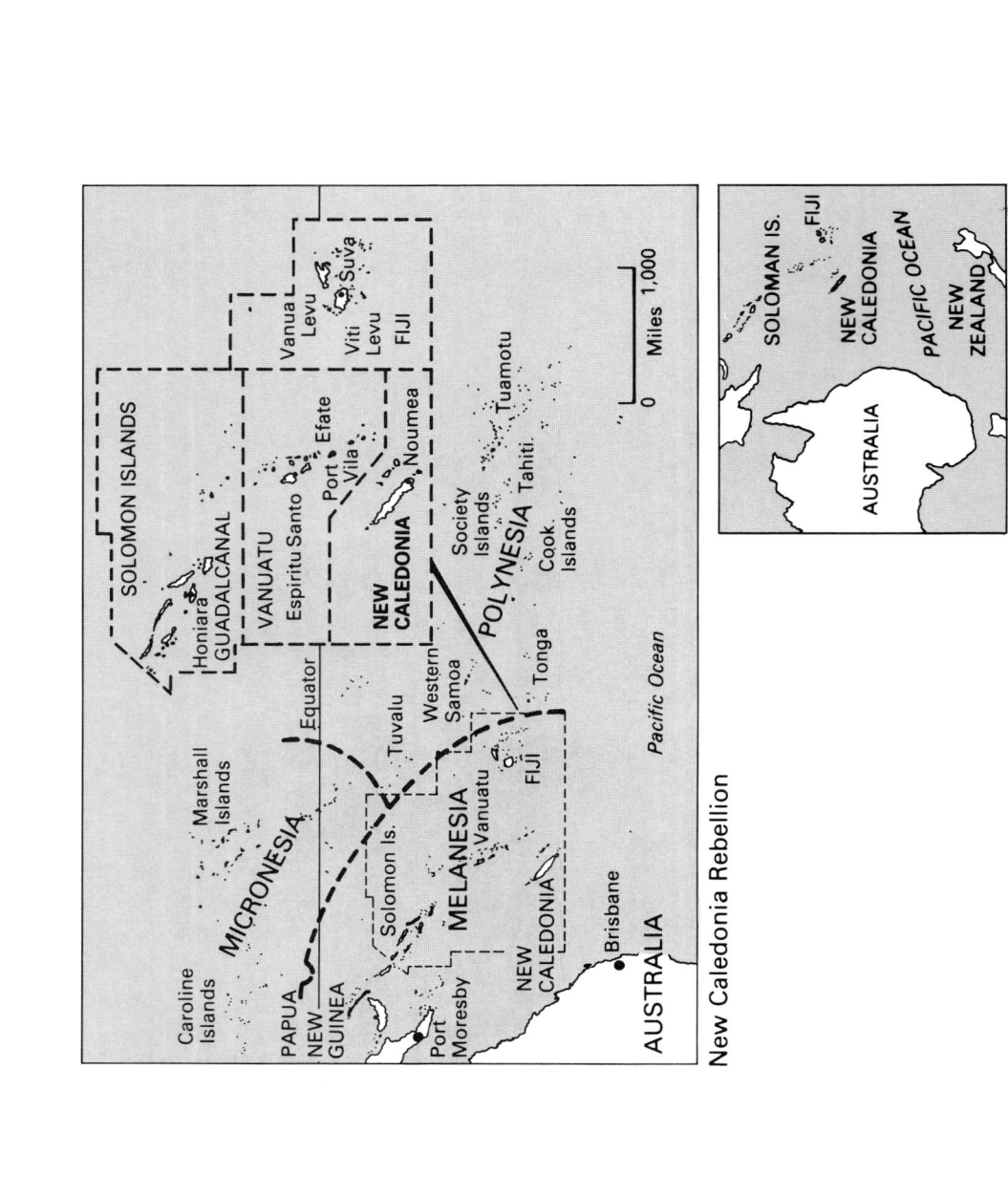

New Caledonia Rebellion

New Caledonia

Whatever the description of the dispute in New Caledonia between 1984 and 1987, by 1988 it was a war and it would be misleading to give it lower status. After all, both sides to the conflict—the French government and army and the Kanak separatists—call it a war.

The native Kanaks in the group of islands, 1,000 miles east of Queensland, want independence from France, even though they do not have an absolute majority. With 62,000 they are the largest group, but there are 54,000 Europeans, mostly French, and 30,000 other Pacific islanders and Asians. Through the Kanak Socialist National Liberation Front (FLNKS), the Kanaks showed that they were ready to use violence to gain independence. The French settlers, known as the Caldoches, were prepared to use violence to oppose the Kanaks.

In Kanak eyes, the struggle goes back to the nineteenth century when the French first arrived in large numbers after the discovery of nickel. They appropriated the best land, herded the Kanaks into reserves, and killed several thousand who resisted.

In August 1983 a charismatic 39-year-old Kanak, Eloi Machoro, a specialist in roadblocks, set up a 'provisional government', with due ceremony, in a village a few miles outside the capital city Noumea. He renamed the French colony 'the Independent State of Kanaky'.

On 30 November 1984 a French settler was shot dead in his farmhouse and from that moment New Caledonia was an 'international trouble-spot'. Machoro was the leader of a group of armed Kanaks in a barn on a farm when it was surrounded by paramilitary gendarmes. They ordered the Kanaks to put down their arms and when they refused a police marksman shot Machoro dead. His faithful lieutenant, Marcel Nonaro, was also killed. Within days Machoro's face adorned Kanak posters, Che Guevara style, and has done so ever since.

On the night of 5 December 1984 a gang of French settlers ambushed seventeen unarmed Kanaks in the valley of Hienghene, 250 miles north-east of Noumea. The Kanaks were stopped by a felled tree while driving home in the mountains. As they alighted from their bus they were caught in crossfire and hunted down by settlers with automatic weapons, dogs and searchlights as they tried to escape across a river. Survivors told how the killers systematically finished off the wounded at pointblank range. Among the dead were two brothers of Jean-Marie Tchibaou, who was soon to become leader of the FLNKS.

A police post five miles away was alerted while the massacre was still going on but arrived sixteen hours later. Seven of the killers gave themselves up but after twenty-one months' investigation, the examining magistrate dismissed all charges, saying that the French had acted 'quite properly in self-defence'. The settlers' newspaper, *Les Nouvelles*, described the killers as 'war heroes'.

Gun battles took place in January 1985 and again in May that year when more than 100 people were killed. As a result, the French socialist government divided New Caledonia into four regions, each with a powerful local assembly, and a territorial assembly in the capital, Noumea. Kanak separatists under Jean-Marie Tchibaou, a former Roman Catholic priest, won control of the three least populated regions.

This policy, supported by President Mitterrand, for a time calmed the resentment of the Kanaks at their alleged domination by white settlers. With Mitterrand's blessing, the government in Paris examined the idea of 'independent association'. This would have given the Kanaks what the socialists called their 'legitimate rights' as the original inhabitants, while preserving a link with France.

A new government, under Jacques Chirac, opposed this. It regarded 'liberation-ist extremists', some of whom were Libyan-trained, as terrorists responsible for murdering settlers and burning farms. Charles Pasqua, the Interior Minister, drew a parallel between New Caledonia and the bombing attacks by Corsican separatists. 'The defence of Bastia [the Corsican capital] begins in Noumea', he said. New Caledonia is twice the size of Corsica.

Chirac's Minister for External Territories, Bernard Pons, wanted the issue of independence to be settled by a referendum in which all islanders would vote. Such a vote would inevitably reject independence, since whites were a majority. Jean-Marie Tchibaou argued that only Kanaks should be eligible to vote.

In a referendum held on 13 September 1987, a total of 58.99% of the electorate turned out to vote, which was 8% higher than in a previous referendum; the vote in favour of staying with France was 98.3%. Australia felt that the referendum vote did not grant France sufficient authority to continue in government of New Caledonia. New Zealand expressed fears about the divisions between communities becoming more pronounced as a result of the referendum. The politicians in Paris believed that whatever attitude they took towards the island micro-states, they would come up against opposition 'fomented' by the regional powers, Australia and New Zealand, which they accused of wanting to eradicate French influence in the Pacific. Prime Minister Chirac described the two countries' attitudes as 'Anglo-Saxon hypocrisy'.

In April 1988 the FLNKS severely disrupted polling for the French presidential election. The movement had already called on the indigenous Melanesian people to boycott the election. Then on 22 April, hooded separatists hacked three gendarmes to death on the remote island of Ouvea and kidnapped twenty-seven others. A fourth gendarme died and eight others were wounded in further attacks carried out at polling stations.

Bernard Pons, as Minister of Overseas Territories, flew to New Caledonia and General Antoine Jerome was sent with reinforcements to strengthen the military presence. Already 300 soldiers, including twenty élite sharpshooters, were deployed across the small island of Ouvea. Two companies of France's Rapid Intervention Force (FAR) were rushed to New Caledonia.

The kidnapped men included Captain Philippe Legorjus, commander of the élite commando unit, *Groupe d'Intervention de la Gendarmerie Nationale* (GIGN), together with six of his soldiers and a magistrate from Noumea. All were held in a cave in a steep cliff in an area which the Kanaks considered sacred.

Pons recommended military action to Chirac, who quickly approved it. General Jacques Vidal prepared an assault force of sixty, with a commando spearhead. Captain Legorjus persuaded the kidnappers that it would be useful for them to allow him to make contact with the army. The Kanaks let him go for several hours at a time but tied up his colleague, Captain Picon, and threatened to kill him if Legorjus did not return. Legorjus smuggled in two revolvers, one of which was kept by Captain Picon.

Two helicopters began the assault. They hovered close to the cave to cover the sounds of troops crawling through the nearby jungle. Most of the Kanaks were outside the cave and began a prolonged small-arms fight with the advancing soldiers. About eight retreated into the cave and were about to turn their weapons on to their hostages when Captain Picon pinned them down with revolver fire.

Troops threw smoke grenades and stun grenades into the cave, forcing out the Kanaks. The hostages escaped through a side passage which had previously been closely guarded. The French troops killed fifteen of the thirty Kanak fighters and wounded three, while two soldiers were killed and two wounded. After the seven-hour fight twenty-four Frenchmen had been rescued.

Despite the French victory, the Kanaks are seen as an effective guerrilla force. By mid-1988 they had forced the French to station 9,000 members of the security forces in New Caledonia, one for every four Kanak adults. The bloodshed in the Ouvea cave made New Caledonia's future even darker.

Independence has become normal in the Pacific. The regional leaders, Australia and New Zealand, accept that they, too, belong to the Pacific and are embarrassed that the French regard New Caledonia as simply a distant bit of France.

The Strategic Implications

The strategic implications of the New Caledonia crisis should be assessed not merely in relation to French interests, but also in the context of an international situation where the leading roles inevitably go to the two superpowers, the US and the Soviet Union. Secondary roles go to the regional powers—Japan, Australia, New Zealand and to a lesser degree, China, whose foreign policy is continental in character.

The Western powers have a threefold aim. First, to ensure that their fleets can move freely in the South Pacific; the US has a particularly clearcut attitude to this proposition. The second aim is to maintain the regional communications and research experimentation considered to be of vital strategic interest. What is true for France in respect of Mururoa Atoll—where it conducts nuclear tests—is even truer for the US. It maintains in the Marshall Islands important test installation for its anti-missile defences, has several satellite ground relay and transmission stations in the region, and co-operates with Australia on research programmes.

The third aim, the most fundamental of all, is to ensure that no hostile power—in this case the Soviet Union—is given facilities by South Pacific countries comparable to those enjoyed by the Western states. On this issue the US determination is clear to all concerned. Only one country, Vanuatu, has let it be known, since obtaining independence, that it would consider allowing Soviet warships into its waters. This has resulted in the Port-Vila authorities being kept under constant surveillance by 'security agencies'.

It is on this last point that the future of New Caledonia is of particular strategic interest. Strategists and politicians wonder what would happen if the Kanak separatist leaders won power and yielded to probable requests by Moscow. They have already shown signs of being sympathetic to Marxist-inclined governments. Soviet warships have been noted frequently in the South Pacific, sometimes on observation missions around Mururoa during French nuclear tests.

Reference

1. A full-page headline in the *Sunday Times*, London, 20 January 1985.

Northern Ireland Terrorist War

'A LEVEL OF BARBARISM'

Background Summary

In modern times, violence in Northern Ireland dates from the late 1960s. The basis of the bitter confrontation is the demand by the nationalist organsation Sinn Fein, whose members are Roman Catholics, for the union of Northern Ireland with Eire (the Irish Republic) and the insistence by the Protestant or Loyalist community that Northern Ireland remains part of the United Kingdom.

Since the split in the organisation in 1969, Sinn Fein's military arm has been the Provisional Irish Republican Army, often known as the Provisionals or the Provos. In practice, Sinn Fein and the IRA have the same command. The IRA wages a terrorist war against the Protestants' 'defence' groups, some of which are also terrorist. The British army's overall objective is to protect Protestant and Catholic communities while at the same time fighting the terrorists.

Since 1977 the British Army has not been responsible for normal law and order. In that year it became the responsibility of the Royal Ulster Constabulary (RUC). Any operations by the army are carried out in conjunction with the RUC.

In the early 1970s the army had 22,000 men in Northern Ireland but this figure was down to 9,000 in 1985. With 6,500 men and women, the Ulster Defence Regiment (UDR) comprised the larger portion of the army presence. In the face of improved defence, terrorists found it more difficult to operate but nevertheless caused numerous casualties with car bombs, mortar bombs and mines set in roads. In October 1984 a massive delayed action bomb blew up the Grand Hotel, Brighton, killing five sleeping guests attending the annual Conservative Party conference. The IRA intention had been to kill the Prime Minister and members of the Cabinet.

The Hillsborough Agreement signed by Britain and Eire late in 1985 was designed to reduce terrorism by improving co-operation between the two countries. The Protestant majority in Northern Ireland—sixty-two per cent of the population—opposed the agreement and resorted to violence against the RUC. The IRA opposed the accord because it threatened their freedom of action. Nevertheless the agreement appeared to be working.

Several court convictions in 1986 put terrorist gangs out of action and other terrorists died in shoot-outs with soldiers or police. However, IRA actions continued to claim innocent lives.

As the IRA improved its bombs with micro-chip technology and electronic

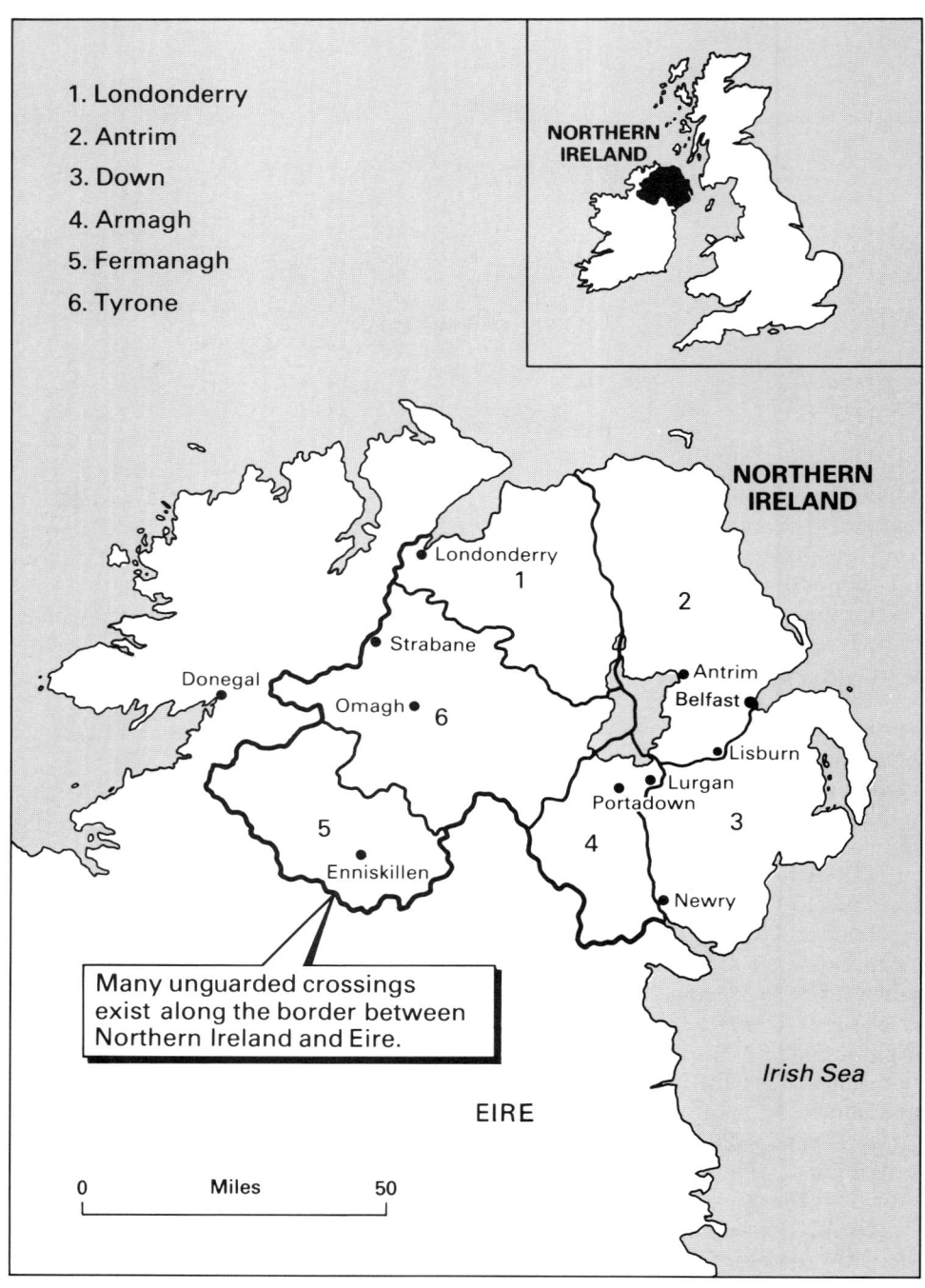

1. Londonderry
2. Antrim
3. Down
4. Armagh
5. Fermanagh
6. Tyrone

NORTHERN IRELAND

NORTHERN IRELAND

Londonderry
1
2
Strabane
Donegal
Omagh 6
Antrim
Belfast
Lisburn
Lurgan
Portadown
5
Enniskillen
4
3
Newry

Many unguarded crossings exist along the border between Northern Ireland and Eire.

EIRE

Irish Sea

0   Miles   50

Main Centres of Northern Ireland Terrorist War

Small arms and rifles remain the favourite choice of urban terrorists in Northern Ireland—but republican terrorists have shown an interest in heavier calibre weapons such as this US Army M60 machine-gun recovered by the police. (John Laffin.)

An officer and men of the Ulster Defence Regiment on night patrol in 'bandit country'. It is tense and tiring work and the officer's face shows it. (John Laffin.)

circuitry, so the security forces met the challenge with ever more sophisticated means.

Summary of the War in 1987

Some members of the terrorist organisation the Irish National Liberation Army (INLA) broke away to form the Irish People's Liberation Organisation. This resulted in a murderous struggle for power in which several notorious terrorists were killed.

The IRA, finding its operations limited in Northern Ireland, extended its field of activity to British services targets in West Germany. In March 1987 a car bomb was detonated near the joint British Army and RAF headquarters at Rheindahlen; thirty-one people were injured.

In mid-1987 the British Army had 10,200 men in Northern Ireland. The principal units were 2nd Infantry Brigade HQ, ten infantry battalions, one SAS unit, one engineer squadron and two squadrons of the Army Aviation Regiment.

On 30 October French customs officers boarded a Panamanian-registered freighter, the *Eksund*, and ordered it into Brest harbour. Here a search of the vessel produced 150 tons of arms and ammunition and explosives. The haul included: ten Soviet 12.77 mm heavy machine-guns with anti-aircraft gun mountings; recoilless anti-tank rifles and ammunition; RPG–7 anti-tank launchers and rocket-propelled grenades; 600 Soviet F–1 grenades; twenty Sa–7 missiles; 1,000 Kalashnikov AK–47 rifles; fifty tons of ammunition and two tons of Semtex plastic explosive. In all, the cargo was worth £15m.

The five-man crew, which included a senior IRA logistics agent, had come close to pulling off the most sensational arms smuggling run in the history of terrorism. Libya was the source of the consignment, which was intended for the IRA. Since the IRA had no need for such a large quantity of arms there was speculation that part of the cargo was intended for the Spanish terrorist organisation, ETA. In fact, the IRA would have stored surplus weapons on the Continent, safe from searches, until they were actually needed in Ulster. The IRA is known to plan for years ahead.

The seizure of the *Eksund*, which came about as a result of an intelligence operation, was a major blow to the IRA's morale and prestige. Its finances also suffered but secret bank accounts could be readily replenished with donations from sympathisers in the US.

In Enniskillen, as several hundred people assembled for Remembrance Day ceremonies on 11 November, the IRA exploded by radio a 40lb bomb. It had been placed in a community centre and against its walls many people were sheltering from a cold wind. The explosion killed eleven civilians and wounded sixty-three others. Of the dead, seven were over sixty years of age; thirteen of the injured were children. The Soviet news agency TASS, which usually supports the IRA, described the bloodshed as 'barbaric'.

The War in 1988

The SAS in Gibraltar—6 March 1988

Three IRA convicted terrorists, Mairead Farrell, Danny ('the Butcher') McCann and Sean Savage, formed an 'active service' unit to carry out a bomb attack in Gibraltar. It was to take place during the parade, held every Thursday, by the Royal Anglian Regiment's band, and watched by hundreds of tourists. The casualties were expected to be very heavy. The bomb of 400lb—ten times bigger than the Enniskillen bomb—was made by Savage, one of the IRA's most expert bomb-makers. The remote-controlled detonating device was ultra-sophisticated. The IRA has used remote control devices on more than 200 planted bombs; a transmitter sends a radio signal to a receiver attached to the bomb which detonates it.

During the preparatory stages of the operation and later, the IRA terrorists were under surveillance by British and Spanish intelligence agents. Six soldiers of the British Special Air Service (SAS) were sent to Gibraltar to be ready to deal with the emergency. In preparation for the attack, on Sunday 6 March, Savage crossed from Spain in a Renault car and parked it in the small square where the Royal Anglian band would halt at the end of its parade three days later. Farrell and McCann followed him in a Ford Fiesta.

The SAS had orders to arrest the terrorists unless their lives or the lives of bystanders were threatened, in which case they could shoot. The surveillance officers believed that the Renault was being planted and activated for Tuesday's parade, when the bomb would be detonated from Spain, only a mile away.

The three terrorists met in the square and then walked into Main Street, shadowed all the time by two plain-clothes SAS men, with four more in back-up roles. Savage separated from the other two and SAS men followed him. Other SAS men closed up on Farrell and McCann and, believing that they had been spotted, shouted a challenge to the terrorists According to the SAS,. Farrell's hand moved towards her large black shoulder bag and McCann appeared to reach for his trouser pocket. An SAS man shot them dead. Almost simultaneously Savage was challenged. He, too, seemed to reach for a pocket, at which point an SAS man killed him.

The controversy which followed the dramatic event—based on why the terrorists were killed rather than taken prisoner—has no place in this book. As an incident in a war the operation was successful. (In fact, the Renault did not contain the bomb; this was found in a car in a parking area in Spain. The Renault was to 'reserve' a space into which the explosive car would be slotted on the day of the parade.)

The decision to send in the SAS was taken with the approval of the Prime Minister, acting on information channelled through the Cabinet's Joint Intelligence Committee. A large number of government agencies were involved. They included the Foreign and Commonwealth Office, Ministry of Defence and Northern Ireland Office, MI5 and MI6, and liaison with the Spanish authorities through the British Embassy in Madrid.

SAS teams use special satellite dishes, small enough to fit into a pack, to communicate with their base. Coded signals can be sent on an even smaller system. Skynet satellites pass their signals to a ground station in Hampshire, from where they go to an army office in Whitehall. A special unit of the Royal Corps of Signals is stationed at the SAS barracks in Hereford and is responsible for maintaining the communications system, which could, in an emergency, put an officer in the field in direct communication with the Prime Minister or her representative.

The Funeral Murders—19 March 1988

Two British soldiers trying to make their way by car from one military post to another in Belfast became trapped in Andersonstown when they met a funeral cortège on its way to a cemetery. The man being buried was Kevin Brady, an IRA mourner, shot dead by a Loyalist gunman during an IRA funeral. The soldiers stopped the car, reversed and were trapped by taxis. The two men were dragged from their car, viciously beaten, stripped and shot dead. The atrocity took place in front of television cameras and every detail was recorded. A number of men were arrested.

The British Prime Minister described the killings as 'an act of appalling savagery; there seems to be no depth to which these people will not sink'. An editorial in *The Guardian Weekly* commented: 'The murders displayed a level of barbarism which shocked and enraged the British public more than anything seen or reported during the Irish "troubles", which have, in nineteen bloody years, taken a toll of 2,647 lives.'

The Murders in Holland—30 April 1988

Three RAF senior aircraftmen based at RAF Laarbruch, West Germany, drove to the Dutch town of Nieuw Bergen to spend an evening in a disco. They left about 1.20am. As they sat in the car for a few seconds it was blown apart by an IRA bomb. Two of the airmen were killed, the third seriously injured. Fifty miles south of Nieuw Bergen, three other RAF senior aircraftmen left their base at RAF Mildenrath for a twenty-mile drive to Roermond, where they began a pub-crawl. About midnight one returned to the car and fell asleep. The other two reached the car later and also slept. An IRA gunman opened fire with a machine-gun, killing one airman and wounding his comrades. An alert to Dutch border posts did not go out until thirty minutes after the shooting and too late to stop the killer in his getaway car.

The Lisburn 'Fun-Run' Atrocity—15 June 1988

The IRA has a network of 'spotters' or information scouts, whose function is to observe the movement of soldiers and their vehicles and report to 'active service units'. In fact, ordinary cars used by army personnel carry no military markings but assiduous spotters can sometimes identify them. On the afternoon of 15 June, six soldiers set out from Erbrington Barracks, Londonderry, to take part in a charity 'fun-run' in Lisburn, County Antrim, where the army in Northern Ireland has its headquarters.

Their van was already on the IRA 'known' list and when the soldiers left it in a Lisburn car park that evening a spotter noticed the registration number and reported it to a stand-by terrorist gang. While the soldiers were jogging with 4,500 other fun-runners a four-man Provo team reached the unguarded van and one attached $7\frac{1}{2}$lb of Semtex explosive of the type supplied by Libya.

The soldiers returned and, without carrying out the regulation security checks, drove off. In theory, the bomb should have gone off as soon as the van moved, since the detonator was the type activated by mercury tilting to one side or the other as the vehicle moved.

Had it exploded, as the IRA must have thought it would, there would have been dozens of deaths among the milling crowds. When the driver hit the brakes at a traffic signals the jolt tripped the mercury and the van was blown apart. All six soldiers were killed instantly and thirty civilians were injured.

Attack on Army Helicopter—23 June 1988

In the 'bandit country' of South Omagh, IRA machine-gunners damaged the tail structure of an army transport helicopter sufficiently to force it down. While no casualties occurred, the incident alarmed the security forces. In some areas of Northern Ireland the roads are so potentially dangerous that all movement of troops and supplies is by helicopter. Also, it is the helicopter which gives the army its mobility and speed of response. IRA machine-gunners had fired on helicopters before the 23 June attack but without causing any damage. Should the IRA use missiles or should their terrorists be in a position to open more intensive machine-gun fire at closer range, the whole of the helicopter strategy would be endangered. One remedy advocated at a crisis meeting was that helicopters should always fly in pairs or trios. In this way one of them, at a greater height than those doing transport duty, would observe enemy on the ground, warn the transports and attack the IRA position.

IRA Arms and Ammunition

During 1988 there was evidence that the IRA had a massive armoury, including heavy machine-guns, rocket-propelled grenades and modern automatic weapons. A large part of the stock is in Eire, where the IRA believes it is safer from discovery than in Northern Ireland. British intelligence believes that a defrocked Irish priest, Patrick Ryan, could have arranged the transfer of about 200 tons of arms and ammunition, including Sa–7 missiles, from Libya to the IRA. Ryan began his IRA involvement in 1969 and became its key agent in Europe and Libya. The Roman Catholic church defrocked him in 1973 and he then devoted himself full-time to working for the IRA. Arrested and expelled from several countries, he went into hiding in 1978. With a new identity, he is believed to be a member of a top secret cell that has organised five shipments to the IRA since 1984. He is wanted by the British police for questioning about several terrorist attacks, including the 1982 Hyde Park bombing in which four soldiers died. Ryan was apprehended in Belgium in June 1988.

In September 1987 the IRA used a new impact grenade. Crude but effective, the grenade is an empty can packed with up to 2lb of plastic explosive and then capped with a hollow copper nosecone. A handle is welded to the base and strips of plastic bin-liner are attached to give the grenade stability in flight. If the grenade hits an armoured car at right-angles it produces a white-hot jet of flame which can bore through the vehicle's 9mm armour-plating. Inside, the grenade explodes with an intense heat and lethal shards fly from the melting copper and armour plated steel.

While the security forces greatly reduced the incidence of IRA attacks in mainland Britain during 1988 and while many terrorists were convicted of earlier crimes and imprisoned, the IRA was active in Ulster and further afield. According to some intelligence reports, the IRA commanders intended to attack British army targets in Hong Kong and Cyprus. It would not be difficult for them to mount attacks in Cyprus since they could count on the help of the Palestine Liberation Organisation which is well established on the island.

Because the identity of most IRA activists is known to the RUC and the army, some senior officers advocated that those known to have killed should themselves be killed. The order to carry out such a policy would have to come from British government ministers. They would be unlikely to give it. During 1987–88 the RUC was criticised for supposedly conducting a 'shoot to kill' campaign against terrorist suspects. Then the shooting of the IRA bombing team in Gibraltar brought Press condemnation, on the grounds that the forces of law and order should not be using the methods of the IRA.

Peru's 'Shining Path' War

General Summary

The Left-wing Maoist movement *Sendero Luminosa* or 'Shining Path' brought guerrilla war to Peru in 1980. Founded by a Professor of Philosophy, Abimael Guzman, it brought together in the Andean town of Ayacucho a strange group of people. The leaders were from the provincial intelligentsia while the followers were rural peasants and city unemployed who found refuge in Ayacucho.

Guzman's lieutenants described him as the 'fourth sword of the revolution'—that is, after Marx, Lenin and Mao. Just what the group's policy might be has always been obscure but its objective was simple and direct from the beginning—total overthrow of the Right-wing system. The group's murderous actions and the ruthless official responses to them resulted in the deaths between May 1980 and October 1987 of about 10,000 people. They included 410 police and military officers and 3,500 guerrillas. The rest were peasants killed either by *Sendero Luminosa* or by the security forces.

Alan Garcia, who became Peru's President in 1985, at the age of thirty-seven, tried to restore order. He showed great courage in dismissing two senior generals after the army massacred sixty-nine peasants in Accomarca in September 1985. It was not so easy to deal with *Sendero Luminosa* or with the urban terrorists of the *Tupac Amaru* Revolutionary Movement. Neither would talk to the government and it was not even clear whether Abimael Guzman was still alive.

Garcia three times declared a state of emergency in 1986. On 18 June 1986 *Sendero Luminosa* prisoners in three prisons rebelled and Garcia put them temporarily under military control. Without his knowledge or approval, the army stormed the prisons and slaughtered 1,000 captive guerrillas. Again Garcia dismissed senior officials.

In January 1987 *Sendero Luminosa* guerrillas hit many economic targets in a wave of sabotage and destruction, intending, as they said 'to turn Lima into a second Beirut'. A week later they blacked out the country with attacks on power-stations and at the end of the month assassinated Cesar Lopez Silva, national secretary of the ruling party, the American Popular Revolutionary Alliance (APRA).

The guerrillas held large areas of the Andes but Garcia built up a people's militia to guard the small towns and villages and tried to tread the difficult path between liberal democratic government and law and order.

The War in 1988

Apart from the 10,000 people killed since 1980, an estimated 8,000 people have become 'the disappeared' or *desaparecidos*. Most of them are peasants captured by the army in its zeal to root out the *Sendero Luminosa* rebels. Marked as suspected collaborators, they are unlawfully abducted and many simply vanish. Others are found dead, their bodies so mutilated that they cannot be identified.

Military officers claim that *Sendero Luminosa* is so fanatically secretive and implacably ideological that the very nature of the insurgency creates excesses in trying to deal with them. Army tactics have terrified peasants in the countryside, who say they are victims of both the guerrillas' brutal revolt and the military's campaign to put it down.

Fearing reprisals, peasants are often reluctant to report the disappearance of friends and relatives. Only 3,200 cases have been officially documented and at President Garcia's insistence, the Attorney General's office spent 1988 trying to investigate them. Nearly twice as many disappearances go unreported and lawyers say that investigating military involvement is 'delicate'. All high-ranking officers use *noms de guerre* which makes it difficult for the investigators to establish the identity of men ordering arrests and killings.

The majority of the 'disappeared' are male, Indian, young and extremely poor and Peru's general public is unconcerned. This is in contrast to Argentina's 'dirty war', in which most of the 'disappeared' were union leaders, students and middle-class workers and where public concern was strident and insistent.

Fernando Silva Santisteban, an anthropology Professor at the University of Lima, says:[1] 'There is a tremendous regional and racial divide in Peru. We have always viewed the mountains as another world. What we are seeing today is civil war'. Ayacucho Province, the base of the war, is the poorest in Peru. The *per capita* income of its 500,000 people is less than $250 a year.

Sendero Luminosa's main victims during 1988 appear to have been members of the self-defence militias set up by the army. They have proved ineffective and as 'collaborators' they are fair game for the guerrillas.

Traditionally one of South America's 'big four', Peru became third ranking, displacing Chile in the so-called ABCP league—Argentina, Brazil, Chile and Peru. In terms of army strength, as distinct from overall power, Peru is the second strongest nation, with 85,000 men of all ranks. The army has six infantry divisions, one cavalry, two armoured, one airborne and one jungle division. The army has more Eastern bloc equipment than any other Latin American army.[2]

In the last few years, the 'working' unit has become the brigade, with three battalion-sized units, an artillery group and a 'service battalion' made up of an engineer company, a signal company, logistical support troops and a medical unit.

Probably the strongest force is in the 3rd Military Region, with its headquarters at Arequipa. In this region, which adjoins the frontiers of Bolivia and Chile, guerrilla activity is rife. Apart from a strong infantry presence, the Puma Special Forces Group is based here, primarily to intimidate *Sendero Luminosa* fighters and, should they attack army patrols or villages and farms, to pursue them and prevent their escape into Bolivia or Chile.

Much of the army's manpower is made up of two-year conscripts who are often lax about fire-arms security. As a result, the veteran *Sendero Luminosa* guerrillas have no difficulty in stealing a variety of rifles, mainly the FN, FAL, G3 and AK-47. The sub-machine-guns are Uzi, the Peruvian MPG-79 and the Argentinian FMK. The guerrillas are also armed with captured machine-guns, including the FN MAG, the Soviet DshK38/46 and the Czech ZB30. While they use all these weapons, many of their attacks in the forests are made with knife and garotte.

By the middle of 1988 President Garcia faced problems so serious that he could give little time to the insurgency dangers posed by *Sendero Luminosa* and *Tupac Amaru*. His country was facing a $23b, unpayable foreign debt, economic stagnation, an enormous increase in drug traffic and a population explosion unparalleled anywhere in Latin America—a net increase of ninety new Peruvians every hour.[3]

The intensified guerrilla war had denuded much of the countryside, causing a rush to the cities which now contain more than 65% of the country's twenty-one million population; seven million are in Lima. President Garcia set in motion a radical birth-control publicity campaign which quickly ran foul of the politically-powerful Catholic Church.

Meanwhile, the spectre of military dictatorships and juntas which have ruled Peru for most of the last twenty-five years is ever present. Garcia's socialist experiment has not brought social justice or placated the Maoist guerrillas who were ruling more of the southern and eastern areas of the country. For the first time in the war there were virtual no-go areas. Even the Puma Special Forces Group did not want to venture into some areas of mountainous forest in pursuit of guerrillas. No insurgency HQ has ever been located and the whereabouts of Abimael Guzman is still unknown.

References

1. Santisteban was speaking to the *Christian Science Monitor.* 28 February 1988.
2. From a study by US State Department.
3. *Intelligence Digest*, Intelligence International Ltd. 22 June 1988.

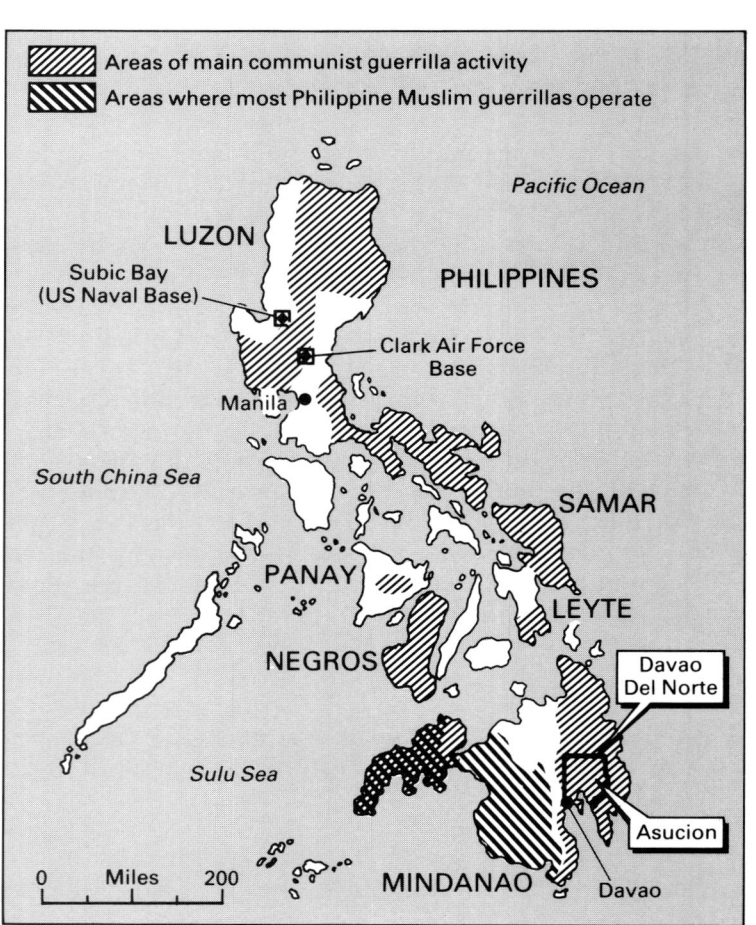

Philippines Guerrilla War

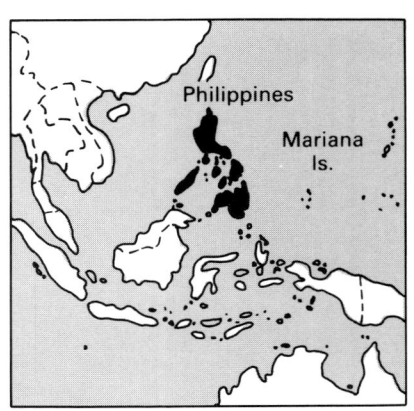

Philippines People's War

Background Summary

The Communist Party of the Philippines (CPP) and its military wing, the National People's Army (NPA), came into being between 1969 and 1972 as a consequence of the oppressive regime of President Marcos. NPA began a 'people's war' against Marcos, whose troops, in 1976, captured its chief-of-training, Victor Corpus. The NPA survived this setback and in 1977 formed a loose alliance with the Muslim rebels of Mindanao, only to split later. By 1984 the NPA was active in sixty of the seventy-three Philippines provinces and the army launched a general but inconclusive offensive against it.

Even after the government appointed the able General Fidel Ramos as Commander-in-Chief of the armed forces, the NPA's 20,000 men and women caused trouble out of all proportion to their numbers. They had popular support from the peasants, many of whom had suffered under army brutality and all of whom were poverty-stricken. In desperation, the government formed the Civil Home Defence Force. The NPA treated its members as traitors and murdered several. With no outside source of funds, the Communists obtained all their arms by theft and capture.

When Mrs. Corazon Aquino was elected as President and the hated Marcos fled the country some observers believed that neither the NPA nor the Muslim insurgents would any longer be a threat. But she was in no position to reform the economic and social system quickly enough for the rebels, and autonomy for the Muslims was out of the question.

Summary of the War in 1987

In 1987 the rebel groups comprised the NPA, the *Bagsa Moro* Army, which is the armed wing of the Moro National People's Liberation Front (MNLF), the Moro Islamic Liberation Front (MILF), the Cordillera People's Liberation Army (CPLA) and some private armies. Their total strength was 33,000, of whom 22,000 were NPA members. They lacked aircraft, vessels, tanks and artillery. Samar Island, 200 miles south-east of Manila, was the NPA's strategic centre. The rebels planned to intensify their operations there so that government forces would have to concentrate in Samar, thus giving rebel groups elsewhere a chance to develop their activities.

Against the numerically weak NPA, the Filipino army, navy and air force had a strength of 113,000, with an additional 42,000 men in paramilitary units, reserves of 48,000 and a Home Defence Force of 65,000. All military activities and all equipment were geared to counter-insurgency work. For instance, the air force had sixty-eight Bell UH-1H helicopters, seventeen Sikorsky helicopters and thirty-two North American T-28D aircraft. Since the Philippines is a country of 7,100 islands, the navy in 1987 had 102 amphibious craft, eighty-six patrol vessels, ten corvettes and seven frigates.

The government was trying to divide the rebels. It wanted both to split them regionally and to separate the rank-and-file from the leadership. It continually emphasized its acceptance of the NPA's 'genuine grievances' but insisted that they could only be resolved if the NPA would accept regional ceasefires. The NPA commanders were not so easily deceived. They knew that if a ceasefire were arranged in Mindanao the government could quickly move troops from there to northern Luzon. Nevertheless, a 60-day ceasefire *was* arranged. It took the parties no nearer a settlement.

Simultaneously with the Communist guerrilla war, the government and army were coping with the Muslim insurrection, mainly on Mindanao island. But for the deep political and ethnic divisions within the Muslim population of five million the danger of the government would be even greater. Some Muslim leaders have their own private army. The strongest is that of Sultan Muhammad Ali Dimaporo, the 'Mad Dog of Mindanao'. His army of 5,000 is strong enough to protect him from any army or guerrilla attack.

President Aquino had to deal with four known military coups during 1987. Some were mounted by supporters of the deposed and disgraced former President Marcos, others by senior officers who resented orders that they must not embark on guerrilla extermination campaigns.

The War in 1988

During 1988, violence by one side was matched by violence from the other. There were 3,000 violent incidents involving government forces and Communist rebels. More than 1,500 NPA guerrillas died, but so did 1,000 civilians and 1,100 from the armed forces.

The constant complaint by the armed forces was that they were forced to fight 'with one arm tied behind our backs'. Officers can now get promotion only if they are cleared of abuses by the National Commission on Human Rights. In contrast, by definition, the NPA fights outside the law and promotion comes, usually, by carrying out a specified killing. Soldiers are expected to follow a judicial code that requires a suspect to be formally charged within eighteen hours of being captured. Experience shows that after masses of paper-work, the suspect may walk free either by bribery or government amnesty. As a consequence, many military men prefer to take no prisoners.

Despite the quality of some of its arms and equipment, the army has basic deficiencies. In 1988 many soldiers had no boots to wear and there were not enough backpack radios to pass on orders in the field. At any one time more than half of the aircraft were out of action for want of spare parts. According to the new Chief-of-Staff, General Renato de Villa, 'this is the poor man's armed forces'.

In theory the Philippine armed forces should be able to defeat the NPA. The Military Academy produces many officers who have studied the successful campaigns against Communist insurgencies in Malaysia and Thailand. Not that the lessons of Thailand could be applied without modification to the Philippines. A

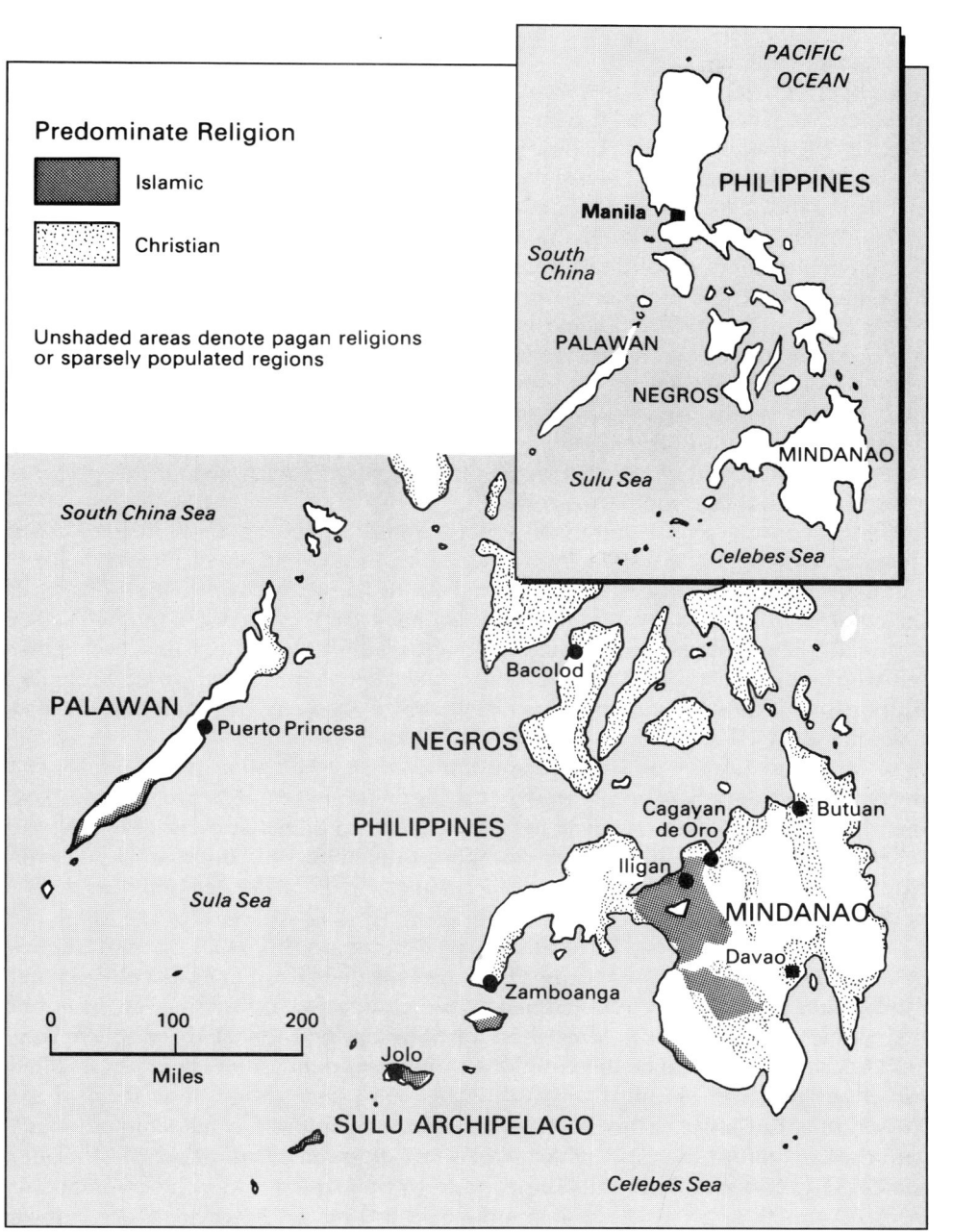

Predominate Religion

Islamic

Christian

Unshaded areas denote pagan religions or sparsely populated regions

PACIFIC OCEAN

PHILIPPINES

Manila

South China

PALAWAN

NEGROS

Sulu Sea

MINDANAO

Celebes Sea

South China Sea

PALAWAN

Puerto Princesa

NEGROS

Bacolod

PHILIPPINES

Cagayan de Oro

Iligan

MINDANAO

Butuan

Davao

Sula Sea

Zamboanga

0   100   200

Miles

Jolo

SULU ARCHIPELAGO

Celebes Sea

director of operations would be needed with power to move men and equipment anywhere, without notice. But no President of the Philippines would appoint a director of operations and give him powers that would enable him to mount a successful coup.

'I expect greater vigour in the prosecution of the war against the Communist insurgency', Mrs Aquino told troops on parade during the hand-over of military control to General de Villa. Calling allegations of military excesses 'total lies', the President told the army, 'I will stand by you through thick and thin, to share the blame, defend your actions and enjoy with you the final victory'.

In April 1988 the security forces achieved great success by capturing three CPP politburo members, including Romulo Kintanar, who was responsible for the NPA's activities. The other two were Rafael Baylosis, who as secretary-general is No. 2 in the CPP, and Benjamin de Vera, head of the party in Mindanao, No. 7. They were among seven rebel leaders caught in a house in Manila.

Despite President Aquino's morale-building parades, the occasional intelligence success and the outstanding active service qualities of a few officers, the Philippines has one of the most ill-disciplined and ineffectual armed forces in the world. One veteran observer of the country considered, in 1988, that the 'entire force presents a portrait of amiable hopelessness'.[1]

The best and brightest graduate officers should be sent to the field against the NPA; instead, they go straight from the academy into staff posts. However, some battalion commanders were showing a new willingness to move their troops from the comfort of fixed camps into the campaigning area. In Mindanao, the Colonel of a Brigade marched his men to hilltops overlooking the jungle valleys where the NPA lurked. He even permitted them to take their wives. From these mutually-supporting hilltops the soldiers moved aggressively through the jungle and the area was practically NPA-free by mid-1988.

In May the Ministry of Defence announced that it had allocated $30m for the purchase of twenty helicopters under the US military assistance programme. This was the start of a major project to equip every battalion operating against the rebels with at least one helicopter. Battalion commanders did not want to go to the trouble of calling for air support. They could act more decisively if they had a helicopter under their own hand.

The Philippines Defence Under-Secretary, Fortunato Abat, said that the Hughes 500-D helicopter gunship was the army's preference. The generals believed that the Hughes was compact and manoeuvrable enough to land virtually anywhere in the country. Until 1988 the forces had relied on ageing UH-1H Huey helicopters.

The Ministry of Defence increased the number of military reservists to be called to active duty from 45,000 to 80,000. This was said to be an indication of the worsening insurgency. The increase in military manpower came simultaneously with the creation of the Citizens Armed Force Geographic Units (CAFGUs). Under the CAFGU concept, active auxiliaries were to be formed under the command of officers on active duty and non-commissioned officers in the regular forces down to platoon level. The active auxiliary units will eventually come under the command of regular military units that have responsibility in their respective areas.

The Communist rebels were decidedly on the run in 1988. In the Cordillera of northern Luzon, where they had ruled in the early 1980s, they were a spent and unpopular force of less than 300 in mid-1988. The Communists had once considered Davao and northern Luzon, at either end of the country, the bases from which they would take over the rest of the Philippines. But by June 1988 only the Bicol area of southern Luzon was an NPA stronghold and only in Negros Occidental were the Communists gaining support.

The NPA should not be seen as the Khmer Rouge of the Philippines and it is guilty of fewer atrocities than the Filipino armed forces. The NPA is unique among guerrilla organizations in that it has lasted for twenty years without any external help. Its leaders have on occasion asked for help from Communist countries but it has been refused, most recently by China. The CPP, and through it the NPA, claims to follow Maoist revolutionary theory but what they really possess is a pragmatic determination to overthrow the rapacious landowners who have kept the peasant classes so poor. About seventy per cent of Filipinos live on the land, earn 75p or $1.50d a day and give seventy per cent of what they produce to their landlords.

A Western television journalist[2] who spent six months with an NPA command on the Bendoc Peninsula, Luzon, in 1987-88, noted that while the guerrillas are determined, they lack physical stamina because of extremely poor diet. He accompanied them on a raid against the official buildings in a rural town. While 140 men and women went on the operation, thirty had no weapons and acted as carriers. Another fifteen had received only basic training. Eleven of the guerrillas, wearing stolen army uniforms, commandeered seven vehicles and the entire party rode into town. Here they made a two-pronged and untidy attack on their target. Having achieved their aims—to kill certain officials who had killed guerrillas and to capture arms, ammunition and documents—the guerrillas took their dead and wounded and vanished into the jungle. While they had been lax in failing to provide a rearguard, they were less inefficient than the army. Soldiers did not reach the scene until the following day.

The fact that the NPA was doing badly in 1988 and that the numbers of its fighting members and of its active sympathizers were decreasing needs to be emphasized here because the army, its American advisers and the CPP all exaggerate the Communist menace. The army has good reason to do so. Already shorn of many of the privileges it enjoyed during the Marcos era, it would lose much of its budget if the rebellion were seen to be declining. The Americans have an extra stronger reason to present the NPA threat as still serious. The US wants good arguments to persuade President Aquino to retain the giant American bases as Subic Bay and Clark airfield after the present agreement ends in 1991. (See **WAR ANNUAL 2**)

The CPP wishes to conceal the failing strength of the NPA, hence its campaign of attacking ordinary policemen in Manila. Forty were shot dead during 1987 and twenty-eight between January and July 1988. 'Sparrows'—so called because they flit in and out—committed most of the murders on the orders of the CPP, whose leadership want to regain support by goading the army into bloody over-reaction to their attacks.[3]

During 1988 the CPP imported scores of small Casio personal computers for groups fighting on the hills and jungles. These 'laptops' are light enough to carry in a backpack whenever their guerrilla operators are being chased by soldiers. They enable party leaders and guerrillas of the NPA to send coded messages to each other via radio transmissions. This greatly helps them to communicate across the nation's far-flung islands. Plans can be co-ordinated and new instructions quickly disseminated. The military frequently pick up computer transmissions but have apparently not cracked the code.

The computer software used by the CPP and NPA has an anti-piracy 'virus' built into it. On many occasions it has eaten whole documents and even the entire memory of cadre computers, according to sources close to the CPP in Manila. The 'virus', as the computer industry calls it, can spread as software is changed.

The software bug flashes a warning before it liquidates a file. 'Watch out for the dungeon' the warning reads. The CPP employs a number of experts to deal with such technical problems but when the code itself has been eaten it is difficult to make contact with distant cadres.

President Aquino sent a personal emissary to Saudi Arabia to seek King Fahd's help in blocking an attempt by Philippine Muslim separatists to gain recognition among Islamic states. The mission was entrusted to the Speaker of Parliament, Ramon Mitre, who told the King that recognition of the Moro National Liberation Front by the Islamic Conference Organization (OIC) would 'break up the Philippine Republic'. The MNLF received observer status to the OIC in 1986 but Mrs. Aquino's appeal prevented it from gaining 'belligerency' status in 1988.

The Moros (the name means Moors) do not consider themselves subversive. They are descendants of the Muslims who were in this part of South-east Asia before the Spanish conquered it in the name of Roman Catholicism in the sixteenth century.

Army Success in Davao City

Between 1983 and 1985 the NPA killed about 800 people each year in the Davao area and in just one slum quarter, Agdao, the killings averaged fifteen a day. By 1988 killings by NPA 'sparrow' gangs were almost unknown. The NPA fighters had been driven out by Lieutenant Colonel Franco Calida and the 3,000 men under his command in Davao. He has gained the praise of President Aquino but the condemnation of human rights groups and churchmen for his ruthless policies.

Calida's success is based on the formation of a citizens' self-defence group, a euphemism for vigilantes, known as *Alsa Masa* (the Aroused Masses). It worked because the NPA had become more like common criminals than guerrillas. Even more important, Calida had induced men and women to defect from the NPA and join *Alsa Masa*. One of the Colonel's offers of amnesty brought in twenty-four 'sparrows' in four days. Later he issued an ultimatum—surrender or be harried to death. This produced the surrender of 3,000 active Communist fighters and 10,000 sympathizers.

Colonel Calida now has these followers for life—which may not be long, as NPA defectors are priority targets for assassination. Human rights groups say that *Alsa Masa* members are guilty of atrocities, but a US State Department report says that they are 'overwhelmingly popular'. Both assessments may be extreme but other vigilante groups are murderous. The *Tadtad* ('Chop'), a fanatical cult, which believes that it is immune to bullets, specializes in beheading its enemies.

The Escape of Gringo Honasan

In February 1986 Colonel Gregario Honasan instigated the military-backed revolt against President Marcos, but then turned against the Aquino Government because it would not permit the military to play a dominant role in government.

Honasan led a coup against the government in August 1987; fifty people were killed and more than 300 injured. He fled but was caught in December, cashiered from the army and sent to a navy prison ship in Manila Bay. His reputation as former senior aide to the dismissed Defence Minister, Juan Ponce Enrile, and his dashing manner soon made him the dominant figure aboard the ship. The naval officer in command, an old friend, allowed Honasan a stream of visitors, including a large group to celebrate his fortieth birthday.

In April 1988, when military intelligence received information that Honasan was planning to escape, two military-powered rubber boats were sent to the ship as one of several precautions against a rescue team storming it. However, Honasan's help came from inside. He took with him two of his closest associates and thirteen military guards, including the officer in charge, and they used the rubber boats to effect their escape.

Apparently, Honasan's glib tongue had induced the guards to join his organization, 'Reform the Armed Forces of the Philippines Movement', which he had established in 1985. It was through the rebellions organized by this movement that the soldiers were given badly needed pay rises and benefits.

President Aquino appeared on television to brand Honasan as a 'traitor and a monster' and vowed that her loyal army would recapture him. However, Colonel Honasan has many influential friends as well as a resourceful wife and it seemed likely that he could stay in hiding. Suggestions that he might join the rebels and lead them were taken seriously but such a course of action was unlikely. Honasan enjoyed killing rebels. In any case, joining them would mean the end of his comfortable and colourful lifestyle.

References

1. Simon Winchester of *The Guardian*, London. He was present, in March 1988, when General Renato de Villa inspected 500 of his troops in Manila. Few foreign military observers in the region share General de Villa's own optimism or his colleagues' belief that he is the man most likely to win the war. 27 March 1988.
2. Nick Downie. A former British regular soldier and an experienced in-the-field war observer, Downie was impressed by the guerrillas' commitment. His film, transmitted in the UK on Independent Television Channel 4 in June 1988, repeatedly showed the NPA's paucity of ammunition.
3. Diplomats in Manila are unanimous in their criticism of the Philippines armed forces as inefficient. One diplomat said: 'The army is riddled with corruption, badly trained, poorly led and completely without motivation.'

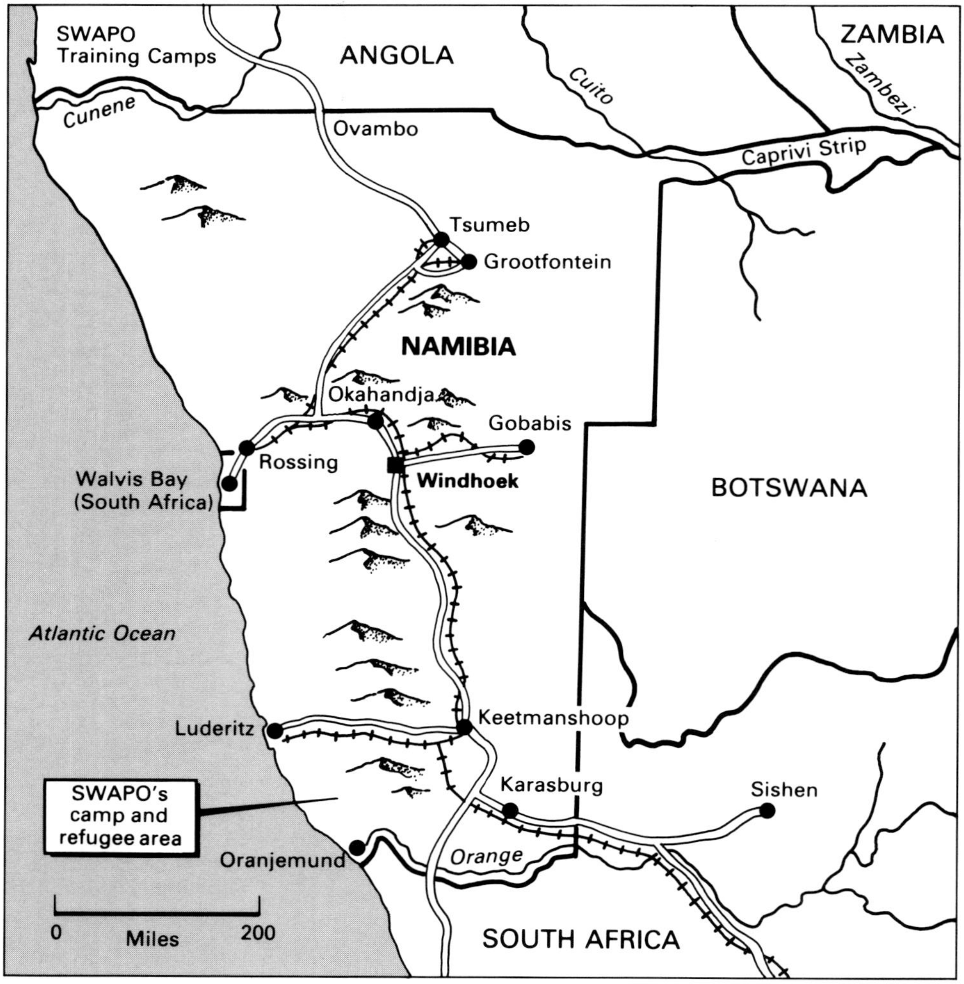

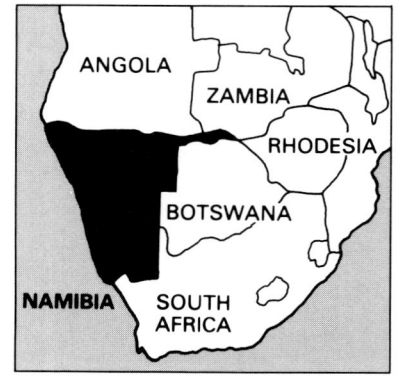

South Africa's Namibia War

South Africa's War in Namibia

TWENTY YEARS OF CONFLICT

Background Summary

(South Africa's operations in Namibia should be studied in conjunction with its campaigns in Angola and its activities in relation to Mozambique).

South Africa, as part of the British Empire, took over the territory known as German South-West Africa during World War I and, despite opposition from many countries, has held it ever since. It is now known as Namibia though in all official South African reports it is referred to as SWA/N.

Half the one and a half million Namibians belong to just one tribe, the Ovambo. Ovambo leaders, under Sam Nujoma, control the South-West Africa People's Organization (SWAPO) which in 1973 the UN declared to be the 'sole and authentic representative of the Namibian people'. The country has 75,000 whites.

SWAPO created a military wing, the People's Liberation Army of Namibia (PLAN). PLAN infiltrated Namibia from Angola and established a base at Ongulumbashe in western Ovambo, where they began local recruitment and training. The South African Defence Forces (SADF) attacked and destroyed the base on 26 August 1966. It was the only permanent base that PLAN ever established in Namibia. Beginning from that date, the conflict is the longest bush war in Africa and it is taking place in Africa's last colony.

The rainy season, December–April, is the combat period. PLAN commanders call it 'the killing time'. During the wet season the tactical advantage lies with the guerrillas, who exploit the downpour and the dense growth.

Since the late 1970s South Africa has stationed between 25,000 and 35,000 troops in northern Namibia. The strategy is to ensure that PLAN does not hold the initiative and during 1985, according to SADF figures, 599 guerrillas were killed.

In March 1986 the South African President, P. W. Botha, announced that a UN plan for Namibian independence, drawn up in 1978, would be implemented in August. However, this would only happen if 'a firm and satisfactory agreement could be reached before that date' on the withdrawal of Cuban troops from neighbouring Angola. Predictably, no such agreement was reached.

For the South African government, the South-West African Territory Force (SWATF) is the basis of the defence force which will protect a future independent Namibia. SWATF provides sixty per cent of all troops in combat operations against PLAN; its mobilization strength is 22,000. The South African High Command knows that SWATF could comfortably hold Namibia against SWAPO-PLAN without army help but the presence of more than 30,000 Cubans in Angola is a constant threat and SADF reinforcement is necessary.

SWAPO resorts to outright terrorism to prevent Namibian groups or tribes from co-operating with the South Africans.

South Africa has never seemed likely to take notice of UN resolutions about Namibia. With the African National Congress (ANC) steadily increasing the strength of its military wing, *Umkhonto we Sizwe,* the possibility of concessions is even less likely. The President of the ANC, Oliver Tambo, has declared a 'people's war' against South Africa and the ANC had 10,000 trained fighters in 1986. During that year groups from ANC carried out several terrorist attacks in South African cities.

South Africa's open attacks on its neighbours' territory began in January 1981 when commandos were sent into Mozambique to kill twelve black South African exiles in a suburb of the capital, Maputo.

The War in 1988

In 1987 Soviet technicians completed air defences across Angola to prevent the South Africans from raiding at will into Angola. In late 1987 the South Africans set out to break the air-defence line, but their forces became bogged down for months outside Angola at a river crossing near the small town of Cuito Cuanavale. The SADF mounted bold diversionary raids into central Angola, behind the line, but they could not dislodge the main enemy front.

Jonas Savimbi, the South Africans' main supporter in Angola, resented the way South Africa took over the leadership of the fight against the Angolan government. He would prefer to get less help from South Africa and more from the US. The Americans said that if the Cubans and Russians left the country they would do what they could, short of using force or sanctions, to eject the South Africans from Angola and Namibia.

Namibia was once rich in minerals and fish. The Russians and others, however, depleted the sardines and pilchards that once swam along Namibia's Atlantic coast. Uranium fell greatly in value and copper has proved too expensive to exploit. Only diamonds retain their worth but the dreams of abundant wealth from Namibia have vanished. For South Africa, by 1988, Namibia was no longer a source of present or anticipated profit.

It has been said that a better strategy for South Africa might be to get out of Nambia altogether, on the assumption that the ensuing government would be too weak to cause much mischief. Withdrawal would also put a vast area of desert between South Africa and black countries to its north. Any invaders from that direction could be readily dealt with in the desert by the South African air force.

But leaving Namibia would limit South Africa's ability to dominate the southern half of Angola either directly or through its UNITA proxy. (See *Guerrilla-Civil War in Angola*). It would lose its forward bases and its air and radar coverage. Most of all, it would reduce South Africa's physical dominance of southern Africa almost up to Zaire.

The South Africans' aim is a 'neutral' government in Angola. They intend to keep bases on its territory to strike against SWAPO. As long as it keeps Namibia under its rule, South Africa needs to have soldiers there and in Angola too. The government has no intention of withdrawing from Namibia unless it can first establish a pliant black government to leave behind.

South Africa's military-initiated regional policy has been one of destabilization. Rather than a prosperous black-governed neighbour, it has preferred a weak and troubled one, prey to and frightened by SADF raids. The South African leadership calculates that it can thus keep SWAPO and ANC guerrillas at bay and demonstrate its own power in ways that will impress antagonistic blacks within South Africa itself.

According to US State Department sources, a deal was reached during talks in London in May 1988 between representatives of South Africa, the US, Cuba, Angola and UNITA. These were the main points:

- Complete withdrawal of the Cubans within one year.
- Namibia to be given independence under UN Resolution 435.
- SWAPO, the new, elected government in Namibia, to be required to sign a non-aggression pact with South Africa.
- No foreign troops, including ANC guerrillas, to be allowed on Namibian soil.
- Namibia to remain within the South African sphere of influence. Walvis Bay, Namibia's only port, to remain in South Africa's hands. It was not part of the former German colony and Resolution 435 states only that an independent Namibian government will negotiate with Pretoria over its future.
- The South Africans to drop their support for UNITA rebels in Angola.

It is unlikely that any 'agreement' on these points will be put into effect.

SADF Intelligence Assessment of SWAPO/PLAN

In January 1988 the SADF's Military Information Bureau, a branch of the Intelligence Section, produced an internal assessment of SWAPO and PLAN. The officers who compiled it considered that, after twenty-one years of armed struggle, PLAN should have at its command 24,000 trained and armed men. However, it had only 8,500 men and of these a mere 1,300 could be made available at the beginning of each year for action against the security forces of SWA/N.

The security forces, the report stated, maintained a loss ratio of seventeen guerrillas for each security force casualty, resulting in a rate of attrition which was having a crippling effect on PLAN's capability. 'The compounding effect of being unable to get volunteer recruits and having to rely on the flow of recruits from SWAPO bases for *untrainables* at Kwanzu-Zul in Central Angola and Nyango in North-West Zambia—where young children abducted many years ago are accommodated—is slowly but surely exacting a heavy toll.'

Parts of the document make particularly interesting reading since they reveal the South African perception of the enemy.

> With the establishment of PLAN, it was given the task of embarking on the political activation of the population in the northern border areas, which represents sixty-six per cent of the people of SWA/N. In this regard each terrorist functions as an armed political activist and the military weapon is

utilised to lend status and authority to the revolutionary idea. The actions of the terrorists are restricted to activities which have high propaganda value, but which are not very hazardous, as their personal safety is of primary importance.

As a general rule, it can be accepted that terrorists only initiate actions which have propaganda value and all terrorist activity of an offensive nature can in fact be regarded as armed propaganda. It is obvious that a military organisation, with such a fundamental approach, does not willingly make physical contact with the security forces at random. The only actions normally directed at the security forces are those with a guaranteed psychological result, for instance stand-off bombardments of bases located in densely-populated areas, or the use of vehicle mines with the intention of inflicting casualties.

The terrorists direct their energy and efforts at undermining the neutral section of the population. They also regard the traditional tribal authority, all respected persons with influence in the community and those who are sympathetic to the existing political order, as their natural enemies. Acts of selective intimidation are used as a political weapon against the target groups, with the aim of creating a leaderless, defenceless, frightened mass which can be manipulated and exploited.

Under the heading *Current Operational Strategy,* the lengthy SADF intelligence analysis continues:

The current basic operational approach of SWAPO can be summarized as one of stimulating an internal revolutionary process by the regenerating of an emotional wave, supplemented by terrorist action within the dwindling capability of PLAN, while simultaneously doing all in its power to restrict the rate of attrition. With the latter it succeeded in 1983-84 in raising its incident rate above its casualty rate. However, in 1986-87 it again failed in its attempt to execute a cost-effective campaign.

The number of contacts and ambushes is still relatively high, but in reality these reflect the ability of the security forces to locate the terrorists and to force them into contact. This could possibly be interpreted as illustrating a basic law, namely that if a military wing is incapable of maintaining its incident rate above its casualty rate, the compounding effect of such a rate of attribution must ultimately lead to the demise of the organization.

The report draws this conclusion:

In order to ensure its continued existence SWAPO will ultimately be forced to return to the democratic political system in SWA/N. As soon as this occurs, the revolutionary wheel will have turned full circle, and SWAPO will have to return to the evolutionary process of development, which it abandoned on 26 August 1966 [the date when SADF destroyed PLAN's only base in Namibia].

Tracker-Fighting Teams

In the same month, January 1988, that SADF produced its assessment of the war in Namibia, SWAPO terrorists exploded a bomb in a crowded bank in Oshakati, northern Namibia.[1] It killed twenty-seven people and wounded many more, almost all of them black. Oshakati is the main military base for SADF in northern Namibia and is only thirty-five miles south of the Angolan border. The atrocity seemed to indicate that SWAPO was a long way from accepting the evolutionary process referred to in the report.

In retaliation, eight Mirage and five Impala aircraft raided SWAPO targets near the Angolan town of Lubango, 180 miles north of the border.

The Oshakati bomb was probably placed by SWAPO sympathisers within Namibia, since, according to SADF commanders, guerrillas entering Namibia from Angola cannot survive long before being tracked down. In a typical pursuit operation the army receives a tip from local people about SWAPO activity in a certain area. A tracker fighting team of ten men in a Casspir armoured car is sent out at once. The key man in the team is the expert black Namibian soldier tracker. Most trackers are members of the 101 Battalion, which is manned almost entirely by locally recruited Ovambo soldiers. SADF officers claim that the tracker teams kill eighty-five per cent of the guerrillas whose trail they find.

SWAPO fighters have attempted to develop anti-tracking techniques. They walk along farm fences, tread in one another's footsteps to cause confusion about numbers, walk great distances backwards, and as far as possible they stay on hard surfaces. The Ovambo trackers are rarely deceived. Their skill comes from having had to track, from boyhood, missing cows and goats, but tracking men brings in more money in the ranks of the 101 Battalion.

South African Arms

In 1977 the UN imposed an arms embargo on South Africa, which at that time imported seventy per cent of its military requirements. As a result the state-owned arms corporation, Armscor, came into being. In 1988 South Africa imported only five per cent of its military needs and was among the world's top ten arms producers. Armscor is South Africa's biggest single exporter of manufactured goods, employs 23,000 people and provides another 67,000 jobs through 975 private contractors.

As the sole weapons procurement authority for SADF, the corporation deals simultaneously with up to forty major weapons systems and another 150 smaller projects. The latest jet fighter, the Cheetah, became operational in April 1988. It is said to be a match for the Soviet MiG 23, which is supplied to South Africa's northern neighbours. From the SAAF's new base at Louis Trichardt, in the northern Transvaal close to the Zimbabwe border, the Cheetahs—with in-flight refueling—have the range to strike as far north as the Tanzanian capital, Dar es Salaam. The main ANC guerrilla bases in Zambia, Angola and Tanzania are all potential targets.

Heavy artillery is a major Armscor product. The G5 155 mm can throw a shell thirty miles with great accuracy. The G6, which is self-propelled on six enormous wheels, is capable of firing nuclear shells and is the only weapon of its type built outside the Warsaw Pack countries.

Iran and Iraq are two of the twenty-three countries to which South Africa exports arms. With G5s—obtained in exchange for oil supplies—they have lobbed tens of thousands of shells at each other. Sri Lanka transports its troops in landmine-proof South African Buffels and Morocco uses South African Ratel armoured personnel carriers. Recent Armscor output includes the Darter shoulder-fired air-to-air missile which can be directed to lock on to its target by a unique look-and-shoot helmet sight. Other products are the Seeker remote-controlled spy plane, the Krimpvark (hedgehog) mine-resistant passenger vehicle, the Jakkals lightweight jeep, and Valkeri multiple rocket launcher and the Nongqai patrol vehicle.[2]

References

1. SWAPO spokesmen denied that their organization was responsible for the explosion. A statement issued in Luanda said, 'The bomb is part of the South African dirty propaganda campaign to smear the name of SWAPO.' The SWAPO statement alleged that a bomb placed in a bank used mostly by blacks was proof that South African intelligence had been responsible.
2. Most of the arms and equipment mentioned here were on display in Johannesburg in April 1988, during the Rand Easter Show.

Sri Lanka Civil War

Background Summary

Sri Lanka, formerly Ceylon, became independent from Britain in 1948 and from that year the ethnic animosity between the Buddist Sinhalese and the Hindu Tamils steadily increased. There are eleven million Sinhalese, three million Tamils and 1.5 million Muslims in a country of 25,332 square miles. The Tamils are mainly in the north but with smaller areas in the centre and on the east coast. From the beginning they wanted a separate state, to be called Eelam.

Open violence between the communities began in 1983. Since the army was wholly Sinhalese, the Tamils organized many guerrilla groups. The best known were: Liberation Tigers of Tamil Eelam (LTTE), the People's Liberation Organization of Tamil Eelam (PLOTE), the Tamil Eelam Liberation Organization (TELO), the Eelam People's Revolutionary Liberation Front (EPRLF) and the Eelam Revolutionary Organization and Supporters (EROS). A wholly political body, Tamil United Liberation Front (TULF), included members of parliament.

Following the killing of an army patrol by the Tigers, about 1,000 Tamils were murdered by Sinhalese mobs in what the Tamils call 'the Holocaust'. All Tamil MPs were forced out of parliament. The government of President J. R. Jayawardene opposes a Tamil state in Sri Lanka, contending that the Indian State of Tamil Nadu, just across Palk Strait, is adequate for all Tamils. It has a population of fifty million Tamils.

Neither side was militarily prepared for a civil war but arms and equipment poured in. The government turned to the United States and Pakistan for financial aid to buy arms. The Tamils looked to Tamil Nadu and to expatriates worldwide. Each side developed a strategy and tactics. The security forces aimed to destroy the Tamils' bases and to prevent arms reaching them from abroad. As guerrillas, the Tamil fighters—generally known as 'the boys'—were opportunist in their tactics. Both sides were guilty of many atrocities.

Unable to find a political solution, President Jayawardene attempted to achieve a military solution by bombing the Jaffna district, where the population is ninety-seven per cent Tamil, and the army embarked on terror campaigns.

The rival Tamil groups were seriously divided and in April 1986 the Tigers turned against TELO, killing 100 of its members, including its leaders, and finishing it off as a guerrilla force. The Tigers, now undisputed masters of the resistance movement, opened an arms factory to produce mortars and grenades.

To end the savage conflict, in which Tamil, Sinhalese and Muslim civilians were suffering, Jayawardene, in late 1986, proposed a genuine degree of autonomy for

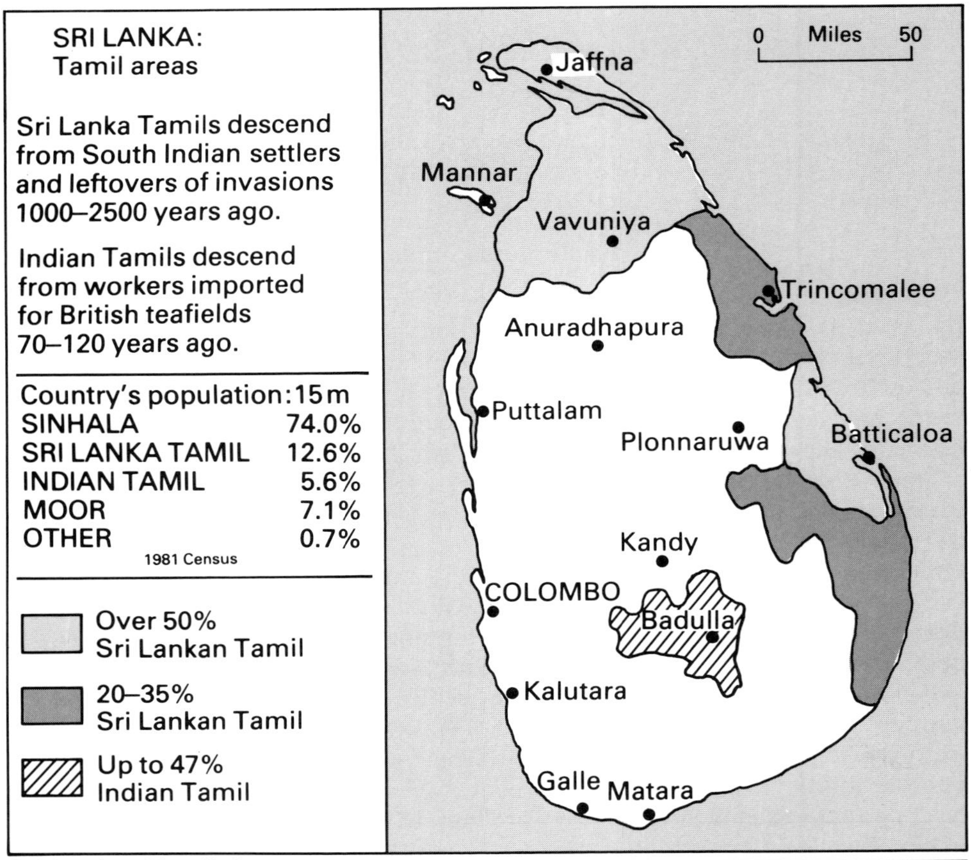

SRI LANKA:
Tamil areas

Sri Lanka Tamils descend from South Indian settlers and leftovers of invasions 1000–2500 years ago.

Indian Tamils descend from workers imported for British teafields 70–120 years ago.

Country's population: 15 m

SINHALA	74.0%
SRI LANKA TAMIL	12.6%
INDIAN TAMIL	5.6%
MOOR	7.1%
OTHER	0.7%

1981 Census

Over 50% Sri Lankan Tamil

20–35% Sri Lankan Tamil

Up to 47% Indian Tamil

Jaffna

Mannar

Vavuniya

Trincomalee

Anuradhapura

Puttalam

Plonnaruwa

Batticaloa

Kandy

COLOMBO

Badulla

Kalutara

Galle Matara

0 Miles 50

Sri Lanka: Tamil Areas

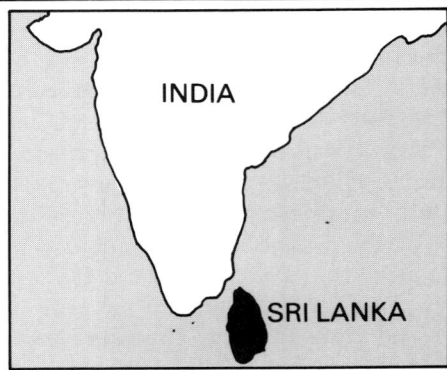

INDIA

SRI LANKA

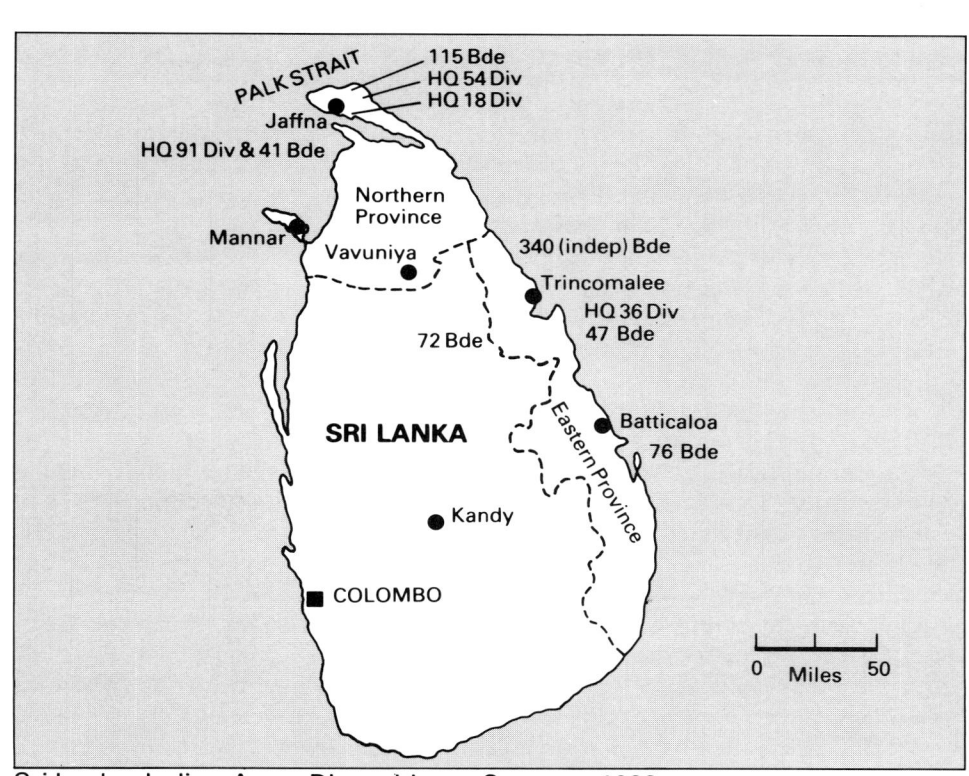

Sri Lanka: Indian Army Dispositions; Summer 1988

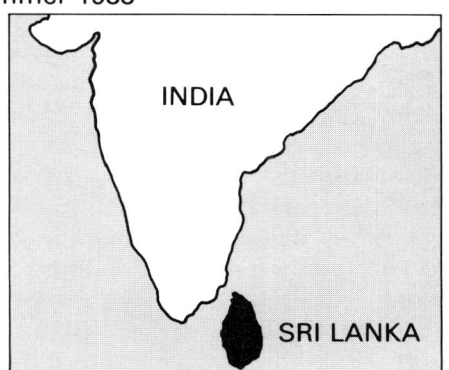

the Tamils in the form of nine provincial councils. TULF liked the idea but it did not go far enough for the guerrilla groups. In contrast, it went too far for the Sinhalese, since the Jayawardene plan would give the Tamils, who formed 12.7 per cent of the population, twenty-five per cent of the land.

Summary of the War in 1987 (to July)

On 6 February 1987 the Sri Lankan security forces began their biggest offensive of the war—invasion of the Jaffna peninsula. As 5,000 troops combed the jungles, gunboats patrolled the coast to prevent guerrillas from crossing to India. Aerial bombing destroyed some Tamil bases.

By 1987 more than 150,000 Tamils had fled from Sri Lanka to escape army brutality. The war became even more bloody and violent, with one large-scale massacre succeeding another. Clearly, there was little hope of an early end to the conflict and no hope at all of a peaceful settlement.

Operation Pawan

In desperation, the Sri Lankan government turned to India for military help in suppressing the Tamils whose acts of massacre and sabotage were in danger of destroying Sri Lanka's economy and causing a break-up of Sri Lankan society. Strive though they might, the Sri Lankan armed forces could obviously never overwhelm the Tamils, while the government, though prepared to go far towards granting them autonomy, had no intention of allowing a new and separate state to be established on the island.

In an accord signed on 29 July 1987, the Indian government agreed to create an Indian Peace-Keeping Force (IPKF) which would operate in Sri Lanka to subdue the Tamils. The Indian navy would patrol the waters around the island to ensure that supplies and reinforcements did not reach the main guerrilla group, the Tigers of LTTE.

Called *Operation Pawan,* the movement of the IPKF began in August, with the High Command under instructions to neutralize the Tigers as soon as possible. In a major airlift, Punjabi, Sikh, Gurkha, Garhwali, Madrasi, Maratha and Mahari regiments were flown to Sri Lanka. Grenadiers and Parachute Regiment units and members of the Reserve Police Force were also sent.

Initially, the Indian army moved slowly while trying to convince the Tamil population that by supporting the guerrillas they were only prolonging a bloody and hopeless insurgency. The Indian troops were ordered to go to great lengths to avoid civilian casualties. The Tigers soon heard of this and adopted the classic guerrilla tactic of using civilians as shields.

The Sri Lankan government, through a massive publicity campaign, informed the Sinhalese population that the IPKF would be on the island for only a limited time but the Sinhalese viewed the Indians with suspicion. The chauvinist Marxist group, the *Janata Vimukti Peramuna* or People's Liberation Front, know as JVP, was particularly resentful of the Indian presence which it feared might become permanent.

Well-trained in conventional warfare, the Indian units had difficulty in countering urban guerrillas in the Jaffna fighting. The troops, operating in

Bodies of Tamil fishermen massacred by the Sri Lankan Navy while the men were at work in Palk Strait. These are the victims of more than 100 massacres carried out by either the Sri Lankan security forces or the Tamil resistance. (John Laffin.)

Tamil 'Tigers' in an ambush position on a road leading into Tamil territory in Sri Lanka. Heavily funded by Tamils living in India, the Tigers have plenty of modern weapons and equipment.

unfamiliar military conditions, were also in cities that were unfamiliar. Patrols in the alleyways of Jaffna suffered heavy casualties. A fundamental problem was lack of intelligence. Because of the order to go straight for the Tigers and overwhelm them, the IPKF had had no time for adequate reconnaissance. Only senior officers possessed maps and few of these contained essential military information, such as position of LTTE strongholds. On 11 October 1987 helicopters landed a platoon only 200 yards from an LTTE HQ and the troops were wiped out.

The Indian officers also underestimated the Tamils' expertise when they transmitted radio messages in clear and not in code. Tamil interceptors understood every word and were prepared for Indian movements.

Having lost men to Tamil mines, the Indians discovered that many mines were detonated by electric cable impulses. Consequently, they cut off the Jaffna region's power supply. The disruption to civilian life was so great that the IPKF allowed power supply to be resumed. The Indians came under renewed mine attack almost at once.

The original order to the Indian troops to be tolerant towards civilians proved fatal for many soldiers. The Tamils made use of children, women and old people to fire sub-machine-guns, throw grenades and plant explosives. When some Indian units shot first and asked questions afterwards, the Tamil propaganda machine was ready to broadcast stories of Indian 'atrocities'.

Gradually, the IPKF commanders co-ordinated their arms and used more and more air support, both to bomb and machine-gun. Artillery and helicopter gunships caused civilian as well as guerrilla casualties. Nevertheless, the majority of Tamils in Tamil Nadu supported the army's operations. In February 1988 a further 15,000 troops were sent to Sri Lanka, bringing the total to 70,000, more than twice the size of the Sri Lankan army. India's 'peace policy' in Sri Lanka was costing it dearly that month. President Jayawardene put the number of Indian soldiers killed at 600-700, with more than 1,000 wounded since the assault on Jaffna.

Indian politicians and others had been trying to negotiate with the LTTE leader, Valupillai Prabhakaran, but they came to doubt and then to distrust his protestations of sincerity. The Indian High Commissioner in Colombo, J. N. Dixit, revealed[1] that India used every possible means to induce Prabhakaran to sign the 29 July 1987 agreement between Sri Lanka and India. At that time the Indians were trying to gain Prabhakaran's support, or just his neutrality, and they were prepared to pay for it. Dixit said that the LTTE leader was offered five million rupees (£212,000) a month by Rajiv Gandhi. In addition, Prabhakaran was paid another one million rupees as a form of bribe to help the future government of Northern Province to rehabilitate the zones destroyed during the fighting. According to Dixit, the money was paid right up to the moment when relations between New Delhi and the LTTE were broken off in October 1987 when fifteen Tigers committed collective suicide.

The chances of a durable agreement with LTTE, the Indians decided, were impossible. The IPKF commanders were told to crush all centres of Tamil resistance in the north of the island by the end of February and establish control in the east by the end of April.

In the east, in particular around the towns of Batticaloa and Trincomalee, where they fell back and regrouped following the fall of Jaffna in November, the Tigers terrorised the civilian population of Sinhalese, Tamils and Muslims, while setting more and more ambushes for the poorly-motivated Indian soldiers. On 31 March the Tigers overran two villages near Batticaloa, burned down more than 100 houses and killed forty people, all Muslims. The Muslim were forming militia units to defend themselves against the Tamils and, like the Sinhalese, they did not hesitate to conduct bloody retaliatory strikes.

In the north nearly all the Tamil guerrilla groups established offices and camps in Vavuniya. The Indian Intelligence Unit, Research and Analysis Wing, trained some groups, gave them arms and supported them in the Vavuniya area to serve as an eventual balance to the Tigers. They tolerated the offices in return for information and the provision of social services for civilians. The groups in Vavuniya were supposed to act as informers in helping the Indians to find the boys in the bush. Besides extorting money from passing buses and trucks, the men of the various groups were killing each other. In Killinochchi, LTTE and EROS were fighting a third group. In Mannar, the fight was between PLOTE and ERPLF. In Vanuniya the killing concerned PLOTE and a revived EROS group.

In the east, the Indians stepped up the pressure. In a single action on 10 April they captured 377 suspected militants, twenty-five of whom turned out to be Tigers. The Tigers' arms supplies were running low. In the period 7-15 April the Indians killed fifty-five guerrillas. The next day three of the local Tigers commanders contacted the Indian army command to seek surrender terms.

The Indian army was behaving very much like an army of occupation. With its military presence and civilian assistance the army was gradually digging itself firmly into Sri Lanka.

In their desperation, the Tigers turned for help to Colonel Gaddafi of Libya. He supplied them with mortar bombs, rocket launchers, explosives and Chinese AK-47 rifles. In April, seventy Tigers were in Libya for 're-training'. This is taken to mean instruction in modern methods of terrorism.

The Sinhalese Opposition accused India of deliberately dragging out its stay on the island. In fact, India wanted to speed up the process of forcing peace on Sri Lanka, if only because of the restlessness of the Tamil population of Tamil Nadu. The Indian government would not have gone ahead with its Sri Lankan intervention without the strong backing it received from Tamil Nadu.

Anura Bandaranaike, leader of the Sri Lanka Freedom Party (SLFP) declared that the Indian soldiers were deliberately turning a blind eye to the massacres still being perpetrated by the Tigers in their efforts to force the Sinhalese and Muslims out of the eastern areas. He argued that the Tamil-dominated government which would then be set up in the Northern and Eastern provinces would be a 'tool' of New Delhi.

The fiercest opposition to the Sri Lanka–India accord had from the beginning come from the *Janata Vimukthi Paramuna* (JVP). Led by chauvinist Sri Lankans, it was founded in 1971 and became the most secretive, most extreme and most feared group in the south. It launched an abortive coup against the government in 1971 and was officially banned after being blamed for the bloody anti-Tamil rioting in 1983.

JVP gained many of its recruits because of heavy-handed tactics by the security forces and the paramilitary Special Task Force, which it accused of executing JVP suspects. In the cause of 'achieving peace', JVP killed scores of people between July 1987 and May 1988, mostly Sinhalese who supported the government. A gunman from JVP tried to assassinate President Jayawardene in the parliament buildings but he was unharmed. On 28 March JVP terrorists lobbed three grenades into a council meeting in Matara, south of Colombo, causing casualties.

However, JVP signed a peace agreement with the government on 10 May 1988. The deal was that the government would lift the five-year ban on the movement if its members surrendered their weapons by 29 May. This appears to have happened.

International comment about the IPKF's activities were generally favourable because of the horrific level of atrocity which the Force was trying to reduce and eventually eliminate. However, political reaction was less favourable, especially after Sri Lanka and India came to an agreement—some time after the July accord—that the great port of Trincomalee would not be made available 'to any country in a manner prejudicial to India's interests'.[2] In addition, India undertook to provide training facilities and supplies for Sri Lanka's armed forces. Even more sinister, in foreign eyes, was the statement that Sri Lanka and India would come to an understanding about 'the relevance and employment of foreign military and intelligence personnel' in Sri Lanka.

All this could only mean that any decision the Sri Lankan government might at any time consider concerning its relations with a third party would be subject to Indian approval. In particular, the strictures were obviously aimed at Sri Lankan co-operation with the US and Pakistan.

In June 1988 India announced that it would start to withdraw the IPKF and that as many as 8,000 troops would leave in the first contingent. Foreign diplomats in Colombo believed that the process would be very slow. After all, the Tamils, though greatly weakened, were still militant and some of their guerrilla leadership cells were intact in Sri Lanka and in Tamil Nadu, where their largest bases are situated.

A Western diplomat in New Delhi, who is familiar with the region, said:

> Delhi has for a very long time been looking for an excuse to impose its presence in the island, which it considers a natural extension of its territory. President Jayawardene offered it on a plate, whereas it was the Indians themselves who created the 'Tamil people' by arming and training the guerrilla movement for years. The Indians will now never let go of Sri Lanka, particularly as this tiny country forms part of a much vaster design, that of India's expansionist role in the whole Indian Ocean region.[3]

Towards the end of 1988 the major result of India's intervention in Sri Lanka was that India's influence was profound and that Sri Lankan foreign policy was controlled from Delhi. Despite its 2,500 casualties, the Indian Army High Command was well pleased with the campaign in Sri Lanka because it had given all levels and all branches of the services experience in combined services operations.

Sri Lanka Army Reorganisation

During 1988 the army's structure, distribution and command system were radically changed. Apart from the capital, Colombo, the country was divided into twenty-one sectors, each with a battalion of troops. Colombo district came under army HQ.

Two new operational divisions were established. Division One, with its HQ at Panagoda, twelve miles south of Colombo, covers the districts of Amparai (Eastern

Province), Kandy (Central Province), Kuruvita (Sabaragamuwa Province), and Matara (Southern Province). Its GOC is Major General Asoka Jayawardene.

Division Two covers the districts of Palaly (Northern Province), Jaffna, Trincomalee (Eastern Province), Vavuniya (Northern Province) and Puttlam (North Central Province). Its GOC is Major General Hamilton Wanasinghe.

The post of Army Commander was filled by a General, rather than a Lieutenant General as before. A new office of Deputy Commander of the Army was created as a Lieutenant General post. The chain of command now runs: Commander, Deputy Commander, the two Divisional Commanders, the Chief-of-Staff at Army HQ.

References

1. The Dixit revelations were an exclusive for *The Observer*, London, on 3 April 1988. An LTTE spokesman in Madras confirmed the deal. He said that the payments had been part of a larger package of guarantees which the Indian Prime Minister had offered Prabhakaran. They included £43m. economic assistance to be provided for the rehabilitation of the Jaffna peninsula.
2. For an analysis of the strategic importance of Sri Lanka in general and Trincomalee in particular see **WAR ANNUAL 2.**
3. This diplomat blames Indian 'manipulation' of'the Tamils for most of the trouble in Sri Lanka. 'It was a major part in Indian strategy to destabilize Sri Lanka and then make a *de facto* take-over in the guise of offering protection', he said.

Sudan Civil War

Sudan Civil War

ARAB MUSLIMS VERSUS NEGRO CHRISTIANS

Background Summary

Animosity between the Muslim Arabs of northern Sudan and the Christian negroes and animist tribes of the south led to a war between 1955 and 1972. Despite a negotiated peace, the southerners were forced to form a guerrilla army to resist oppression from the state security forces and against Islamic pressure which was intended to subdue the Christians and turn them into a *dhimmi* people—second-class citizens.

The guerrilla army, known as *Anyanya*—'venom of the viper'—developed into a more conventional military force, the Sudan People's Liberation Army (SPLA). Western-educated Colonel John Garang became its leader in 1982. Abdullah Chol formed *Anyanya II* in opposition to SPLA. While the SPA wanted to secede from Sudan, *Anyanya II* was ready to co-operate with the Khartoum government of President Gaafer Nimeiri.

By 1985 Garang controlled two of Sudan's three southern provinces. His forces, 10,000-strong, disrupted Nile river traffic and closed down work on oilfields and irrigation projects. SPLA long-distance raids continued after the despotic Nimeiri was overthrown in a military coup. *Anyanya II* collapsed when Abdullah Chol was killed while fighting against SPLA.

During 1986 the civilians of the south suffered at the hands of both the SPLA and of the Sudanese army. The government set other tribes against the Dinka tribe, to which Garang belongs, by encouraging them to raid, steal cattle and burn crops. The SPLA retaliated by starving government-held southern towns into submission, though sometimes they stormed fortresses, as at Rumbek on 5 March 1986.

In April 1986 the nation's foremost political figure, Sadiq al-Mahdi, became Prime Minister. Garang had hoped to negotiate with al-Mahdi but the Prime Minister backed the army and accused Garang of being the tool of neighbouring Marxist Ethiopia. Garang insists that SPLA is neither Marxist nor Christian, nor is it an African movement but a Sudanese nationalist movement. Nevertheless, his links with Ethiopia are strong and he receives most of his weapons from there.

Summary of the War in 1987

Garang concentrated on weakening army garrisons, even if this meant disrupting Western food aid to starving civilian populations. For instance, SPLA troops prevented food from reaching Malakal, 600 miles south of Khartoum, on the Nile. This did little to weaken the army garrison, which was supplied by air, but it resulted in the deaths of many of Malakal's population of 80,000.

Neither side appeared to have a strategy likely to bring about a decisive end to the war. With Muslims making up two-thirds of the population of 22.5 million, the government would never be short of manpower. Also, Sudan was receiving military and financial aid from Saudi Arabia and the Gulf states. But bringing the SPLA to battle or destroying it from the air was beyond the Sudan armed forces' capability. In their frustration they carried out massacres of people from the Dinka and Nuer tribes considered to be in alliance with the SPLA. For his part, Garang seemed convinced that siege operations combined with crop destruction and starvation of the people would bring the government to the point where it would concede independence to the Christian southerners. When his army captured two localities in Arab northern Sudan, Kurmak and Gizen, much of the Arab world became alarmed. Algeria and Iraq joined the nations already helping the Sudanese government.

Garang's incursion was mainly to win new recruits for the SPLA but the psychological impact of the Kurmak and Gizen operations was profound. The ensuing panic in Khartoum was used by rival northern political groups to gain advantage. The SPLA raid was represented as an 'advance' and a 'slight on the integrity of the north'. The hydro-electric power stations which supplied the capital with electricity were said to be in danger and it was rumoured that before long the SPLA fighters would attack Khartoum.

Libya sent troops to help the government recapture Kurmak and Gizen. However, the SPLA raiders withdrew and, contrary to Libyan and Sudanese government claims, no battle took place.

The War in 1988

The war changed direction in 1988. It moved northwards towards the Arab region and Khartoum and seriously undermined the political and economic stability of al-Mahdi's coalition government. The governing classes had been accustomed to referring to the war as 'the southern problem' but the arrival in Khartoum of more than a million desperate southern refugees made it a national problem.

In spite of emergency laws and frequent police raids and roadblocks, smuggling, hoarding and robbery increased. In Khartoum gunfire could be heard at night. In the provinces, where tribes have been armed by Libyans fighting against neighbouring Chad, the situation was more critical. Murderous freebooting armies roamed the western province of Darfur.

Racial and religious tensions increased steadily throughout 1988. The northerners blamed the non-Muslim southerners who had fled to the north for the deteriorating economic situation, for low wages and high rents and for pressure on all public facilities. Arab *agents provocateurs* alleged that many of the refugees were actually a fifth-column sent by the SPLA, ready to attack when Garang sent a signal.

Until May 1988 Westerners in Khartoum believed that they were safe in the city. They realized their mistake when Islamic fundamentalists attacked Western Christians in the Acropole Hotel and the Sudan Club, killing five Britons. The attacks were taken to be warnings to Western aid agencies that they should leave Sudan. Many northern Sudanese believe the fundamentalists' stories that the rebels, the Christian Church, foreign missionaries and relief agencies are in collusion against the Muslim majority.

Many relief workers in Khartoum reported that Prime Minister al-Mahdi was using starvation and a scorched-earth policy against the tribes who supported the SPLA. Aid workers said that large quantities of food being sent by the US, EC and other agencies were being stolen by the army and sold at exhorbitant prices. Relief agencies reported increasing human rights violations, including torture by government troops.[1]

On 25 January 1988 SPLA units captured Kapoeta in eastern Equatoria province, 800 miles south of Khartoum. The SPLA's radio stations, monitored in Nairobi, claimed to have shot down a MiG-23 fighter-bomber and to have hit and badly damaged another. The Sudan air force is not known to have MiG-23s but Libya has more than 150 and some are known to have been on loan to Sudan.

Reversing the usual policy, the SPLA then held Kapoeta, thus forcing the army to build up a military force strong enough to recapture it. This caused immense effort and expense. When SPLA spies reported to Garang that the army was ready to begin its offensive, he quietly withdrew his troops and carried out two lightning strikes against garrisons elsewhere which had been weakened by having to send reinforcements to Kapoeta.

Armed Forces

Sudan's armed forces totalled 59,000 men in 1988, 54,000 of them in the army. The army has 205 tanks, but tanks have yet to play a part in fighting the rebels. Few of the 206 armoured fighting vehicles have managed to get close enough to the SPLA units to enable the infantry to come to grips with them, though their tactical presence inhibits Garang from engaging in field fighting against the army. The army's reconnaissance vehicles are of greater use but some have been captured in SPLA ambushes.

The Sudan air force has only forty-three combat aircraft and lacks armed helicopters. Nominally, it has one squadron with three BAC-167 Strikemaster aircraft but their serviceability is questionable. There are forty-four ordinary helicopters but as they are divided among the ten regional commands most generals refuse to run risks with them. Helicopters are considered so precious that in some areas pilots are under orders never to fly more than 20 km from their base.

The navy has only three river boats and two of these were reported to have been damaged by SPLA artillery fire while escorting food relief ships along the Nile.

By the middle of 1988 the SPLA had grown to a strength of 21,000, organized in battalions. Individually well armed with AK-47s, the units also had 60-mm mortars, 14.5-mm artillery and SA-7s. The force's mobility was greatly increased with the acquisition of trucks from Ethiopia and some relief agency workers reported that armoured cars had been sighted.

The War as an 'External Problem'

The Sudanese government decided upon a new public relations line. Its spokesmen said that the war was mainly an external problem, the chief cause of which was Ethiopia's support for the SPLA. The government's greatest propaganda success was to allege that Ethiopian and Cuban troops were directly aiding the SPLA. This created a wave of patriotism among northern Sudanese.

The government therefore concentrated on securing a dialogue with the Ethiopians, not on studying the demands of the SPLA, among which the abolition of the Islamic law—the hated *sharia*—was crucial.

Most of the pressure to keep the *sharia* came from the Islamic fundamentalist movement, the National Islamic Front (NIF). It is well organized, wealthy and confident of taking power in Sudan. The movement is inspired by extremist religious sentiments and is convinced that the many disasters which have struck Sudan in recent years are an indication of Allah's wrath. In particular, Allah is said to be angry that the *sharia* has not been even more strictly applied.

The NIF organizes massive demonstrations in support of the *sharia*. It controls student unions, missionary and relief work and five of Khartoum's ten daily newspapers. The NIF's leader is Hasan al-Turabi, who has a cogent political and economic programme and strong connections with Egypt and Saudi Arabia. Through Turabi, the NIF has the support of many Sudanese middle- and high-ranking army officers. One of them is General Adb al-Rahman Siwar al-Dhahab, who led the transitional military council before handing over power to Prime Minister al-Mahdi.

That a growing number of Sudanese appear to see the NIF as the answer to Sudan's dreadful problems is an indication of the ever-widening gulf between north and south. Neither the SPLA nor any other southern group would ever negotiate with Turabi. All southern politicians believe that the NIF's ultimate aim is to suppress the south into submission to Islam.

A few northern politicians support the idea of partition. However, in 1988 the SPLA's attitude to partition has changed. Garang and his colleagues now appear to want an equal share for the south in the government of Sudan. If the north wants partition it may have to fight for it; and it may be an easier war to win than a war to subjugate the south.

Sadiq al-Mahdi was re-elected Prime Minister on 20 April, not surprisingly considering the undemocratic nature of the elections. Whether he could continue to hold power against the ever more influential Turabi—who happens to be al-Mahdi's brother-in-law—was doubtful. It was certain that he could not win the war against the SPLA but neither could he lost it.

Resurgent Slave Trade

With more and more automatic weapons in the hands of tribal militias, there has been an eruption of slave-trading in central Sudan that may have few precedents in this century. The mounted Arab raiders, armed by the government, have tacit approval to steal all the Dinka people and cattle they want.[2]

Tribal slavery, an ancient institution in Sudan, was greatly reduced by British rule at the turn of the century. Until recently the scale of tribal fighting was limited by the available weapons—spears and clubs. When fighting got out of hand the army was quick to intervene. Tribal traditions have been destroyed by the power of the new weaponry.

Most of the abducted people are women and children. Several have escaped and reported that they were used as porters and field workers. The girls and women were first raped by the Arab slave dealers who captured them and then by the men to whom they were sold. The dealers generally shoot the men and older youths of the tribe but young boys are considered the best workers and bring high prices.[3]

Northerners claim that SPLA patrols kidnap Arab peasants and force them to work as porters for the SPLA's columns. There is some evidence that armed Dinkas have raided the Arab Rizeigat tribe to obtain slave porters.[4]

Sadiq al-Mahdi admitted that the government has armed Arab tribal militias but insisted that they operated under the 'strict control' of the Sudanese army. This had unfortunately led to an increase in tribal slavery but this did not have government approval.

References

1. Relief agency workers are the only reliable source of information about social conditions. Mark Duffield of Oxfam said that malnutrition in 1988 was worse than at the height of the 1984-85 famine. 'One third of all the children are skeletons', he said. 'They're dying—quite literally on the way out.' Kamel Shawgi, Sudan's commissioner for the Relief and Rehabilitation Commission, said that the RPC faced 'impossible difficulties' in getting food shipments through the conflict areas. Stein Villunstad, an official with the Norwegian Church Aid, said that 500,000 people would need food relief for most of 1988 and much of 1989. John Patel, field controller of Save the Children, said: 'The southern refugee children are as near death as possible. A lot of people have died and a lot more will soon join them.'
2. According to Suleyman Baldo, a researcher at Khartoum University and author of a report on tribal massacres and the revival of slavery in Sudan.
3. Reliable information on slavery comes from Cole Dodge, director for Sudan for the UN Children's Fund; also, from Jacob Akol, a Dinka from Gogrial who is a spokesman in Kenya for World Vision, a California-based relief agency.
4. According to Abdullah Suliman, director of the Islamic-African Relief Association in Khartoum.

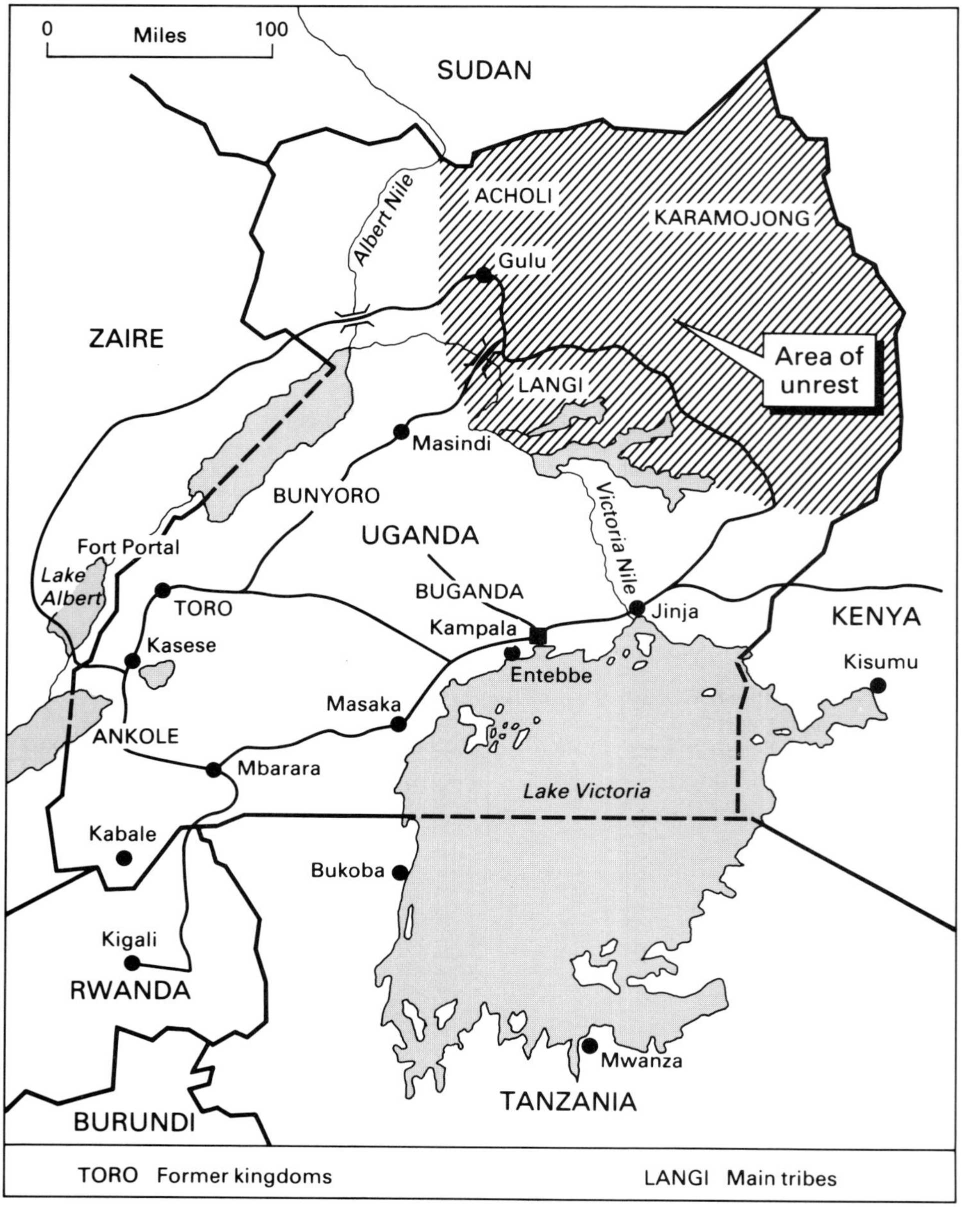

0	Miles	100

SUDAN

Albert Nile

ACHOLI

KARAMOJONG

Gulu

Area of unrest

ZAIRE

LANGI

Masindi

BUNYORO

Victoria Nile

UGANDA

Fort Portal

BUGANDA

Lake Albert

TORO

Kampala

Jinja

KENYA

Kasese

Entebbe

Kisumu

Masaka

ANKOLE

Mbarara

Lake Victoria

Kabale

Bukoba

Kigali

RWANDA

Mwanza

BURUNDI

TANZANIA

TORO Former kingdoms   LANGI Main tribes

Uganda Civil War

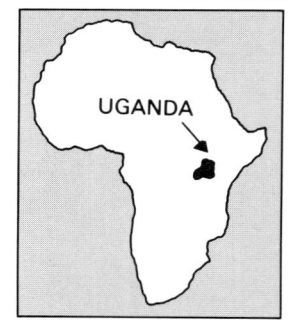

UGANDA

Uganda Guerrilla War

BACK FROM THE BRINK

Background Summary

Milton Obote became President in 1980 after the brutal Idi Amin was overthrown. The Defence Minister, Yoweri Museveni, alleging that Obote's election had been rigged, took to the bush to wage a guerrilla war against him. Creating the National Resistance Army (NRA), Museveni gathered 6,000 fighters, who were largely armed by Libya. The Ugandan army, in its pursuit of the NRA, committed countless atrocities against civilians, butchering at least 300,000 people. During 1985 most fighting took place in the Lowero Triangle, where the army shot any peasant suspected of helping the NRA. Tribal fighting added to the national chaos.

In July 1985 Brigadier Okello overthrew Obote and asked General Tito Okello (no relation) to become President. The army, now little more than a looting rabble, slaughtered still more people in many centres. Museveni, with the NRA strengthened to 8,000, moved out of the Triangle and promised to restore order to the whole of Uganda. On 26 January 1986 he captured Kampala, deposed Okello and had himself declared President.

Even as Museveni set about trying to bring order and discipline to the army, which he planned to integrate with his NRA, he faced dangers from the north where General Basilio Okello, with his HQ at Gulu, raised an army to fight him. He recruited from the 800,000-strong Acholi warrior tribe. Simultaneously, the Uganda National Liberation Army (UNLA)—formed mostly of men from the disbanded armies of Obote and Okello—took the field against Museveni.

Summary of the War in 1987

On 18 January 1987, at Corner Kilak, the NRA won a battle against the 'Holy Battalion' of the UNLA. In the seven-hour fight more than 350 rebels were killed and the NRA—now really the national army—lost thirty-eight dead and 116 wounded. The NRA had other triumphs. For instance, near Kaberamaido trading centre, 235 miles from Kampala, NRA soldiers fought their way out of an ambush and killed fifteen rebels. However, peace seemed to erode the NRA's discipline and Museveni disbanded some mutinous regiments.

Museveni suffered a setback in April when the Uganda Freedom Movement (UFM) withdrew from the government following the murder of its leader, Andrew Kayiira. The UFM returned to the bush, with 1,000 trained fighters, to become yet another of the President's enemies.

The War in 1988

Despite President Museveni's many problems, by early 1988 he had re-established security in Kampala and most of Uganda's south and west, which were the hardest hit by war. Kampala had commonly been regarded as one of the world's most dangerous cities but in 1988 women vendors could remain safely in their roadside markets well after dark. People who in 1985 refrained from painting their houses for fear of attracting looters, were again decorating them. Many small businesses started, some of them with capital from a UN $18m loan.

Museveni still faced serious security problems in the north and east, despite the assurance of his speech in February that the NRA had 'broken the back of the bandits'. Heartened by the surrender of about 6,000 rebels under the government's amnesty offer, he appealed to other rebels to follow their example.

International observers in Kampala commented that Uganda's six rebel movements lacked co-ordination and a clear political programme. Even so, they said, continued military operations would be a serious drain on government resources. The existence of these groups indicated Uganda's deep regional, ethnic and religious divisions which the government would at some point have to reckon with.

That point came in April 1988 when rebels of the Uganda People's Democratic Army (UPDA) had an amicable meeting in Gulu with Major General Salim Saleh, the President's twenty-eight year old brother-in-law. He offered army posts for properly trained soldiers who had become rebels. Exiled rebel spokesmen and government politicians were left out of what Saleh described as an agreement between combatants in the field. 'Soldiers are the ones who die', he said, 'and I think it's better for them to find their own solution'. Saleh himself has been a soldier since he was fifteen. The agreement was denounced by the political leader of the UPDA, Otema Alimadi, who is resident in London.

Saleh and other leaders from Kampala also met leaders of the UPA, who asked if they could join the national army or form local militias to defend the UPA area from cattle raiders. Rebels from two other factions who were afraid of being isolated in any peace deals also approached government leaders. By the end of April, according to a government spokesman, 20,000 rebels had surrendered under the amnesty and another 20,000, though still armed, were honouring a cease-fire arrangement. The country appeared to have stepped back from the brink of another ruinous phase of civil war.

Military Aid from Abroad

During 1987 Museveni had the service of soldiers from North Korea, East Germany, Cuba and Libya. About 400 Libyan military staff arrived at Nakasongala, sixty miles north of Kampala, in March and another 750 were welcomed in December. Thirty 76 mm and ten 120 mm field guns, apparently from North Korea, reached Uganda through the Kenyan port of Mombasa.

Museveni claims to be a friend of the West and during 1988 solicited American economic and military support. He asked the US to put pressure on neighbouring Zaire and Kenya to stop them from destabilizing Uganda. The reason for his problems with the two pro-Western countries is that he has allowed his territory to be used as the site for Libyan-financed bases and military training camps to accommodate people opposing Presidents Mabuto of Zaire and Daniel Arap Moi of Kenya.

Uganda is also supplying facilities to African volunteers from both countries on the way to training schools in Libya as well as to Libyan-sponsored terrorists and agitators travelling to the two countries and other parts of Africa.

Several prominent Ugandan dissidents have found refuge in Zaire and Kenya but there is no evidence that the countries are giving any material support to these politicians and their movements. This may change as Zaire and Keyna have been consulting on how to stop the attempts of Libya and Uganda to overthrow their governments. To counter Kenyan and Zairean moves, Museveni told the West that although such camps existed in Uganda he was trying to close them down and that he was distancing themself from Colonel Gaddafi. Late in 1988 there was no proof that either claim was true.

At this time the NRA numbered 20,000 and was absorbing the men of the Federal Democratic Movement. The army was loosely organized in brigades and battalions and was mostly equipped with small arms. It had only ten tanks of uncertain reliability and 150 armoured personnel carriers, mostly in a poor state of repair. The Ugandan air force exists in name only, having no more than one transport aircraft and a few helicopters. The country has no money to buy arms and is not considered creditworthy by arms dealers.

Alice Lakwena and the Holy Spirit Movement

Uganda is plagued by witchcraft cults which have a profoundly damaging effect on law and order. The most notorious cult was the Holy Spirit Movement, founded by a twenty-seven year old herbalist and 'priestess' Alice Lakwena from Gulu.

In October 1987 she led an army of peasants and ex-soldiers against the NRA. Smeared with Alice's 'magic oils' which they were convinced would protect them against bullets and shellfire, Alice's warriors charged the NRA positions. About 7,000 were killed and the movement appeared to collapse. Alice fled to Kenya, where she was sentenced to four months in prison for entering the country illegally.

Other cult leaders, all of them vicious and murderous, set up private 'armies'. Joseph Kony, with about 1,000 men, seems to be the most powerful. Escaped rebels reported that he wanted them to go into battle shouting 'James Bond! James Bond!' although they did not know what this name meant. Diabolically cruel, Kony arbitrarily executes his own men when they displease him, breaks down friendships among others and forbids the sharing of food. He enforces fasts to the point where his men became desperate. Kony tells them that if they take food a snake will bite them on the mouth. His followers believe this.

Another cult group, known as the 'Red Commodores', chop their enemies to death with *machetes* and according to foreign relief workers are responsible for about twenty murders a night. Millions of Ugandans believe in the existence of spirits with names such as 'What? What?', 'Who are you?' and 'Star Snake'. When a spirit incites men to fight against the NRA or any other group trying to impose law and order they will do just that. A new movement calling itself Lakwena Part Two appeared in June 1988 and the government regarded it as a serious menace.

When Alice Lakwena finished her prison sentence in Keyna she was deported to Uganda where she is said to have been murdered. No responsible authority has confirmed her death.

War Trends

The Dangers of Chemical Warfare

Perhaps the most important military trend of 1988 was the growing importance and use of chemical weapons. At least sixteen nations probably already have 'the poor man's nuclear bomb', as gas of various kinds has been called. Another forty nations have the capability to make military chemicals.

The attraction is not merely economic. Such 'armaments' can be developed with relative ease and are readily disguised and hidden. The potential psychological effect on an enemy is considered to be so great that the morale of troops subjected to chemical attack would collapse. At least this is the assessment of military leaders in Iran, Iraq, Libya and Syria, all of which have large stocks of chemical weapons.

Even in a world swollen with sophisticated weapons, chemical arms are still generally regarded as among the most horrible agents of war. One droplet of nerve gas can send a victim into paroxysms and uncontrollable vomiting, followed by paralysis and asphyxiation.

The chlorine and mustard gases used during World War I were considered so monstrous that in 1925 the major nations banned their use by international protocol. In 1969 President Richard Nixon unilaterally stopped US production of chemical weapons, calling their use 'repugnant to the conscience of mankind'. However, in December 1987 workers at the US army's arsenal at Pine Bluff, Arkansas, resumed nerve-gas production by filling, sealing and storing artillery-shell components related to the pesticide malathion. When combined with a simple industrial alcohol, the chemical turns lethal. The US army is believed to have already loaded the two components into hundreds of thousands of shells at Shreveport, Louisiana.

The American return to chemical weapons production results from more than ten years of Defence Department efforts to persuade Congress to fund binary weapons—devices in which two comparatively harmless components of a deadly compound are stored and transported separately. When the components mix, during the flight of a shell perhaps, they become toxic.

Pentagon planners claim that chemical weapons are needed to deter a Soviet Union nerve-gas attack in Europe. According to what looks like conclusive intelligence, the Soviet Union has a larger and more modern stockpile than the US. Also, it has 100,000 men trained to fight in chemically-contaminated situations. The Americans are alarmed that much of the US stockpile is outmoded.

The Soviet Union admitted in April 1987 that its forces did have chemical weapons in store but gave an assurance that they were no longer being made. This was seen as a ploy to induce the Americans not to resume production. The Russians have now permitted Western experts to inspect their chemical weapons factory at Shikhany, but Western intelligence agencies have detected similar factories elsewhere.

Some NATO defence ministers agree with the US that chemical weapons are

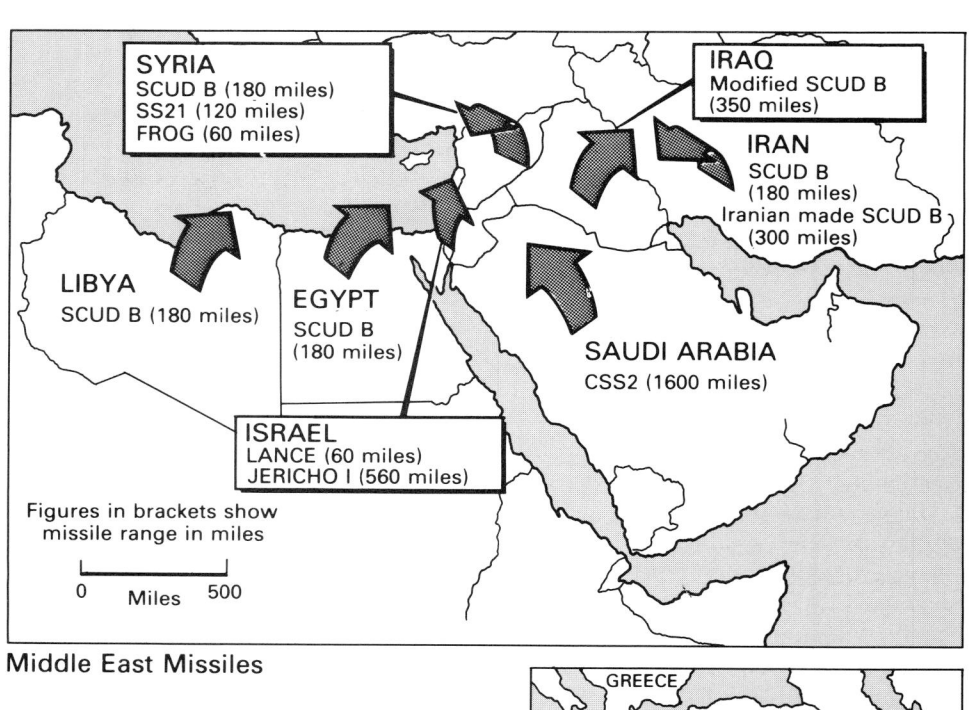

SYRIA
SCUD B (180 miles)
SS21 (120 miles)
FROG (60 miles)

IRAQ
Modified SCUD B
(350 miles)

IRAN
SCUD B
(180 miles)
Iranian made SCUD B
(300 miles)

LIBYA
SCUD B (180 miles)

EGYPT
SCUD B
(180 miles)

SAUDI ARABIA
CSS2 (1600 miles)

ISRAEL
LANCE (60 miles)
JERICHO I (560 miles)

Figures in brackets show
missile range in miles

0   Miles   500

Middle East Missiles

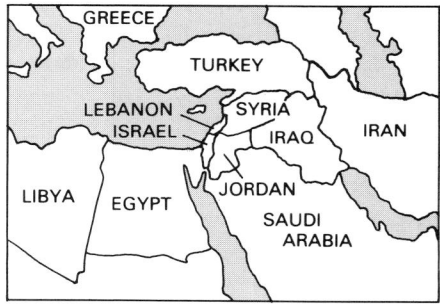

GREECE
TURKEY
LEBANON
ISRAEL
SYRIA
IRAQ
IRAN
LIBYA
EGYPT
JORDAN
SAUDI
ARABIA

necessary as a reserve but all fear that deployment of such weapons in their countries would be politically unacceptable. Technical opponents of the 'gas-is-best' theory say that it is not necessarily superior to other kinds of arms. By producing a new generation of toxins, the critics say the Pentagon will begin a dangerous chemical arms race. The American Chemical Association claims that the US alone already possesses more than 5,000 times enough nerve gas to kill everyone on earth.

The Pentagon experts retort that they plan to spend nearly three-quarters of 1988's chemical warfare budget of $970m on detection and avoidance, not on production. The army, after many trials, wants less bulky protective gear for soldiers and more emphasis on sensors for locating chemical weapons launchers and improved decontamination methods.

The Regan administration has negotiated with the Soviet Union about eliminating production and stockpiles. However, Pentagon thinking is that Soviet co-operation is best achieved by convincing the Russians that the US intends to modernize its weapons. Only then, will the Russians be ready to talk seriously.

For seventeen years negotiators in Geneva have sought to produce a convention to ban the development, production, stockpiling, transfer and use of chemical weapons. Draft convention followed draft convention until some basic principles were agreed in 1984. Since then the committee on chemical weapons which forms part of the UN Conference on Disarmament has been unable to agree on a definitive text. Another session of the Conference ended on 28 April 1988, with all parties admitting that nothing could be achieved for another two or three years. The subject of chemical weapons did not appear on the agenda of the Reagan-Gorbachev summit in June 1988.

Senior generals see certain benefits in the use of chemicals, not least because they do not destroy ports, airfields, factories and equipment. In warfare it is the tactical use of chemicals which most interests the generals. Using precision guidance together with an accurate weather forecast—since a change in wind could blow gas to the 'wrong' area—a small amount of lethal gas could be fired at an enemy airfield or other installation. Tasteless, colourless and odourless, it would leave no marks on the victims' bodies and enemy generals might even believe their men had been killed by blast, since high intensity percussion bombs could be dropped with the gas. In this way, according to one school of thought, the possibility of chemical retaliation could be avoided. In any case, relatiation by gas would be preferable to a nuclear strike.

Chemicals have been used in modern war more than is generally realized. Italy used blister gas against Abyssinian tribesmen during its colonial war of 1936. Japan used gas against Chinese soldiers and civilians in 1937-39. Egypt fought its North Yemeni enemies with gas in the 1960s, Vietnam spread nerve gas in Laos and Kampuchea, the Soviet Union used it in Afghanistan and the Angolan government, with Cuban connivance, has used it against UNITA rebels in Angola. Iraq has employed chemical weapons against its Iranian and Kurdish enemies from 1983, most recently at Halabja in March 1988. The US was guilty of waging chemical warfare in Vietnam, if herbicides and riot-control agents constitute chemical weapons, a point still being debated by the Conference on Disarmament in Geneva.

The US and the Soviet Union have by far the largest stockpiles. In 1987 the Soviet stated that it held 50,000 tons, but this was too absurdly low a figure to be believed. The Russian stockpile could be as high as 500,000 tons and is certainly not less than 200,000 tons. The US admits to stocks of 30,000 tons, also too low for credibility.

France has sophisticated chemical weapons as well as the best security about their precise form. Apart from the countries already mentioned, Egypt, India, Pakistan, North Korea and Taiwan have chemical weapons stocks and Israel may also have them. Considering the massive stocks owned by neighbouring hostile Syria it would indeed be surprising if Israel did not have nerve gases and other chemical weapons. The Israel Defence Forces certainly have advanced protective, detection and decontamination techniques.

Proliferation of chemical weapons is only one aspect of concern. Another is the involvement of the world's chemical manufacturers, traders and engineering contractors in the supply of raw materials, technology, plans and equipment to make the chemical agents. Some are easy to produce. For instance, crude mustard gas—as used by Iraq—can be produced by stirring two chemicals, hydrogen chloride and thiodiglycol together. This results in a volatile liquid which can be poured into shells. When they explode after being fired from guns the gas is widely flung. Even nerve gas can be produced in a plant no more complicated than one producing conventional weapons. A small number of trained specialist chemists working in a small and readily disguised factory could produce enough nerve gas to wipe out an army. A pesticide factory can be converted into a plant for making lethal chemical agents, as Iraq showed. In 1988 Iraq had three plants producing nerve agents, yet all of them had been originally built by Western European companies to manufacture pesticides. Iran's war gases came from similar sources.

Verification is the main problem for any prohibiting convention which might eventually be signed. The US negotiators in Geneva are pressing for 'challenge inspections'—that is, inspections at virtually instant notice to detect cheating. Britain and the Soviet Union agree to such a form of inspection but many Third World countries object to them. India strenuously opposes 'intrusive monitoring'. Any form of inspection other than a 'no-notice' type would be virtually useless. A plant producing lethal chemical war agents could change to making something innocuous in a matter of hours.

The trend towards the use of nerve agents is strong. In Syria, in 1982, the army used gas in Hama to exterminate thousands of enemies of the Assad regime. They were members of the Muslim Brotherhood and their families, all living in large apartment blocks. Gas was introduced into these buildings and into mosques where other 'rebels' had congregated, through long pipes. According to one report, the gas did its work 'quickly and efficiently'. Many of the 40,000 people who were killed at the time died in shootings and bombings so it is not known precisely how many were the victims of lethal chemicals What is known is that the administration and the army considered the chemicals much more cost-effective than quelling an uprising by conventional means, which are often destructive.

Dictators and desperate guerrilla leaders opposing them are likely to feel an ever stronger compulsive urge to achieve quick and decisive results by the use of chemical weapons. Beleaguered countries might be tempted to make pre-emptive chemical strikes against powerful and belligerent enemies known to be on the verge of invasion. Invaders long thwarted in their campaigns of colonial conquest—such as Colonel Gadaffi in his attempts to subdue Chad—might well decide that chemical warfare was the only option left to them. After all, Libya possesses stocks of at least three types of gas.

No matter what type of convention against the use of chemical weapons is finally produced in Geneva, it cannot restrict their use by the desperate, the unstable, the ruthless or the poor among nations and leaders. The lack of effective condemnation of the use of gas by the Soviet Union, Iraq and Cuba–Angola will encourage others.

Iraq's Chemical Warfare Against Kurds

Iraqi aircraft began to drop gas bombs on Kurdish settlements late in August 1988 and soon after this the artillery fired shells against civilian and military targets. As a result, for some weeks the Kurds attracted more attention than any other people involved in a current war. Many of the victims fled into Turkey where army doctors confirmed that they were indeed suffering from chemical injuries. Turkish politicians who visited the refugees said that chemical weapons had certainly been used and their claims were supported by regional governors.

Amnesty International reported on 2 September that the Iraqi army had used chemical weapons and declared that massacres committed by the Iraqis were part of a deliberate and systematic policy aimed at wiping out a large number of Kurdish civilians.

Iraqi's use of chemical weapons spread such terror that many of the refugees fled from fear of gas bombs rather than actual attacks.

Iraq denied that it was using chemical weapons but this was rejected by the US administration and Congress pressed President Reagan to cut off $800m in credits to Iraq. Other international reaction was muted, despite overwhelming evidence of the Iraqis' actions. At the end of September, ten nations finally called on the UN to send a team of experts to Iraq to investigate and report. Iraq at once rejected UN inspection and instead invited journalists to tour the area. This was seen as a ruse by Iraq, since journalists might not see signs of chemical-weapon use that would be detected by experts.

In any case, Marie Colvin of the *Sunday Times*, London, had already seen Kurdish sufferers who had crossed into Turkey, and had taken photographs of their injuries.[1] The symptoms which she described were consistent with gassing, according to medical specialists.

Turkish official sources, including an army general, as well as three foreign diplomats, reported that many hundreds of gas victims died in Iraq and that hundreds more reached safety in Turkey.[2] Iraq's willingness to use chemical weapons on such a scale and despite international uproar disturbed all the nations of the Middle East.

References

1. *Sunday Times*, 11 September 1988.
2. These statements were made directly to the author.

Background Reading

The books here listed have been published since War Annual 2, in which other titles were recommended.

Afghanistan

The Fall of Afghanistan—An Insider's Account by Abdul Samad Ghaus; Pergamon Press, Oxford.
Afghanistan: The Great Game Revisited edited by Rosanne Klass; Freedom House, New York.
War in Afghanistan by Mark Urban; MacMillan Press, London.
Three Women of Herat by Veronica Doubleday; Jonathan Cape, London.

Angola

Southern Africa in Soviet Foreign Policy International Institute for Strategic Studies, London.

Bangladesh

The Chittagong Hill Tracts: Militarisation, Oppression and the Hill Tribes. Anti-Slavery Society, London.

Central America

Comment—Central America Catholic Institute for International Relations, London.
A Thousand Times Heroic a report by a delegation of the Catholic Institute for International Relations, London.

East Timor

Timor Link quarterly magazine published by the Catholic Institute for International Relations, London.
East Timor: A Christian Reflection the Catholic Institute for International Relations, London.

Guatemala

Guatemala: False Hope, False Freedom by James Painter; Latin America Bureau, New York.
Prophets in Combat by Bishop Pedro Casaldaliga; Meyer Stone Books, New York.

Holy War

Holy War—Islam Fights by John Laffin: Grafton Books, London.
Islamic Fundamentalism by Dilip Hiro; Paladin Books, London.
The Assassins: Holy Killers of Islam by Edward Burman, Crucible, London.

Iran–Iraq War

The Spirit of Allah, Khomeini and the Islamic Revolution by Amir Taheri; Alder and Alder, Bethesda.
The Gulf War by Edgar O'Ballance; Brassey's, London.

Lebanon

War and Intervention in Lebanon: The Israeli-Syrian Deterrence Dialogue by Yair Evron; Croom Helm, London.

Middle East

The Nuclearisation of the Middle East by Anoushirvan Ehteshami; Gulf Centre for Strategic Studies, London.
Nuclear Rivals in the Middle East by Shyam Bhatia; Routledge, London.

Mozambique

Struggle for Mozambique by Eduardo Mondlane; Zed Press, London.
Mozambique: Cry for Peace by Julian Quan; Oxfam publication.

Namibia

History of Resistance in Namibia by Peter H. Katjavivi, J. Currey, London.

Nicaragua

Nicaragua: Revolution in the Family by Shirley Christian; Random House, New York.
Fire from the Mountain: The Making of a Sandanista by Omar Cabezas, Jonathan Cape, London.
Blood of the Innocent by Teofilo Cabastrero; Orbis Books, New York.

Northern Ireland

The Provisional IRA by Patrick Bishop and Eamonn Mallie; Heinemann, London.

Philippines

Land, Poverty and Politics in the Philippines by Mamerto Canias et al; Catholic Institute for International Relations, London.

Sudan

John Garang Speaks edited by Mansour Khalid; KPI, London.

Uganda

Uganda Now: Between Decay and Development edited by H.B. Hansen and M. Twaddle; J. Currey, London.

Western Sahara

Western Sahara: Roots of a Desert War by Tony Hodges; L. Hill, London.
War and Refugees: The Western Sahara Conflict edited by R. Lawless and L. Monahan; Pinter, London.

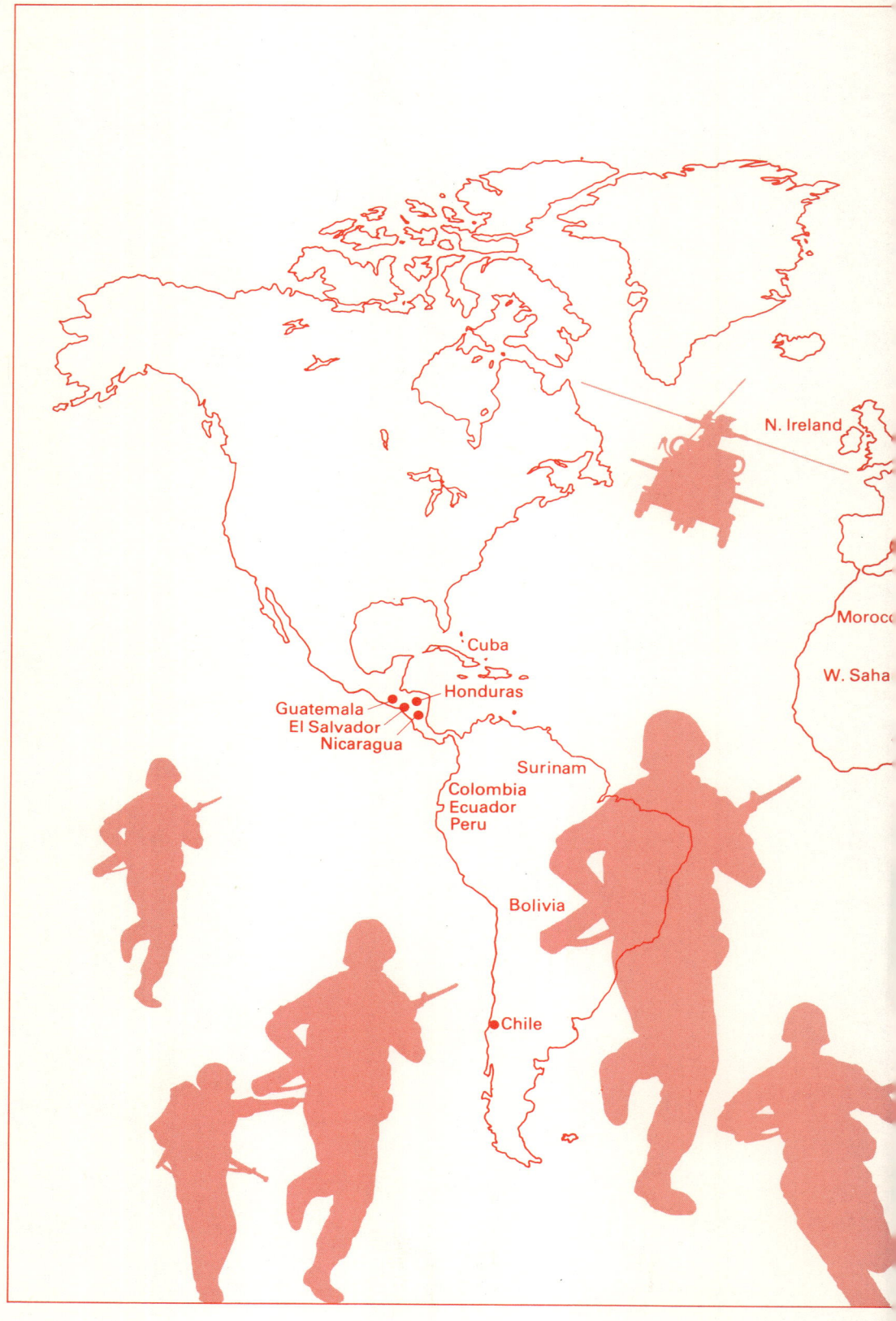

N. Ireland

Morocc[o]

W. Saha[ra]

Cuba

Honduras

Guatemala
El Salvador
Nicaragua

Surinam

Colombia
Ecuador
Peru

Bolivia

Chile